WEEDS

CONTROL WITHOUT POISONS

When you find weeds invading your grass sward, fertilize. Weeds are a lot like human beings and civilizations. Make them too prosperous, and they perish.

An old Vermont farm saying

WEEDS

CONTROL WITHOUT POISONS

Charles Walters

Acres U.S.A.
Greeley, Colorado

WEEDS

CONTROL WITHOUT POISONS

Acres U.S.A., Inc.
P.O. Box 1690
Greeley, Colorado 80632 U.S.A.
1-800-355-5313 • 1-970-392-4464
info@acresusa.com • www.acresusa.com

Walters, Charles, 1926-2009
    Weeds: control without poisons / Charles Walters – 2nd ed.
    xvi, 352 p., 23 cm.
    Includes index.

    1. Weeds–Control. 2. Soil science. 3. Agricultural ecology.
    4. Sustainable agriculture.   I. Title.

SB611.W35 1996   632'.58
                                          QBI96-83
ISBN: 978-0911311-58-7
Library of Congress Catalog card number: 90-084508

*Dedicated to the memory of James A. McHale,
former Secretary of Agriculture, Commonwealth of
Pennsylvania, a farm leader who made a difference.*

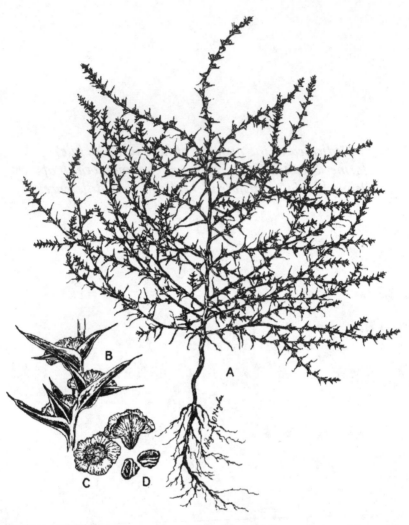

The Russian thistle, sometimes called tumbleweed, would stair-step tumble into the loft of a western Kansas barn when the wind did its thing. Its classical name is Salsola kali, *after Carolus Linnaeus, variety* tenuifolia. *This Regina Hughes art from USDA's* Selected Weeds of the United States *does not illustrate the ball-like nature of the weed when it starts tumbling before the wind. Shown here is the weed itself (A); flowering branch (B); fruiting calyces (C); and seeds (D).*

CONTENTS

Redroot pigweed came up without too much of a struggle, but hand removal resulted in blisters just the same. This weed could annihilate a potato crop if left unchecked. There is a symbiotic relationship between redroot pigweed, Amaranthus retroflexus, *and lambsquarters and most commercial plants. In fact, both weeds are the best possible laboratory analysis for phosphate availability on a daily meal basis. Above, the weed (A); the pistillate spikelet (B); the utricle, or small, thin-walled, one-seeded fruit (C); and the seeds (D).*

A NOTE FROM THE PUBLISHER

During the late 1930s, when the author of this book first took an interest in weeds, it seemed inconceivable that the world would be long content — like a blind horse — to starve knee deep in corn, to endure want when there was abundance, and to destroy food while women and children perished for want of it. Truth, it seemed to this future editor, had some rights simply because it was the truth. Yet the economic breakdown system, and the practitioners of the art that harvested wealth from imbalance, relied not on truth, but on continuance of pretense that things were different than they really were.

This thought comes to mind as *Weeds, Control Without Poisons*, moves into press. In fact, the historian has always had to point to some utter unreason that in every season occupied the minds of men. He has not been able to explain why men once believed in the mystical significance of numbers, or why they studied the gizzards of birds as omens of the future, or enticed young men into flames or atop an altar where a stone knife would remove their hearts. We pride ourselves on having outgrown such primitive childishness and yet we leave alive the superstition that weed control is not possible without a suitable propitiation to a chemical company. Each year the battle against Johnsongrass, quackgrass, shattercane, foxtail, fall panicum, and dozens more, is joined by a call to arms, as though use of Ala-Scept, Ignite, Freedom, Pinnacle, Pursuit, Passport, Verdict, Bullet, Beacon, Tough, and all the rest was equal to a march down the tabernacle aisle to the mourner's bench. A vote for post-emergence chemistry is to be considered a vote for the Good Book of Science. Farmers are promised burndown efficiency — in the words of one university scientist — "something that will burn down a fence post . . . and get the wire too." And yet this toxic technology, this murderous alchemy, has corrupted science, farming, the soil and water, and offended humanity as well, and it is on the way out. For the past fifty years, weed manuals have held to giving nomenclature and prescribing chemicals of organic synthesis for weed control. In this book, *Acres U.S.A.* founder Charles Walters has taken a different tack. First he asks, *What is the weed telling us?* and then he wonders, *What are we doing to worsen the problem?* The bottom line, when it has been figured out, prescribes the remedy without poisons. There is a chapter that answers the question, *Why not poisons?* and it will not likely leave an untroubled conscience in anyone with the mental acuity to project the implications.

Phil Callahan, the author of *Ancient Mysteries, Modern Visions* and *Paramagnetism*, has called this the best book on weeds ever written. He came to this conclusion because *Weeds, Control Without Poisons* is well into the business of asking the right questions, often staying on for definitive answers. The questions and the answers make up the pages of this entertaining and valid book.

The Publisher

FOR THE RECORD

The so-called conventional agricultural system of the United States is falling apart at the seams. Its intellectual advisers in the university hardly know what is going on in the countryside. Their advice has created extensive soil erosion, universal environmental contamination, and a degeneration of the health of almost every living species on this planet. Public outcry is growing in proportion to its awareness. Politicians are mocking their shared concern in order to sway votes. Legislation to curb or banish the current agricultural system of toxic warfare on man and nature is becoming more plentiful. Caught in the middle of this political football is the farmer. One by one, his toxic crutches are being eliminated from the market. He is told that he must farm without these "magic bullets" which he has become so accustomed to using. This use has been sanctified by constant insistence of the USDA, land grant universities, and Extension personnel. Now, however, he is being told by the politicians that he cannot use these materials anymore, but is not being told by the lords of agriculture what to do or what to use in their place. The farmer feels lost and frustrated. And he is lost and frustrated until he realizes that the solution to his dilemma rests with his own intuition and common sense. Farming is not a desk job nor the work of a laboratory technician. It is a natural experience. It is an understanding and appreciation for all life on this planet. It is an attitude of living, of peaceful coexistence, not an attitude of kill or be killed or of constant conflict.

The first step in building a system without toxic chemical war games with nature is to change your attitude. Become a farmer rather than a miner of the soil. Decide to leave the farm in a better condition when you depart than it was last year or when you started farming. Decide to accept responsibility for the health of this country, yourself, and your family.

Weeds, Control Without Poisons is an original, even though it leans on the scholarship of many in the identification of weeds. It does not pretend to have all the answers, yet it has furnished a beginning in asking the right questions. Many minor weeds have still to be evaluated, and there can be no doubt that answers will be forthcoming. As far as the major crop weeds are concerned, this book hints, then sledgehammers the answers into place.

Weed manuals published since World War II have simply identified weeds, the implication or actual direction being that use of this or that poison is the only rational advice. Charles Walters questions this, and he has used most of his journalistic career to gather in support for dealing with weeds without poisons. Hopefully, this little book will be a turning point away from our rush toward perdition.

Arden Andersen, Ph.D., D.O.
author of *The Anatomy of Life and Energy in Agriculture* and *Science in Agriculture*

PREFACE

Some few years ago, I tripped to Houston, Texas and environs for the purpose of visiting a rice producer who, once upon a time, knew my old mentor, William A. Albrecht, then emeritus professor, Department of Soils, University of Missouri. This rice grower had a small plane on his farm for the purpose of monitoring the crop — and, not least, the weeds. He had a small laboratory on his farm because he had been trained to compound things like DDT, and — also once upon a time — he chest-thumped this fact to the good professor Albrecht, adding that "this stuff works." Albrecht responded, *Yes, it works today and it will probably work ten years from now.* And with that Albrecht shot a finger into the rice grower's chest. *But ten years from now you won't know where it is!* Much of the toxic genetic chemistry spilled into agriculture over the past several decades is still out there. I know where some of it is. Richard L. Penney is an Iowa scientist who spent several years at the U.S. South Pole station. He took the biopsy specimens that revealed DDT in the fatty tissue of all the examined penguins. Apparently this toxin has established itself in the migratory food chain that travels to the South Pole and back.

In order to strike down dicots such as balloonvine, bindweed, Indian hemp, common milkweed, Canada trumpet creeper, a veritable cauldron of toxic brews has been developed, and sold by the republics of higher education, USDA, Extension and state departments of agriculture, each acting as a free sales arm for a faulty idea. For it is a fact that large seeded annual broadleaves — bristly starbur, bur cucumber, cocklebur, woolly croton, crotalaria, dayflower, Jimson weed, sickle pod, velvetleaf and wild cucumber — and small seeded annual broadleaves — beggarticks, carpetweed, Florida beggarweed, groundsel, lambsquarters, all the pigweeds and ragweeds, Pennsylvania smartweed, wild mustard — can be rolled back best with fertility management, and not with herbicides. According to Madison Avenue copywriters, weeds are easy prey to Tough, Stomp, Dual, Prowl and Select — to name a few weed killers — but first rate science sees the proper control of weeds seated in fertility management, and not in inventory from the shelves of the devil's pantry.

In the pages that follow, I have put together extant knowledge on controlling, without poisons, small seeded annual grasses, perennial grasses and sedges, as well as exotic weeds. The weeds all have names, common and scientific. If the reader wants to know the scientific name for watergrass, broadleaf signal grass, the foxtails, red rice, stinkgrass or witchgrass, whatever, there is a common name directory and there is a scientific name directory after the last chapter.

Withal, weed lore is no hard-to-digest subject. It has insight to offer, not a little fun and lots of excitement, and I have elected to insert all this into a readable narrative. My objective has been to kick open the door to the airtight compartments into which academia has filed the weeds of the world. A little air and light so far have worked wonders, delivering a new level of weed comprehension to production agriculture. After several chapters of general discussion, I have presented over one hundred weeds as a cast of characters. For approximately half of these there is a definitive bottom line, one that reveals to all who wish to see the fact that high science is about to take over weed management exactly as suggested nearly 20 years ago in *Acres U.S.A.* and in *Eco-Farm, An Acres U.S.A. Primer.*

Charles Walters

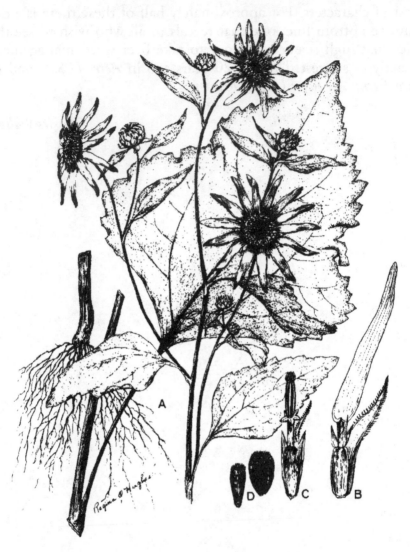

The state flower of Kansas, the sunflower, Helianthus annuus. *It provided a dash of color to an otherwise bleak landcape in the 1930s, and gave Alf Landon a campaign symbol that is remembered almost as much as the 1936 presidential candidate himself. The plant stands tall (A); has a yellow ray flower (B); a disc (C); achenes, meaning a dry one-seeded closed fruit, two views (D).*

1
LEAVE HER ON A STORMY DAY

When I was a boy in Western Kansas during the Dust Bowl days, the weeds were my friends, especially the Russian thistle. On long barefooted walks across wind-rippled fields of dust near our home, they provided companionship when everything else had been scoured from the soil. They piled up where fences intercepted them on their march across the countryside, and then the dust blasted itself under and around this stately, beheaded plant, until finally I could walk right over barbed wire enclosures as if they didn't matter. I figured there was something sacred about this plant because, once, I heard Grandpa call it a name that sounded like something in the old church tongue. Grandpa said the tumbleweed came to Kansas with the arrival of the Volga Germans in 1876. "We brought it along with our wheat seed," he said, and I always figured it must have had something to do with the religion the immigrants introduced to Ellis County. It contained awesome rituals and Latin songs set to the music of masters — Beethoven, Bach, Mendelssohn, Mozart — and at Easter, bits and pieces of Handel's Messiah. I often sang parts of the High Mass and the Litany of Saints to our pony, Brenny. It was a strange chant that I memorized, words that sounded like *Oh, Robert Nobis*, and a refrain, *Leave her on a stormy day*. It was years before I learned that the real Latin was *Ora Pro Nobis*, and *Libera nos, Domine*.

That is where the tumbleweed came in. Grandpa got scientific one night and recited genus and species, *Salsola kali*, and there was a reference to *enuifolia*, or something to that effect. The next morning I hollered at the top of my lungs, *Oh Salsola kali*, and then the litany refrain, *Leave her on a stormy day*. I was imitating the baritone voice of the rotund Capuchin who intoned hell-fire with the trap door open during Lenten sermons, and I figured my voice would one day land me at the Met, or possibly on the stage of La Scala in Milan, but my brothers and sisters said I sounded awful.

My forebears understood how the high plains were as twin brothers to the chernozem or black earth of the Russian steppes. The same crops flourished in both areas. Before the Volga Germans arrived, Kansas and the high plains had no Russian knapweed, goatgrass, Russian olive, corn cockle or summer cypress. My mother disliked corn cockle worst of all. Stone ground with winter wheat, it made her bread taste bad. It too was a weed the emigrants of 1876 failed to leave behind. Dad had his pet antipathy, cheatgrass, a sticklike weed that ruined his steppe by crowding out calcium-rich native pastures that once supported the world's biggest buffalo herds.

It is said that on the high plains as on the Volga steppes, plants that thrive love weeds. The grand champion, in the survival game, was the Russian thistle. It had its aliases — Russian cactus, saltwort, prickly glaswort, wind witch, but the moniker we used most of the time was simply tumbleweed. There were other tumbleweeds of a pigweed stripe, but we considered Russian thistle the real thing. You'd find them in soil so dry it baffled the imagination how they endured. For a few weeks in the spring the cows would eat these tumbling balls of vegetation, but with warm weather the plant parts hardened and set up like sawmill splinters, crowding out other vegetation. And then they broke from their anchorage and raced before the wind, dropping seeds that remained viable for years. Someone has computed that a single tumbleweed plant produces three million seeds. Hoofs and tractor lugs — and later, tires — trampled them into the soil, but nothing so much helped that love-hate relationship between the farmer and the tumbleweed to grow as did tillage, especially tillage once over and not disturbed after that. The seeds from a single tumbleweed could well populate a square mile if they all came to fruition. Computerwise, theory could have one plant cover the entire United States in three years. Proliferation that way has become a reality in some counties.

We had prickly pear in western Kansas, but they didn't run wild the way they did in Australia. In 1839, a single prickly pear came to Australia in a flower pot. Farmers planted them to create borders around homesteads and used them in certain areas of outback cattle and sheep stations. Less than a century later, the prickly pear had spread — without too much human assistance — to cover sixty million acres. This plant, much like the rabbit, came down under without its natural predators trucking along. Australia's terrain and dry climate did the rest.

Move east of Ness County, Kansas, the locus of my youth, and the normal eighteen inches of annual rainfall becomes twenty-seven inches at approximately the Topeka meridian. The tumbleweed couldn't stand that. So even if that roller derby could march across the country along the highways and scatter seeds by the billions, actual growth remained back in its home territory.

The poet Anselm Hallo once wrote that a tumbleweed looks like the skeleton of a brain. In Russia they had a word for this walking weed — *perekatipole*, literally, "roll across the field." And when the winds blow, the tumbleweed does that, not only on the high plains of the United States, but in Turkestan, in the Crimea, in Kazakhstan and on the Kirghiz Steppe along the lower Volga.

I admired those tumbleweeds. They endured when all else failed. They endured drought and grasshoppers and dust storms, in that order, but not in that order of importance. The drought of the 1930s is among my earliest memories. It was not a drought such as I was to see during grownup years, where farmers complained and excused themselves for bad farming at town cafe talk sessions, but a grinding dryness that stressed beyond endurance everything that grew. Yet the tumbleweed endured. It pulled in its lifeblood, so to speak, so that farmers had only a few days to turn the grown plant to silage.

And then the grasshoppers came. There were millions of them, perhaps billions and trillions, and Dad once computed that there might be septillions of them. They settled on the roads to make a dangerous slime as cars rolled over them. In less time than it would take to pluck a pullet, wingless, small-winged and giant grasshoppers would take the lacework out of a corn leaf, consume the silk before it could pollinate, eat every kernel out of a grain head and annihilate grass to the root level. On some Sundays at Sacred Heart Catholic Church in Ness City, hoppers would bite holes in the silk stockings women wore. At home they chewed the curtains in the windows. And in the barn they made sizeable dents in pitchfork handles.

Not a leaf on our big cottonwood down by the pond survived during the worst of the plagues, and in a few days the bark itself fell victim to nature's own eating machine. The hoppers took the fun out of the great outdoors. Every fence post became a living, writhing staff, and barbed wires took on the texture of living rope, there were that many grasshoppers end to end on the iron spans.

And yet, the tumbleweeds remained. They withdrew their juice into their roots, broke off, and raced across the fields, usually to pile up at the fences as if to send an indecent message to the invaders. They had a government program to distribute a poisoned bait, but Dad swore the hoppers thrived on it and spit out a stronger venom as one generation replaced the next. But the grasshoppers ignored the Russian thistle just as later the Russian thistle ignored the dust storms.

The dust storms followed the grasshoppers the way a condor follows death. The actual spawning ground was small. Without breaking any speed laws, you could circle it in a day. Traveling south out of Ness County by way of Dodge City on Route 283 to Minneola, then moving southwest on Route 40, you'd go through Meade and Liberal, the gateway to the Oklahoma Panhandle. The roadmaps have their blue highways intersect Hooker, Guymon and Goodwell on terrain as flat as a well cooked pancake, before taking you down a lonely road to Stafford, Texas. From there a state road takes you north — Route 287 — back into the Oklahoma Panhandle to Springfield and Lamar, Colorado, then back to home territory. You have now covered the heart of the Dust Bowl. These high plains rise gently from two-thousand to five-thousand feet above the sea. Here the soil graduates from chernozem to blow sand, some of it rich in potassium, phosphates and nitrogen. The Volga-like chernozem in the eastern half faded out somewhat to become the dark brown soils of the western half of this area, with Colorado and New Mexico's brown soil bringing up the rear. The last were most subject to wind erosion. Calcareous and sandy clays washed down the Rockies by glacial water to be joined by wind-blown loess. They made the area survive and prosper because they had paramagnetic qualities. Paramagnetic stones and soil particles attract, dimagnetic particles repel. The term of choice is *flocculation*, that property that causes soil particles to cling together. Flocculation is destroyed in such soil by long periods of drought.

There was nothing new about the dust storms of the 1930s. The cycles discerned from tree rings tell us that dust storms have visited the area for periods of five or more years no less then twenty-one times between A.D. 738 and 1934. On the average these droughts presented themselves every thirty-five to thirty-six years. Moreover, some of the droughts lasted more than ten years and came every fifty-five plus years, much like the

Kondratieff commodity cycle. The tumbleweed lasted through them all, even through the most recent era, which has seen farmers dump chemicals of organic synthesis on the soil with reckless abandon.

That is to say, their seeds lasted. Even as children we learned that some weeds start from seed each year and complete their life cycle within that crop year. This was true for both summer and winter annuals. The summer annuals actually germinate during every season except winter. They grow to maturity, cast off their seed and die with the first or second frost. They have a root system that is simple in the extreme and produces an abundance of seeds, as I have noted for the Russian thistle, or tumbleweed. Pigweed is another example of a summer annual.

Winter annuals come to life in the fall. They usually develop a small rosette of leaves and then stay alive throughout the winter. Growth picks up the following spring, producing flowers and showering seeds. The next fall these annuals are dead. Shepard's purse and mustard are good examples.

The perennials are usually more bothersome. They grow from seeds or underground root parts, frequently from both. The roots often exhibit deathless properties, living on from year to year. In most cases the above-ground part of the plant quietly passes away each fall and new growth issues forth again the following spring. Such plants almost always produce flowers and seeds each year. They grow in great circular patches and defy annihilation with a defensive root system that creeps all over the place. Lateral roots from buds give rise to still more plants above ground. Bindweed is a superb example of the perennial.

In considering these classifications, garlic and wild onion are outlaws. They reproduce by means of bulbs that are grown either above or below the ground, or from seeds.

The darling of the lawn, the dandelion, is in a class by itself, yet it must be considered a simple perennial. It actually produces from seeds, but is long-lived because of its fantastic taproot system.

Biennials require two years to complete their growth cycles. Seeds germinate in the spring. A rosette or crown of leaves and a fleshy taproot are developed during the first year. Biennials live through the winter, then produce new stalks or stems the following spring. Later on they flower and mature their seeds, this business being completed by the end of the second year, hence biennials. Good examples are wild carrot, mullein and burdock.

For the purpose of crop production, farmers have come to view the guardians of the soil as three veritable Musketeers — each as different as Aramis, Porthos and Athos — each a nutrient thief. It is true, weeds are a drain on soil moisture and rate attention as non-economic competitors to the commercial crop.

Arden Andersen, writing in *The Anatomy of Life and Energy in Agriculture*, scrutinized weeds in terms of the Biological Theory of Ionization, as taught by the late Carey Reams. He concluded that "Each weed species is genetically keyed to replace a specific deficiency." He divided cropland weeds into broadleafs, grasses and succulents. "Generally speaking, broadleaf weeds are present to correct imbalanced ratio between phosphate and potash. The ratio should be two parts phosphate to one part potash for row crops and vegetables, and four parts phosphate to one part potash for grasses . . . .

"Grasses such as foxtail and quackgrass are generally present to correct a calcium deficiency. In permanent crop areas such as orchards, grasses can be effectively used as a fertilizer simply by keeping them mowed and allowing the clippings to compost back into the soil. In areas where the clippings will not compost back in the soil but rather create a thatch buildup, there is a lack of aerobic microorganisms, an excessive salt concentration, and poor aeration."

Succulents are usually present to replenish the carbonate ions in the soil as well as to increase its water holding capacity. Succulents also act as a ground cover to protect fragile soil from erosion and dehydration.

In Greek mythology, Sisyphus was sentenced to roll a stone uphill repeatedly. It was an easy sentence compared to weeding quackgrass, sometimes called couchgrass. Agropyron repens is shown here (A); its spikelets (B); the ligule (C); and florets (D). Rhizomes from quackgrass have herbal properties useful in treating urinary disorders. Decay systems are at fault when this weed appears. Excess aluminum also is a problem for the crop, albeit not for quackgrass, which can live with it.

The state flower for Kansas is a common fence row weed, the sunflower, a dry weather survivor capable of splashing superb color all over a sometimes stark terrain. The designation *fence row* does not mean the sunflower couldn't take over entire fields, but Dad did not see this as much of a problem. A little clean tillage kept that colorful crop to its road corners and ditches. Alf Landon developed his famous sunflower campaign for the presidential election of 1936 using the state flower as an insignia. But this was long before the tribe had become domesticated and enlarged, like steriod-fed basketball players, and sanctioned as a regular oil seed crop.

Both the sunflower and the tumbleweed faded from view during what I now call the unpleasantness with Germany and Japan, but they have never been entirely out of mind. Nor have many of the other weeds that added so much character to the landscape. And so, when the time came and I was writing *An Acres U.S.A. Primer* some twenty years ago, it seemed only natural to dust off a bit of arcane knowledge and mix in workaday findings, almost always with rewarding results.

These little nuggets fell into my larder softly and stacked up until there was something to talk about. One had to walk carefully in those days. After all, the great professors had decreed killer technology for weed control, and anyone who demurred was downgraded to intellectual underworld status, or ridiculed as a weed quack. This killer technology theory period came hard on the heels of academia's discovery that chemical companies had grant money.

One day, in Idaho, a man named Ed Weldman thought he had cutworms. He had driven down the gravel road bordering one of his cornfields and discovered some few corn stalks down and out for the season. At one time Ed had used Furadan to control cutworms, but the arrival of some clear reporting on eco-agriculture had prompted him to leave that crude concept behind. And yet when he saw those corn stalks down he experienced that sinking feeling in the pit of his stomach that goes with hanging thousands of bucks in a dry well. Bluntly stated, farmer Ed Weldman worried himself into considering the toxic stuff again.

His windshield diagnosis was wrong, of course. Cutworms simply could not survive in that field because the soil had a proper calcium level. The pH was near perfect and in equilibrium. He knew exactly the state of the humus complex in the soil. All seeds had been treated, not with Captan, but with amino complexes that attached an extra nutrient package. No, there was no way cutworms could live in a healthy plant, or weeds in a healthy soil. On-scene inspection revealed that machine damage had caused row ends to ape the look of cutworm damage. There were no weeds, of course. Weeds and insects often go together.

Within a few weeks after I launched *Acres U.S.A.*, I met up with the late C.J. Fenzau, then of Kentland, Indiana. C.J. taught me how to walk the fields and how to see what I looked at. Later on he moved west to Boise, Idaho, and I got to be a regular on the airplane to and from Boise or Twin Falls. C.J. had experimental plots, ostensibly for the purpose of repeating some of the experiments William A. Albrecht of the University of Missouri had accounted for some decades earlier. Albrecht had proved that he could have weed-free plots without poisons, even though nearby broom sedge scattered its seed progeny like dandruff year in and year out.

On one experimental plot, C.J. Fenzau caused excess water along a diagonal line to stress several crops in as many plots. Aphids appeared only where stressed plants permitted them. Furthermore, weed patterns picked up the stress signal. Nutritional limitations inevitably brought on disease, insect and weed response, or production shortfalls. One plot with corn in thirty-eight inch rows had a section on which two tons per acre finished compost had been used. The other section had two tons of halfway house compost, or material not quite finished. This variable translated into 61,000 ears per acre for the finished compost plot, 45,000 ears per acre for the halfway finished compost.

Quackgrass soils hold water because of the extra tension and because they do not have enough air. This inventory of circumstances gives quackgrass a chance to dominate without being subject to fungal attack. "The key to controlling quackgrass," said Fenzau, "is to invite fungus infection of the rhizomes. Wetting agents should make a tremendous difference — again relating to quality calcium availability."

To put it another way, the soil has to have enough calcium to be able to manage aluminum. Aluminum toxicity is a serious problem in a lot of plants. Quackgrass is not susceptible to aluminum intake. Since calcium is a good governor of aluminum and regulator of it, adequate calcium on the soil colloid is a prime requirement in effecting control of this weed system.

Counting the years I spent with National Farmers Organization (NFO), I figure I have visited more farms in more U.S. counties than most Americans, ag consultants included. I have seen good horrible examples, fields so complexed they could no longer insoak water, if this coined word will do. And I have seen those same fields bounce back, almost always on the basis of an adjustment in calcium and an input of compost or change the structure of the soil. I heard from one of the old NFO crowd not long after *An Acres U.S.A. Primer* was published. Keith Emenhiser of Monroeville, Indiana wrote that bull thistles literally owned his farm, a hog farrow to finish operation with some cattle, but a few *Primer* notes took care of that. "I just added manganese (Mn) at the rate of twenty to forty pounds to the acre, and my thistles have almost completely disappeared." Keith was good enough to note that my "book is worth many times the price you charge for it." I liked that remark and hoped it would become a susurration, maybe more a shout than a murmur, because it was the devil to pay keeping *Acres U.S.A.* alive in those days. Now it would seem almost criminal not to pass along the many things learned in this enterprise.

Some people like baseball cards, even when they don't chew gum. I like weeds. And on hikes across someone's acres or along a country stream, when I am alone, I still like to belt out the refrain I sang as a youth in homage to the lowly tumbleweed, *Oh Salsola kali, leave her on a stormy day!*

Common cocklebur tells the farmer that his soil has a high level of available phosphate and a reasonable pH level. These high levels of phosphate tend to complex zinc, which activates the cocklebur's hormone system. Xanthium pennsylvanicum *is shown here with its root (A); seedling (B); bur (C); seed (D). One look at cocklebur should tell a farmer not to fertilize with phosphate.*

2
OBSERVING WEEDS GROW

Andre Voisin, the great French farmer and scientist who wrote *Soil, Grass and Cancer* and *Grass Productivity*, once declared that most of what he knew came not from the university, but from observing his cows at grass. And so it is with much of what we know about weeds. Walking the fields with the late C.J. Fenzau in areas as separate as Indiana, Iowa and Idaho, I was able to take note of what weeds were trying to tell us during the early days of the *Acres U.S.A.* publication. Admittedly, this knowledge has been fleshed out since then. And recent findings build on, rather than tear down, those field observations.

Weeds are an index of what is wrong — and sometimes what is right — with the soil, or at least with the fertility program. In every field on every farm, there are different soil types, and each has a potential for producing certain weeds, depending on how a farmer works the soil. Fall tillage, spring tillage, tillage early or late, if it takes place when the soil is dry or wet, all these things determine the kinds of weeds that will grow that season. As far back as the Dust Bowl days, it became transparently obvious to my Dad — after viewing rainbelt territory near Conway,

Missouri — that dryland weeds generally don't grow in territory that has rain pelting the soil with a steady squall. Thus the presence of salt grass, iron weed, tumbleweed and all the wild sages in soils where flocculation is gone, and wind wafts dust skyward. There are soil conditions that almost always have restricted amounts of water, and consequently they do not require and cannot grow weeds that thrive when there is plenty of water.

In high rainfall areas of the United States, where irrigation is paper thin and where farmers depend on rainfall for their crop moisture, broadleaf weeds — lambsquarters, pigweed, Jimson weed, buttonweed, and so on — often proliferate. These special conditions appeared classic when C.J. Fenzau and I walked several farms near What Cheer, Iowa one summer. Where the soil structure was poor and farmers worked the soil under wet conditions, they usually built compaction or set up sedimentary levels in the soil from filtration of silt. This set the stage for a lot of grassy weeds. And in only moments, it seemed, the corn farmer is forced to endure the vicious effects of foxtail and fall panicum. The soil's potential might remain. For the season, this pattern of weeds indicates a degenerated soil structure. That's the signal foxtail and fall panicum send out loud and clear — that there is an imbalanced pH condition in the soil, that tight soil is holding water in excess and refuses to permit it to dry out. As a consequence, the farmer is always working his soil system on the wet side and creating clods. When he gets done planting fields with clods, they accumulate excess carbon dioxide. Foxtail and fall panicum like carbon dioxide. This triggers certain hormone processes that wake up the foxtail seed and say, *It is your turn to live and multiply.*

To control the foxtail, it now becomes necessary to change the structure of the soil, and this means tillage, fertility management — not least, pH management, efficient use of water, development of capillary capacity and aeration of the soil. This much accomplished, there is no need for atrazine or other chemicals of organic synthesis.

I recall that in one corn field, planting had been delayed — sure enough, a pattern of rye grass made its stand. Here the crop was planted too long after cultivation. By the time seeds went into the soil, weeds were on the way. I recall one alfalfa field that had been the victim of poor soil management for seven or eight years. The soil was waterlogged and distressed. And weeds of several types increased and multiplied. It became standard procedure to recommend pH adjustment according to the gospel of Albrecht, and well digested compost. Compost contains its own nitrogen in perfectly available form. It often acts as a precursor of bacteria-fixing nitrogen in the field. Even then it was axiomatic that you never get blue-green algae with N, P, and K.

This business of management, or lack thereof, figured everywhere the *Acres U.S.A.* pencil and camera went. At one western dairy, it was practice to cut hay and treat it on the spot with an enzyme hormone complex, bio-cultured by Albion Laboratories out of Clearfield, Utah. In a matter of hours, the crop was put up as part of silage or hay bales. Before nightfall the same field got its shot of irrigation water. Weeds rarely got a toehold in such a well managed field, even though herbicides weren't used.

Weeds seem to have a pecking order. Once the conditions that permit foxtail and fall panicum are erased, there will be other weeds, but none of them will be as difficult to control or as hazardous to crop production. They have names, both Latin and common. Lambsquarters is one. Pigweed is another. But now the message is different. Both lambsquarter and pigweed say soil conditions are good and fertility is excellent, and there is no reason to come unglued when they appear, for they are as Joe Cocannouer says in *Weeds, Guardians of the Soil*, a message that the crop will thrive and insects will stay away.

Cocklebur also indicates that the soil's phosphate level is good. Lambsquarters, pigweed and cocklebur suggest a trio of superlatives, namely wholesome, highly productive, good quality soils. They are not hard to manage with clean tillage, and do not call for inputs of chemistry from the devil's pantry.

In watching crops grow, other clues have surfaced over the years. There are relatives of grasses that reflect wet soils and wet conditions. Barnyard grass and nut sedge warrant mention. On the other side of the equation, the same soil that produces each of these nemesis can produce ragweed, a dry weather phenomenon. This is particularly true when the crop is one of the small grains. Often the soil tends to dry out as the crop matures. With soil moisture low, bacterial systems do not function too well because, of course, they require water. They do not function to release or convert potassium in a proper form. When the potassium supply from the soil is restricted for whatever reason, or held in a complex form, ragweed reveals itself inside the grain crop. With harvest, contamination in the grain bin becomes apparent.

Ragweed tells the farmer that he has poor quality and a wrong form of potassium during the dry part of the crop season. In the cornbelt, when there is too much rain after fall plowing, and in early spring when cold, cloudy weather holds on for a three-week period, then fall-tilled fields still open will generate a whole new crop of bitterweed or smartweed. These arrive under wet soil conditions and grow early in the season. They are related to poorly structured and poorly drained soils. More important, these weeds shout out in understandable terms that something is wrong with the direction of decay of organic matter. Soil that is not in the proper equilibrium will put the decay process into the business of manufacturing alcohols and formaldehyde — in short, embalming fluids.

A good example is often the progenitor for morning glories and other rhizome crops that defy destruction. Picture cattle being fed out on the edge of a field. A lot of waste hay and straw piles up, cemented into place by urine and manure. Two or three years later this mixture is turned under, usually in an effort to return the area back to crop production. The problem is that Jimson weeds and buttonweeds, not crops, will grow. There is a reason for this. They are growing in soils with an excess of organic material that is not decaying properly. A hormone-enzyme process of a different bent takes over. It wakes up weed seeds and allows them to flourish.

The solution is not an overdose of herbicides, but manipulation of pH, distribution of the pileup of organic matter, which in any case must be mulched in more completely. When decay starts to go in the proper direction, Jimson weeds and buttonweeds simply stay dormant and no longer grow in that area. The same principle applies to morning glories and field bindweeds. The last two weeds grow in sick soils, in eroded soils, and in each case they increase and multiply because they are started by an improper decay of organic material.

Sometimes the decay process produces formaldehyde, and at certain stages there is methane, ethane and butane production. These byproducts of decay stimulate the birth of the hormone systems that penetrate ubiquitous weed seeds and tell them to come alive and establish the growth kingdom for that season. Generally, these processes do not occur throughout the entire field. Almost always, it is a spot here, an eroded hill there, always areas in which something has gone wrong in the past. These are dangerous weeds, and they are very destructive. They climb up plants and drag them down. They short-circuit yields and confer harvest problems on the best of machinery, and often account for farm accidents. Many farmers are maimed for life because they have tried to unplug harvesting equipment, the missing hand or arm a legacy of improper soil management.

There are many factors that have a bearing on weed patterns and crop performance. They're all interrelated. The ideal is to have pH control, good loamy soil texture, enough decaying organic matter to set the things in motion for better crop and changing weed patterns. These things diminish the frictions of stress and myriads of things that happen. Every year conditions are different and there has to be different timing. Variables invite changes. There is no way you can machine the process. You can have watergrass come into a waterlogged soil. The next year you waterlog it early and let it dry, and in the early part of the season you get smartweed, a variable of stress reaction. Different conditions invite a different echelon of life to come in. There is a variable in man — his operating style. I recall a farmer who had everything going perfect. But this year instead of taking a spiketooth rake and dragging it over the corn as it was emerging, the worker assigned the task. By the time he got around to it, the weeds were three inches tall. Corn was coming up puny. It was enough to make one shudder. Physical management mistakes can undo everything.

These few observations from the field already suggest that the topic of weeds is a very complex subject. The best weed manual in the world can only hint at solutions to the many problems related to weeds. Unfortunately, those who have taken the weed situation by the nape of the neck and the seat of the pants over the past fifty years have done little more than shake out poisons, not results. Here our objective is to establish a positive viewpoint so that we can analyze what weeds are and accept the Creator's plan while we appreciate the romance of the tribe.

There are many mansions in the house of weeds. For example, there are swamp weeds, the cattails and the rushes. There are desert weeds. There are weeds that grow in sand and weeds that grow in silt, and there are weeds that grow in gumbo so tight it resembles modeling clay. Foxtails grow in gumbo, but they also grow in sand when such soils are out of balance and the electrical tension on soil particles is so tight that even sand can build clods and restrict air in the soil enough to set free the hormone process that wakes up foxtail seeds.

There are subsoil weeds. There are weeds that grow in acid conditions and — in the West — there are weeds that like alkaline conditions. Up in Wisconsin and Minnesota there is a weed called devil's paint brush by the locals. This one joins the daisy in having a love affair with sour soils. Almost always, such soils have an excess of iron and flush out a lot of trace minerals and rock minerals that support the hormone processes that give permission to live for these weed species. It is impossible to grow a high yielding crop when such conditions prevail. It is possible to grow red clover, mammoth clover instead of alfalfa because alfalfa simply won't have much of a chance as a quality foliage crop. There are sour soils, neutral soils, alkaline soils and salty soils, and there are weeds that identify with all of these conditions. There are weeds that relate to wet soils and weeds that embrace hot conditions and others that like colder conditions. The degree of sunshine and the length of day and night figure in nature's equation.

There are weeds that get a head start on the farmer and those that emerge only after the farmer has done his job. All of these weeds have a biography and all seem to share their prophecy with those who look and actually see.

Take rotten weeds, weeds that actually exhibit rotting conditions in the soil. Take stinky weeds and fungal weeds. All reflect the sour, sick, dead excess toxic level of soil components. There are even herbicide indicator weeds, weeds that grow too well after an accumulation of a certain level of herbicides, usually over several years. Such weeds build up a negative effect on the desirable biological things that have to happen if crop production is to be successful. These weeds tell the United States Department of Agriculture that a measure of madness is afloat when spokesmen make their annual pronouncement that without herbicides and chemicals fifty million U.S. citizens would starve. There is a damning finality to the evidence that has piled up since *Acres U.S.A.* began publication twenty-five years ago, because this evidence proves that soils subjected to herbicide use year after year have now achieved a negative depressing effect and gifted degeneration to the soil system, with resultant shortfalls in crop yields. Once such soils are cleansed of herbicide residues, yields can be increased as much as 50 to 75% without the addition of more fertilizer inputs. Moreover, once these soil conditions are corrected, there is a chance to manage the weeds without the use of toxic genetic chemicals.

Every weed, generally within twenty-four to forty-eight hours after germination, has the ability to emit auxins. These are growth factors that come off the seed via rootlets and penetrate out into the soil, sometimes as much as a half-inch from the seed itself. That auxin tells every other species in the immediate neighborhood to stay asleep. There are hundreds and thousands of seeds in every square foot of soil, and yet only so many germinate and grow each year. They seem to know better than to crowd each other out. Another year, other seeds get their chance. As we will see in the next chapter, there are enough seed deposits in most soils to last fifty, one hundred, even five hundred years, and some seeds live that long. As long as the chemistry and biology and environmental conditions are there, certain species will wait. The dust storms did not annihilate the tumbleweed seeds or terminate the prickly pear, and all the laws passed to proscribe noxious weeds or prevent seed transport from farm to farm, county to county or state to state are merely so many monuments to the stupidity of man.

There is a lesson in all this. As the weed seed germinates, it emits those growth factors. Astute farmers can use weeds to their benefit. In the spring, when preparing the rootbed, watch the warming and the curing and the ripening and the germinating capacity of the soil system being established. Always, certain weed seeds will start to germinate. The day that you go out and scratch the soil and see germinated weeds with roots about an inch long, that is the time to change the concentration of carbon dioxide and oxygen in the rootbed, and place the desired crop seed. Within the first twenty-four hours that little weed seed has done its job. It has given off auxins enough to dormatize every other weed seed next to it. It is nature's form of population control. It just allows certain weed seeds to come alive and stake out a proper domain, meaning space to ensure enough light, air, drainage, ventilation and carbon dioxide to prosper and produce new seed, the Creator's purpose for a plant. At the stage of its growth when it germinates, that little weed seed is very susceptible to dying. It can be killed easily simply by taking light tillage equipment through the soil to change the oxygen content. Cation balance, pH, the phosphate level, moisture, air — all determine how long an auxin system will endure in the seedbed. Soils that are completely dead and have no biological capacity, no balance, no equilibrium, soils abused to death with hard chemistry or imbalanced inputs of salt fertilizers, make it possible for the weed crop to hit the ground running, so to speak. Auxins from weeds can endure in the soil for as long as six to eight weeks. Unfortunately, in most soils managed under the precepts of mainline agriculture, crop auxins can endure only three or four days. That is why partial and imbalanced fertilization usually becomes a sales ticket for insurance spraying, a benchmark for the chemical amateur.

Thus the equilibrium established in the soil determines how long growth factors can endure and exercise a dormatizing effect on a crop of weeds. If good biological management gives the crop seed time enough to send out its hormones and say, *I command power over this domain for this generation*, weeds cease to be the grower's boogeyman and coffee klatch excuse for bad farming.

No one need accept my word for this. As Rudolf Steiner often said, "Experiment, experiment!" Almost every corn grower finds that certain rows were missed or that there are gaps in certain rows. The instant impulse is to replant, sometimes one seed at a time. But it never comes to anything. The new and later plants lack vigor and seem deprived of the potential they ought to have. The reason is simple. The other rows out there have already taken command over that soil domain and do everything they can to shut down the come-lately arrivals. They have sent their hormones out into the soil, and injected a negative effect for the replants to field.

That is why it is necessary when planting any seed crop to control the depth of planting and the spacing of the seed, so that they all come up on equal footing.

Any seed that germinates one or two or four days later than the seed placed next to it never has the potential for producing a high-yielding, field-ripened harvest. Weeds have the most serious effect on crop production during the first week or ten days of their life. That is why a small weed, one only a half inch above the surface of the soil, has such negative effect on the yield and quality of the crop.

C.J. Fenzau, my consultant for *An Acres U.S.A. Primer*, was so adamant on this point he sometimes repeated it several times in the same conversation. "We must control weeds in the early stages," he would say. "Once the crop is this tall [indicating a foot or more] and a few weeds arrive underneath, they aren't going to have much of a chance to do a lot of damage."

Across more counties than most people see in a lifetime, this has been the lesson I learned "watching crops grow." You can live with these weeds because they have less effect on yield and quality than when the corn crop is emerging from the soil with weeds arriving at the same time. In theory some of the pre-emergent herbicides set up this condition, but their legacy of damage is worse than the problem they presume to solve.

The bottom line is simply that good soil structure, good soil drainage and good aeration can control biological activity in the soil. In turn, the farmer can increase the nutrient supply and grow a high-yield crop even if a few weeds are supported underneath. But a sick soil with inadequate nutrient release and conversion will have a depressing effect on the yield potential. This allows the weeds to have a more negative effect simply because there are not enough nutrients to feed both the desired crop and the weeds. It also allows weeds to impose water limitations.

Weeds can set up severe competition for water, plant nutrients, air and light. If a crop is dominating and restricting the amount of light, then the light that filters through to the weeds underneath is subdued. Thus the weed is not able to grow as fast as its programed genetic potential might otherwise allow. Instead of having a fat stemmed plant with a lot of root capacity, it is restricted because it failed to get enough light, and thus becomes a weak, thin-stemmed plant, one with smaller heads. Any farm reporter who travels from one end of the country to the next can observe how weeds reflect reasonable variables such as altitude, sea level conditions, the amount of light and the angle at which the sun is exposed to that part of the earth. All these things have a bearing on establishing the character and the form and the potential of various weeds. You see some weeds that are short and blocky and thick-stemmed with great leaves, and others that are tall with thin stems and small leaves. These are all reflections of growing conditions. That is why weeds are an indicator of the limitations that exist. Farmers who learn how to read them find that this knowledge confers an ability to make better management decisions on how to live with weeds and still grow a good crop.

Our journey in this little book will take us into that gigantic mix-master of names and styles of weeds. For now it seems appropriate to walk through farm management practices worthy of consideration. How they fit soils in any area and how they dovetail with crop systems projections becomes all important for the grower who wants to minimize the hazards of weeds so that he does not have to depend on the obscene presence of herbicides to control them.

Fall tillage has to be considered *number one*. It is the first thing a farmer should want to do, yet every fall when the crop is harvested, that bad weather always seems to arrive. Often the fall work does not get done. The farmer is too busy harvesting and he can't get in there and do the tillage. Moreover, most crops are harvested late because schoolbook technology has given us degenerated soils. We do not convert and use fertilizers, nitrogen and other fertility factors locked up in the soil to properly grow field-ripened crops. Proper fertility management would see to it that harvest can take place a month earlier and thus permit time for that fall work. That is when compaction could be best removed, when trash could be mulched in. That is also the time when pH modifiers could be applied. That is when lime and other nutrients could be used to influence the quality and character of the soil's pH, all in time to meld into the soil during fall and over winter.

It is this procedure that would make the soil come alive in spring and get the growing season underway so that crops can germinate a week or ten days earlier.

Fall tillage is an important key to weed management. It is certainly one way to diminish the chances for foxtail and grass type weeds. If fall tillage is used to put soil systems into ridges, those ridges will drain faster in spring. They will warm up a week to ten days earlier. They will have germinating capacity restored earlier and permit planting earlier so that the economic crop can get a head start on weeds. Once the soil is conditioned, it won't be necessary to turn the soil so much in spring. Obviously, every time the soil is turned, more weed seeds already in the soil are exposed to sunlight and warmth and other influences that wake them out of dormancy. Soil bedded in the fall, with pH modified so that the structure does not permit crusting when spring rains arrive, will permit rain to soak in faster, bringing air behind it. Such a soil will warm faster and therefore determine the hormone process that will take place. Good water and air entry into the soil will not likely set the stage for foxtail, nut sedge, watergrass and other debilitating influences on the crop.

When the cash crop is germinated under these conditions, that is when your little pigweeds and lambsquarters, your broadleaf weeds — which require a good quality available phosphate — hand off their message. They say the phosphate conversion is good and the fertility release system is more than adequate to grow a high-yielding crop. Such broadleafs are easy to manage. When they germinate and achieve growth of an inch or less, and you tickle the soil before you insert the seed, they are easily killed off. As a consequence, the hormone process gains the upper hand for four to six weeks, a time frame that permits the crops to grow big enough to be cultivated.

Needless to say, the bio-grower has to depend on proper decay of organic materials in the soil. Root residue and crop stover are always present, and these have a direct bearing on how prolific weeds might grow. This means farmers, one and all, must learn how to manage decay of organic matter better.

As we incorporate it into the soil, preside over proper decay conditions by pH management and regulate the water either present or absent, we achieve plenty of air and good humid conditions that will allow organic material to decay properly and in the right direction to provide the steady supply of carbon dioxide necessary for a higher yield. While adjustments are being made in the soil — soils are sometimes out of equilibrium for years — it is unrealistic to expect the situation will be corrected in a single season or a single month. We can speed the process with the application of properly composted manures. The point here is that there is a difference between quality of various composts, just as there is a difference between predigested manures and manures sheet composted in the soil itself.

Readers of *Acres U.S.A.* in general, and those who have enjoyed the short book, *Pottenger's Cats*, will recall how that great scientist planted dwarf beans in beach sand at Monrovia, California as part of an experiment. Cats had been raised on that beach sand. Some had been fed evaporated milk, others raw meat, still others meat that had been cooked to achieve near total enzyme-destroying potential and some had been fed on raw milk. Cats fed evaporated milk, cooked meat — dung going into the beach sand — produced a dilapidated, depressed crop of beans. Cats fed whole milk — their dung also going into the beach sand, produced a prolific and extended crop, the dwarf bean variety growing to the top of a six-foot-high cage. The quality of manures used in composting have a direct bearing on the performance of that compost.

Experience has taught all those who wish to see that the kind of compost Fletcher Sims of Canyon, Texas introduces into the soil has many desirable fungal systems of bacteria and molds. These have the capacity to attack rhizome roots of quackgrass, Johnsongrass, and those type of roots so far under the top of the soil they cannot be reached with physical tools. Compost tells us that we have to set in motion an environment with antagonistic fungi that will attack the rhizomes when they are in a dormant phase as the season begins to close.

In late August and early September, the length of the day shortens. Everything starts to go into fall dormancy. If at that time we can apply a wholesome, properly composted material to the soil and have it working for thirty days before the soil freezes and becomes inactive, a lot of weed cleanup work takes place at that time. Compost will simply digest most of the dormant weed seeds, and in two or three years of this approach seeds are literally vacuumed up, like soil particles on the family room carpet.

The key is timing. When weeds go into dormancy, they are subject to decay. They can be turned into fresh humus, rather than a charge of gunpowder ready to explode. Quackgrass in particular responds to the compost treatment. With calcium-adjusted pH, compost will attack quackgrass roots and rot them out in one season. The same principle operates with deep-rooted rhizomes, Johnsongrass and thistles.

If the character of the nutrient that went into Pottenger's cats had a bearing on the quality of the dung, the same thing applies to the manure sources used in making compost.

This last statement should send up a warning sign. Commercial feedlots — the late William A. Albrecht called them *bovine concentration camps* — have too much medicated material, too many salts, too many steroids flowing into the animal manure. Animals cannot digest these materials. It takes judgment, brains and high science to turn such manure into fit compost.

The simplest way to start a biological weed control program, then, is to adjust the pH. This affects the intake of water and makes it possible to manage water. In the cornbelt, where rain often comes at the wrong time and where droughts frustrate the best of intentions, this management of water and its capillary return is front burner stuff. pH management directly relates to so many desirable things, there is justification for referring the reader to the several volumes of *The Albrecht Papers* for background insight.

Each weed has a direct bearing on the track record of the farm. Each reflects back to what the farmer has done correctly or incorrectly over the years. Too often — in this age of super mechanization — we have large fields with soft spots and hard textured soils. The farmer moves across one then over the next area because he feels impelled to farm big fields with big machinery. All the low soil is too wet, and so a pass through sets the stage for wild oats or foxtail in corn, or fall panicum. Some soils get the wrong treatment simply because they, not the weeds, are in the wrong place. It may be that the eco-farmer will have to redesign the shape of his fields, or plant in strips so that similar types of soils can be planted at the same time, with due regard being given to the need for soils to dry out and warm up and drain properly. It might be better to wait a couple of weeks. A little delay is better than wet soil work which leaves no chance at all for a crop.

Elsewhere in this volume, we'll cover the business of weeds as related to insects. The great Professor Phil Callahan has given us a roadmap that cannot be ignored. He called it *Tuning In To Nature*, and in it he related how the energy in the infrared that is given off by a plant is the signal for insect invasion. It stands to reason that a plant that is subclinically ill will give off a different wavelength than the one with balanced hormone and enzyme systems. That these signals match up with the signals of lower phylum plants is more than speculation. While writing *An Acres U.S.A. Primer*, I often made field observations that supported Callahan. It became obvious that when farmers did certain things in the soil, the crop could endure the presence of insects because they seemed incapable of doing much damage. I didn't know how the mechanism worked, at least not before the release of *Tuning In To Nature*.

Weeds are going to tell about the nutritional supply, and they therefore rate as a worthy laboratory for making judgments about the soil's nutritional system. They can often reveal the nutrients that must be added to the foliage of the growing crop to react with the negative effects of stress. After all, all growing seasons have variable degrees of timing and stress. It is not only necessary to arrive with nutritional support in time, it is mandatory.

The many mansions in the house of weeds all have family histories. They tell more about gene splicing and DNA manipulation than all the journals of genetic engineering put together. And if we pay attention during class, weeds are our greatest teachers. To learn our lessons, we have only to get into the business of watching weeds grow.

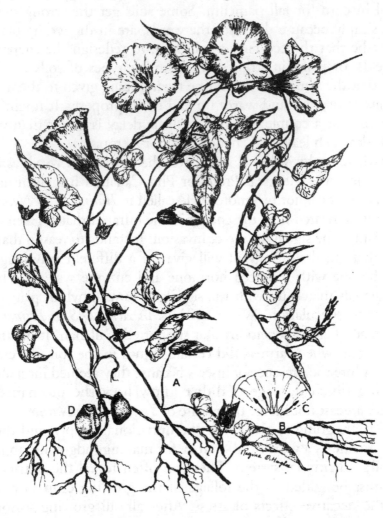

Hedge bindweed, Convolvulus sepium, *is both a terror and an educational text. So is field bindweed, a blood brother. All the bindweeds dominate when there is a short circuit in the energy release of fouled decay systems. These soil limitations have to be corrected via pH management. Microorganisms in well digested compost help attack the shallow creeping rhizomes that make bindweed such a crop destroyer. Pictured here is the plant (A); rootstock (B); the flower showing structure (C); and seeds (D).*

3

FIELDS OF UNKRAUT

According to scholarly studies that parade each genus and species across their pages in acres of print, the names of certain
plants now called weeds go back to the Egyptians and the
Greeks and the Chinese, but these ancient peoples usually
thought of plants like mustard, pond weeds, and castor beans in
terms of their extracts as medicinal remedies and not as nuisance
plants. It would take an etymologist with lots of patience to iso-
late this word history, a task I never considered necessary. In
western Kansas we had a word for weeds and weed killers. The
first was the German word *unkraut*, and the second was *un-
krautvertilgungsmittel*, which said it all. There was no need to
worry about a weed being a plant out of place, and it would be
decades before a terminology committee of the Weed Society of
America would come up with its whiz-bang definition, "A plant
growing where it is not desired."

Nature would be shocked at such childishness. Plants have a
right to grow where conditions are right. Schoolmen might
decide that one of God's own is "of wild and rank growth,"

known for its "persistence and resistance to control or eradication," "useless, unwanted and undesirable," but the fact remains that few weeds are worthless, and whether they are unsightly and disfigure the landscape — as some believe to be the case with the dandelion — well, beauty or the lack thereof is indeed in the eye of the beholder. One has only to turn to *Medical Botany*, a text that examines plant sources for well known remedies such as digitalis, strychnine and aspirin, and *Use of Plants*, a special compendium that covers the findings of those who reached beyond the fringes of accepted science over the centuries, to discover nature's secrets locked in plants.

USDA's *Selected Weeds of the United States* covers two hundred twenty-four weed species, usually cropland and pasture weeds, but with emphasis on weeds prevalent in croplands and aquatic sites. No less than ninety-three — not quite half — surface in *Medical Botany* and *Use of Plants*. There is lore here that could fill the pages of this book, and never allow a side departure into the business of understanding cropland weeds. For now it is enough to note that *Selected Weeds* contains one hundred thirty-one weeds not a matter of entry in any of the texts on useful plants commonly available.

One of the best books on weeds I've ever seen, *Report of the Kansas Board of Agriculture, Weeds in Kansas*, came out of the Kansas state printing plant. It was written before WWII by Frank C. Gates, Ph.D., when J.C. Mohler was Secretary of State. My Dad's copy somehow survived the great Missouri Valley and Neosho River flood of 1950, and became my personal property when that gentle gentleman passed from the scene at age ninety-two. Coverless and stained, this manual has yielded some of the art and a good part of the technical nomenclature used here in extract and abstract form, leaving me and my associates free to concentrate on newer insight into fields of *unkraut*.

There are weeds that many farmers see as truly noxious, a terror to crop production and a steady reminder that life could be lovely if somehow these invaders were eliminated from the face of the earth. These are, in a word, *unkraut*. They prompt normally placid farmers to curse a blue streak and they cause legislatures, in their wisdom, to write laws proscribing them. Kansas became so incensed at the spread of field bindweed in 1937 that the state legislature officially went to war with this pest, with promoters of the law holding out the idea that one after the other various noxious weeds could be eradicated. Farmers were required by law to take on this responsibility on their land, and state agencies were charged with the same responsibility on public lands. Such laws proliferated, state by state, the hope being that a dollop of the right poison would accomplish this eradication chore. Legislators forgot, if they ever knew, that nature never disobeys her own laws, and rarely obeys those created by man.

With the right programming in each weed's DNA, the plants would have hooted aloud at the lawmakers' threats in any case. Weeds must be considered the world's first travelers. For eons of time they have traveled on the wings of the wind. They have tagged along on the furs of animals and meandered cross-country in the gizzards of birds. Long before commerce took to hauling basic storable commodities around the world, weeds walked with the nomads and the military, and like other camp followers often left their progeny behind. Weed scientists have a name for this, *tribethe synanthropes*. And thus we are told about seed migrations across the Mediterranean in hay bales used by armies for animal fodder. Weed detectives have turned up a single synanthrope on the Isle of Lero and two dozen near the Acropolis of Athens. The Confederate violet has been associated with Civil War camping grounds, and certain weeds where the Indians camped are now a part of frontier lore. One can trace Oriental and Siberian trade and migration routes by the weeds that were dropped and fertilized by human beings and animals on trace and trail. There is irony in this travel record. Many weeds leave their country of origin, where they are held in check by insect predators, only to find a clime so congenial that they spread and become, in a word, noxious. The oat crop provides an excellent example. Indeed, it has been possible to determine the country of oat seeds simply by cataloging the weed seeds that came along as unwanted fellow travelers. Oats and wheat from the lower Volga in Russia conferred on the American high plains corn cockle, wild vetches, the tumbleweed and field bindweed. It has been recorded that seeds from Turkey can be expected to truck along *Rapistrum rugosum*, an unidentified Medicago, as well as darnel and sweet clovers. Ball mustard, blue bur and prairie sunflower came from Canada. And the British sent over black bindweed and charlock as contaminants with oats that also contained wild oats. Of some seventy weeds described in *Farm Weeds of Canada*, forty-seven are earmarked as coming from Europe, one from mainland Asia, one from tropical America, with only twenty-one being rated as indigenous.

Once they cross the oceans, weed seeds defy any man born of woman to stop their spread — if conditions for their growth are right. Drummers moving from farm to farm have exposed their clients to more than a new line of merchandise. Indeed, an inventory of weed seeds in trampled mud between a public road and a field of chalky Boulder clay revealed the following:

Arable weeds from the field: slender foxtail, scarlet pimpernel, charlock, lambsquarters, dwarf spurge, knotgrass, groundsel, field speedwell.

Grassland plants from grass by the side of the road: ryegrass, cattail, greater plantain, broadleaf dock, and quackgrass.

Weeds from both situations: silverweed and creeping thistle.

Farm wagons and vehicles take arable weeds into grass fields for temporary residence, and many a farmer has registered both surprise and consternation to find a once clean field suddenly infested with things like shepherd's purse, swinecress, camomile, mayweed, spurry and poppies — all of them tracing the tracks of wheels long after the vehicles have gone back to the pole barn. Such experiences have suggested laws to achieve eradication, it being the conventional wisdom that a law or a war will solve everything.

Storm columns have been credited with moving everything from wild onion to tufted vetch, including roots, to sites miles and even counties down track. Cut fragments of yarrow have impregnated the soil that way, and rooted plants of bird's foot trefoil, horseshoe vetch, mouse-ear-chickweed and shepherd's purse have done the same. Wild chervil and autumnal hawkbit, both move across jurisdictional lines on the violence of storm columns, and there is very little a legislative chamber can do about it. Restharrow will infest a new field from broken pieces that way, as will tufted vetch. The same is true of yellow rattle and sheep's sorrel. Chickweed often leapfrogs across the country-side. These are only a few samples. More details will be provided with individual weed biographies in another section of this book.

For now it is enough to cite a few mechanisms that are of maximum interest. First in line are specialties such as wild carrot, goosegrass, corn buttercup, plants provided by nature with various types of hooks that fasten to the coats of animals and clothing of human beings. Some — such as shepherd's needle — have less discernable hooks, but they have this capacity to cling, ride along, then drop just the same. The bent awn is in a class all its own, being blessed with a hygroscopic character. The awn twists and untwists depending on the humidity in the air.

The most persistent weeds are those that creep under the soil, send up shoots, mosey inches further, then repeat the process. When rootlets are given off from creeping stems, and when such weeds are mascerated or cut, the pieces fight it out on their own, striking roots for themselves when they can. Some, such as bindweed, horsetail, quackgrass and sheep's sorrel have thin underground stems. Corn sowthistle is usually stouter, whereas coltsfoot is often thick as a finger, somewhat fleshy, and goes down several feet into the soil before turning horizontally to creep away immediately below the surface. Then branches are sent up at a regular intervals.

One has to be amazed at the ingenuity used by weeds to obey the Biblical injunction to increase and multiply. Wild onion provides a good horrible example. It reproduces by seeds and also by underground bulbs, but since these systems might fail, the wild onion relies on its insurance mechanism. It has small bulbils at the base of the flower stalks. Often flowers are missing, which means the flower head simply has a main stalk with a cluster of small bulbs. The bulbs ripen and shower the soil with an onion squall, and of course the wild onion proliferates. This triple whammy for reproduction is hard to control, whatever the method.

Withal, most weeds are nevertheless reproduced from seeds and the plants almost always have seeds a'plenty. Hundreds of thousands of seeds are more the rule than the exception. Fat hen, knotgrass, bindweed, field pansy, persecaria, chickweed, speedwell, goosegrass plantain, black bindweed, spurry, sandwort, scarlet pimpernel, toadflax and mayweed not only produce an abundance of seeds, they also provide nourishment to birds. These birds then pass seeds through their digestive tracts, and as nature would have it, some few survive digestion and are unloaded, their shells humbled by digestive acids and ready to grow. Deposited on the soil, they increase and multiply, defying the wiles and laws of men, and mocking those of little vision who would legislate biology. Fortunately, nature has decreed that no weed should have a free reign. Like government, they need checks and balances, which they have in abundance if we have the wit to see.

Maybe this unwillingness to be governed helps weeds turn outlaw and take on aliases. Weeds are not only the world's greatest travelers, they are perhaps the world's most practiced con artists. They change their names as they march across county, state and national lines, and pretend to be members of families to which they don't belong. Even the practice of giving weeds a somewhat Latinized moniker hasn't made the tribe turn entirely honest. The idea of genus and species for each plant in a sort of coined Latin was born — not without umbilical cord — in the fertile mind of Carolus Linnaeus. Historians tell us that his name was really Carl von Linne, but Latinizing his own name seemed a suitable precursor to naming each plant from a classical tongue. Carl Linnaeus was born in Sweden in 1707.

In those days people chose a Latin name as part of the Christian baptism ritual. "Linnaeus or Linne are the same to me," he once said, "One in Latin, the other Swedish." Since he bylined his writings Linnaeus, naturalists came to know him by that name. He wrote some one hundred eighty books in his lifetime, which ended three years after the American revolution started, or 1778. Archivists refer to *Genera Plantarum* and *Species Plantarum* as his *magnum opus*. In those literary outpourings, he mined everything in print from the works of Pliny the Elder on, including the massive three volume work of Tournefort with its name that can hardly be translated to English unless we accept a compromise and call it *Principles of Botany*. There were others too numerous to mention, most of which recited descriptions rather than giving plants names.

Linnaeus was the first to define kingdoms — animal, vegetable, mineral. All plants belong to the kingdom called *plant*. Each kingdom has a phylum, which is a division of the kingdom. In turn, a class is made up of lesser groups called order, and these in turn are made up of families. Families are made up of genera — genus — and finally species. Here's how the complete classification of the Russian thistle, except tumbleweed would read:

Kingdom . . . Plant
   Phylum . . . Spermatothyta
      Class . . . Dicotyledoneae
         Order . . . Chenopodiales
            Family . . . Chenopodiacae
               Genus . . . *Salsola*
                  Species . . . *kali*
                     Variety . . . tennuifolia

Corn cockle was a pet antipathy of the Volga German immigrants who created the greatest bread basket of the world in the U.S. high plains. They cursed this weed in Russia, then brought it over in their wheat seed and cursed it again. Stone ground with winter wheat, it made bread taste bad. Agrostemma githago is shown here (A); its flower (B); the calyx or outer part of the perianth — corolla of a flower (C); fruit capsule (D); and the seed (E).

Not everyone agrees, but I like to write genus and species with the first word capitalized, the second word lower case, both italicized. Genus by itself takes a capital letter, sans italics. That's the way my mentor, Dr. Robert L. Anderes, taught me when I handled an editorial pencil at *Veterinary Medicine* magazine and, like most things classical, I consider it a sacrilege to change.

Some of my readers wonder aloud how it is that I love idioms and the vernacular while still insisting on the flavor of the old church tongue for certain purposes. I won't argue that the Requiem Mass by Wolfgang Amadeus Mozart is the most beautiful piece of music ever written — which it is — because we have to allow each his own. Some people prefer music that is to sound what a bran-stuffed Holstein's issue — backed to a barn door after a heavy clyster — is to art, and this is their business. But Latinized names for each weed make it possible for competent persons in every language to communicate and understand. In this sense, Latin is a living language. The craft of the systematist requires it. Linnaeus saw that there were simply too many vernacular names in any case, each weed, each alias masquerading as the real thing — except there was no real thing. Geographical names meant little. Cherokee rose, widespread in the American South, actually came from China. Arabian jasmine didn't migrate from the Mideast at all, but from India. Spanish cedar has nothing to do with Spain. It actually ran its roots in West Indies soil as home base, and is not a cedar or even a conifer. The list of deception is endless, with a Jerusalem designation leading the list. The Jerusalem artichoke is really a North American plant, and has nothing to do with the Mediterranean region. And the first name, Jerusalem, in this case is actually a corruption of an Italian word some might feel should not be printed. Suffice it to say that Bethlehem sage is not Judean and French mulberry is neither French nor a mulberry. Since few plants had common names, Linnaeus figured he'd supply the much needed common denominator. He'd invent names and bring plants together according to kind or character, which journalists soon distorted to the *genus* we still use today. He must have been an erudite humorist, this Linnaeus. He used a term for ragweed, *ambrosia*, usually reserved for wine sniffing, possibly so followers of weed lore could get a snootful of really rank odor when checking him out. Sometimes he bowed to tradition and used a Latin word that was a literal translation.

The English language is in a dilemma nowadays because of the drive to desex the sentences and paragraphs we use. Any editorial desk receives constant advice to use bastardized terms like *chairperson* and *womanager* instead of chairman and manager, for instance. This has never been a problem in Latin. It may be considered a dead language but it has lively expressions. It is an inflected language, meaning words change form to denote different genders. If the ending is *us*, it means the noun is the subject of the sentence. If it ends in *um*, it means the noun is the object. All nouns are masculine, feminine or neuter. *Ceanothus americanus* is a masculine name, for instance. *Cimicifuga americana* is feminine. And *Narthecium americanum* is neuter.

This much said, we must now face the reality that certain weeds have too many folk names, and sometimes different weeds claim the same common name. Two weeds lay claim to being the genuine tumbleweed, although each has a distinct Latinized name. This accounted for an agonizing decision in writing these chapters, whether to recite the scientific nomenclature each time a weed is mentioned, or to rely on an index so that readers can look up the scientific name if the folk name was not adequate for total communication. Too much Latin can make a sentence almost unreadable. For instance, here are a few of the weeds mentioned in chapter two of this book, except that now those cited weeds have been fleshed out with scientific names attached: salt grass, *Distichlis stricta*; tall ironweed, *Vernonia altissima*; tumbleweed, *Salsola kali*, or *Amaranthus graecizans* (white pigweed); lambsquarters, *Chenopodium album*; green amaranthus, *Amaranthus hybridus*; Jimson weed, *Datura stramoni-*

um; buttonweed, *Diodia teres*; foxtail, *Hordeum jubatum*; fall panicum, *Panicum dichotomiflorum*.

I have concluded that sometimes the mention of the Linnaeus-style name is indicated, sometimes not, the matter being a judgment call. After all, who really knows that the Rhododendron has a common name, rose bay? I am equally at a loss to explain why the public wants to trill names like Chrysanthemum, Amaryllis, Hydrangea, Ranunculus, or Calceolaria over its collective tongue, genus names, all of them. At the same time, few would agree to say Agrostemma instead of corn cockle, or *Andropogon virginicus* instead of broom sedge.

There is an *Acres U.S.A.* office saying that there are only three absolutes in this world: never march on Moscow in the winter, never engage in a land war in Asia, and never question the authority Bargyla Rateaver — a frequent contributor to the journal — on matters of plant nomenclature. Rateaver would prefer instant Latin identification for every weed, but I think farmer readers will prefer the way I handle this knotty problem.

One thing is certain: weeds are sublimely indifferent to man's problems. They have their marching orders — a built-in computer that tells them when to sleep, when to wake up, how to tap into nutrients and how to concentrate plant food for the construction of strange molecules. Their coded DNAs largely have yet to be broken by science, biological propaganda to the contrary.

When weeds grow, there is always a good reason. When they travel and propagate themselves, there is always method to their madness. They are born teachers, if we have the wit to learn. They have character, sometimes more character than the production crops we cherish. They share the plant kingdom and maintain a connection that requires appreciation, not condemnation. Of this connection to every form of life we sing during the rest of our journey through the fields of *unkraut*.

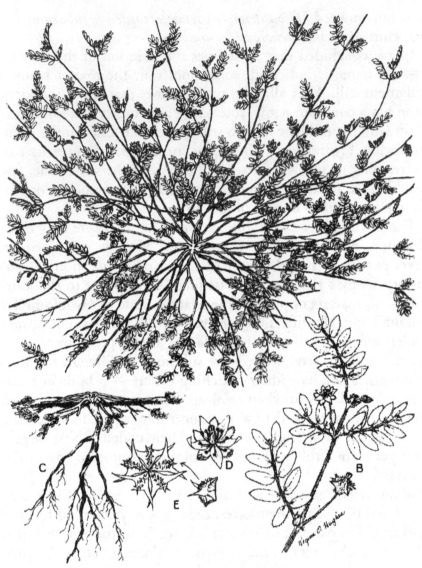

Puncture vine, Tribulus terrestris, *harbors blister beetles, which in turn strike out from their home base to torment commercial crops. The helicopter view (A) tells a part of the story. Its burs are a menace to man and beast. Its horns penetrate tires. Here is the flowering branchlet (B); the taproot system side view (C); a flower (D); and fruits (E). There's one seed to each fruit compartment.*

4
THE WEED-INSECT CONNECTION

Nature never violates her own laws. This was stated as an axiom in an earlier chapter. And it comes to mind again when we review the record of attempts to set insects against weeds with the expectation of the first annihilating the second. *Biological Control of Weeds* designates a world catalog of agents and their target weeds, most of the agents being insects. It lists exotic invertebrates and fungi released over half a century, and records the mixed bag of results. As often as not the tag line seems to be, "Established, but effects negligible," or "Not effective in terrestrial habitats," and so on. This has prompted me to wonder what it is about the weed-insect connection that keeps one from prevailing over another. Obviously plants have coexisted with insects through eons of time, each with a defense mechanism against the other.

Insects have a genetic code locked in their hormone systems. This can be best illustrated by examining the gypsy moth caterpillar. This insect has three types of hormones, one governing the larval stage, another for the pupa, one for the adult. The minute an egg is hatched, brain hormones put in motion a hormone called ecdysone. At this moment in the life cycle, a gland near the brain touches off the so-called juvenile hormone, and this hormone represses all but the gene group controlling larval development. During the larval stage, the juvenile hormone acts like an anchor on cellular activity, meaning that it prevents the insect from maturing too fast. In the life cycle, the juvenile hormone disappears. This pulls up the anchor and turns on the full force of ecdysone. Come winter, or a change of diet, the brain secretion is shut off and life goes dormant.

This general process is complicated in the extreme. For a long time entomologists found the source of hormone generation most elusive. It was, in fact, a matter of serendipity that accounted for the discovery of a principle folk gardeners knew all along. The paper toweling used to line cages seemed to act on larvae exactly like juvenile hormones. Finally it was narrowed down to the fact that fir trees from which the paper towels were made contained a juvenile hormone-like material. Nature has caused fir trees to grow their own defense mechanism against insects, in this case the gypsy moth.

As word got around the scientific world, investigators found what they called analogues of ecdysone in yew trees, evergreens, in lots of places. A Harvard man named Lynn M. Riddilford discovered that mere contact with a juvenile hormone fatally deranged embryonic development of life in insect eggs. Nature apparently created this device so that plants could protect themselves and shut down the danger of insects gaining an upper hand and annihilating all vegetable growth on the planet.

This check on insects suggested a new commercial enterprise. By juggling hormones, and by making use of analogues of hormones, entrepreneurs hoped to create a super-sterilization effect as a chain reaction, much as when venereal disease races through a human population. And with that vision in place, research seemed to vanish as each of the companies raced to develop salable products ahead of the competitors. All seemed to forget that plants had to grow with balanced hormone and enzyme systems, and that the defense potential could not be conferred via spray or genetic engineering without reference to plant and soil management. In eco-agriculture, many farmers realized that they could grow crops with the defenses researchers found in those fir trees. The symbiotic love-hate relationship between weeds and insects must be viewed with the above inventory of information in mind.

On balance, weeds can defend themselves against insects to a marked degree, which probably explains why the *Biological Control of Weeds* roster suggests only marginal success in many cases, with notations such as "large populations developing" generally reserved for programs that bring in an entirely new insect agent, a procedure often fraught with dangerous consequences. Nevertheless, insects and plant diseases rely on weeds for over-wintering in many cases, and it can be stated fairly that each weed has its parasites and associates. We've mentioned the prickly pear, a denizen of western Kansas that was transported to Australia, where it proceeded to run wild. When *Cactoblastis cactorum* was introduced into Australia it provided excellent control for the prickly pear cacti then ruining millions of acres of good grazing land.

The parasites that keep weeds in check may be few, according to species, such as in the case of poison ivy. Or they may be many, as is the case with lambsquarters, tumbleweed (*Salsola kali*), ironweed and sunflower. Insects utilize weeds as food and shelter. It is axiomatic that when weeds proliferate, outbreaks of insects follow. When the Russian thistle became the only crop that would really thrive during a forage failure in the mid 1930s, an outbreak of the beet webworm became a consequence. It has been known for a long time that many insects fall back on weeds when crops they favor are gone. Many aphids and flea beetles downscale their standard of living this way. Wireworm, white grub and stalk borer seem to increase and multiply when weed grasses thrive. As I pointed out in an earlier chapter, the best way to cope with these insects — and weeds that support them — is to clean the field so that crop plant auxins can determine the kingdom for the year. So-called safe seeding dates are of no value if the rootbed is full of weeds and volunteer wheat.

Parasites are both the enemy and the friend of the farmer. Prickly pear in western Kansas covered thousands of acres during the late 1930s, but that crop receded, not because toxic chemicals drove it into retreat, but because the common cactus borer, *Melitara dengala*, and a plethora of other insect pests gave the prickly pear a severe setback, albeit not to a point of annihilation. Farmers have long wondered how insects know just which plant provides the fare they want. Watching greenbugs invade one field and ignore another, one could conclude that some sort of communication signal invites the bugs to where the feast best suits their needs. Otherwise, how would a codling moth know where to go? Philip S. Callahan, then of the USDA

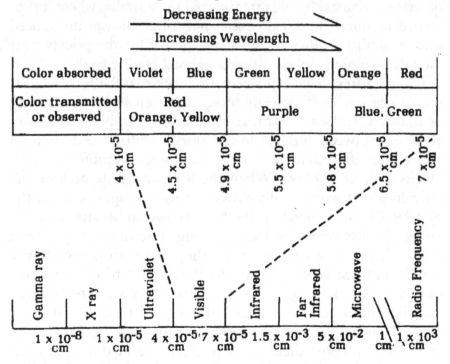

Electromagnetic spectrum in order of decreasing energy and increasing wavelength.

and University of Florida, Gainesville, was among the first to recognize the fact that insects and plants in effect broadcast short-wave, and communicate with each other.

In order to understand this, it might be well to illustrate the full electromagnetic spectrum. The diagram on the previous page illustrates the division in order of decreasing energy and increasing wavelength. The bottom scale has the whole package. Dotted lines take the reader into a breakdown of the visible part of the spectrum — the one we're all more familiar with.

Note that the most energy is concentrated in the gamma ray, x-ray and ultraviolet ray breakdown, just before the visible section of the spectrum. The visible part of the electromagnetic spectrum is what it is — the part that rods and cones of our eyes can pick up. As energy decreases and wavelength increases, there are the infrared, microwave and radio frequency wavelengths.

Callahan touched on the subject in *Insect Evolution*, in a few dozen scientific papers, and then he issued a popular broadside called *Tuning In To Nature*. In *Tuning In To Nature*, he spent quite a few pages proving that "all things natural to the earth radiate naturally in the infrared. If we could see in that region of the IR spectrum, the whole corn field would appear by moonlight as a vast array of fluorescent light bulbs sticking up out of the soil."

In Callahan's way of thinking, it is not possible to understand ecology without understanding something about "the part of the world in which life can exist." There is in fact an infrared window — seven to fourteen micrometers — that allows IR radiation in all day and all night. The gas makeup of the atmosphere figures in all this, as do humidity, weather and climate.

The recorded beginning of this line of thinking goes back to 1863, when an Irish genius from Leighlinbridge in County Carlow wrote a book, *Heat Considered as a Mode of Motion*. His name was John Tyndall. In well-cadenced Victorian language he explained how molecules of scent from flowers and plants absorb radiation. Phil Callahan had been thinking along the same line without ever hearing Tyndall — to use Callahan's words — "for the simple reason that Tyndall's elegant work was ignored by the modern chemists and olifaction physiologists."

Wrote Tyndall: "The sweet south that breaths upon a bank of violets stealing and giving odor, owes its sweetness to an agent, which though almost infinitely attenuated, may be more potent, as an interceptor of terrestrial radiation, than the entire atmosphere from bank to sky." I covered this in *An Acres U.S.A. Primer*, but it needs reiteration here, otherwise the weed-insect connection will not be entirely meaningful.

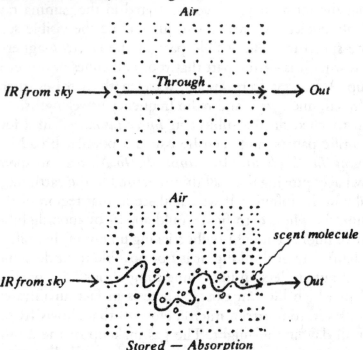

This simply means — again to use Callahan's words — that "air space is made up of many, many specified molecules of oxygen, nitrogen, argon, ammonia, etc., but that scattered thinly among those billions upon billions of air molecules are spread very few molecules of scent substances that block infrared light better than air alone." That is why it can correctly by said that John Tyndall invented the instrument now called the absorption spectrophotometer.

Callahan's explanation of all this can be read in a hauntingly beautiful book called *Soul of the Ghost Moth*. In it he explains how Tyndall "used his absorption spectrophotometer to demonstrate that when a very few molecules of a scent are released into air space the scent causes the character of the air to change so that it absorbs far more infrared radiation from the sun, or night sky, or stars than it would if the scent were not scattered thinly in the air. The combination of thinly spread scent molecules, plus the gases that compose the air act together, so to speak, to trap the radiation within itself."

Now the plot thickens. The air and the blackbody conspire to send out coherent waves, much like a radio transmitter. Scientists call such heated bodies as the earth *blackbodies*. A radiating blackbody is any heated body that absorbs all radiation and radiates infrared wavelengths in a range that depends on its peak temperature. Different blackbodies have different peaks of radiation wavelengths, depending on their temperatures. In general, the hotter the body, the shorter the peak-radiation wavelengths. The cooler the body, the longer the wavelengths. Since the sun is very high, it emits frequencies that peak at very short wavelengths in the visible spectrum. The earth's temperature seldom reaches an average temperature of more than 70° to 100° F and therefore peaks at a wavelength of approximately ten micrometers in the seven to fourteen micrometer window. It is this curve of the peak earth temperature that reradiates back out into space.

"Besides the natural hot and warm bodies of nature, there are, of course, man-made hot objects. Hot automobile engines, factories, tungsten-filament light bulbs, the heated pavement of cities — many more. All are blackbodies emitting an infrared radiation peak at the peak of their own temperatures."

There is a mathematical expression for instant identity of peak radiation for any hot body. It is called Wien's constant — after the German physicist, Wilhelm Wien — and that number is 2,897. When this figure is divided by the absolute temperature of any hot body, the dividend is the wavelength. Absolute here has a special meaning. Zero on the absolute scale is -273.16° C. For ease of calculation, Callahan rounded off that number to -270° before writing this passage.

"A human body with a skin temperature of 96° F will equal 31° C plus 270°, or an absolute temperature of 301° K. The symbol for an absolute temperature, now called Kelvin's (after Lord Kelvin), is K. Therefore,

$$(\text{wavelengths} = \frac{2,897}{301° \text{ K}} = 9.62 \text{ micrometers})$$

or waves 9.62 micrometers long."

In other words, a human being emits infrared radiation at a peak of 9.62 micrometers. The same computation can be made for "all things natural to the earth," again quoting Callahan, since every "insect, mammal, tree, weed, and living creature" emits its own characteristic blackbody radiation.

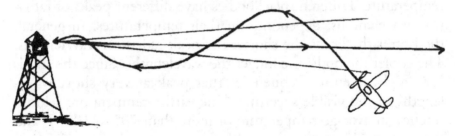

It is equally well known that night flying moths track a phero-mone (sex scent) as if they were following a radio beam.

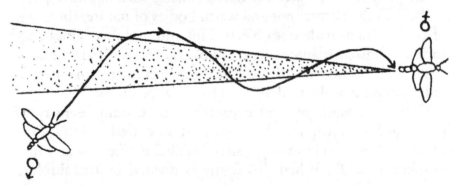

Insects do emit a coded infrared signal, and it contains a unique navigational message. When insects fly, they vibrate their antennae at the same frequency that they flap their wings — and those antennae are indeed antenna, just as are the man-made devices that pluck a radio signal out of the air.

Without knowing it, electrical engineers discovered and put to use what nature has been doing all along. The earliest tracking system for bringing in an airplane during inclement weather relied on Morse code — dot-dash (A), dash-dot (N) — signals riding each other to create a beam. If the signal got weak, the pilot knew he was moving off beam, and accordingly corrected his course.

"Every entomologist also knows that the sex odor of the female emits from the scent gland at the top of her abdomen as she vibrates her wings. During emission her temperature increases 6° to 18° F above that of the air space. This means, of course, that as the scent drifts through the air pushed by the gentle breeze, it cools and decreases concentration. The scent flows along in the water vapor of the gaseous atmosphere which is the carrier gas." The important thing to remember here is that insect antennas are, indeed, antennas.

As a matter of fact, every antenna ever built by man has its counterpart on insects. Callahan has observed that the pheromone signal (chemical released by a female insect to stimulate sexual attraction) is much better than the old-time radio transmitter because it tells the flying male moth how far he is from the pheromone-releasing female as well as the direction. Close to the female, wavelengths are long. A few hundred feet away they are short. In electronics the system is called "concentration tuning."

Insects use short spines (sensilla) to resonate at short wavelengths, longer sensilla to read the signals as they close in. There are spines for tuning in to sex scents — a part of nature's mating game. There are sensilla for detecting infrared radiations from the food supply. Plants, after all, have odors, and odors are governed by health or the lack thereof, regardless of whether pathology is gross or, say, the corn plant is simply subclinically ill. Apparently the weed can call in the insect only to the extent that its health-illness quotient releases signals in tune with the insect's receiving equipment. It is well within reason to suggest that a subclinically sick plant will have an altered wavelength. Is this why insects attack the undernourished plant, commercial crop or weed, the one with missing trace nutrients? If so, then the questions have been answered by the eco-farmer who has discovered the biochemistry of immunity not only in nature's genetic engineering, but also in fertility management.

Callahan has proved that the moth is programmed like an orbiting satellite to respond to a series of frequencies. There are seventeen-micrometer pheromone lines present in a candle. "Thus a candle mimics the moth body-wing-modulated signal because the flickering of the flame in the air modulates the candle blackbody radiation between six and twenty-five micrometers — exactly what the moth is programed to respond to."

Picture the scene. A cabbage looper moth releases a pheromone scent from the tip of her abdomen. It is a complex molecule composed of alcohols and acetates hitched together as a long chain. Free in the atmosphere it is a complex trace element in solvent because of water vapor in the night air. This pheromone is pumped along by other trace elements in the air. Insect sensilla pluck these signals right out of the air. "The drifting plume of pheromone not only gives direction to the flying male but also distance from the female by reference to the wave-lengths at specific concentrations and temperatures in the air," says Callahan.

Are we saying that weeds are unhealthy? To ask the question is to suggest that there is an answer. And the answer may have more to do with what weeds concentrate and how this uptake affects the signals they send out. We know that the poison ivy plant can be annihilated via the feeding of a caterpillar, *Epipaschia zelleri*, which eats the leaves. Whole areas of sumac often fall prey to the sumac flea beetle, *Blepharida rhois*. Indeed, a whole raft of insects have been imported for the purpose of eliminating unwanted plants with mild success, but the practice fell into disfavor with the arrival of chemicals of organic synthesis. Here are a few weeds and insect pests they harbor.

ANNUAL GRASSES
- Cutworm
- Army worm
- Common stalk borer
- Webworm
- Flea beetle
- Wireworm
- White grub
- 12-Spotted cucumber beetle
- Billbug
- Chinch bug
- Corn leaf aphid
- Corn root aphid
- English grain aphid
- Colorado potato beetle
- Green bug (Toxoptera)

BARNYARD GRASS
- Sugar cane rootstock borer

BINDWEED
- Tortoise beetle (gold bug)
- Sweet potato flea beetle

BULL NETTLE
- Colorado potato beetle

COCKLEBUR
- Pale striped flea beetle

DOCK
- Melon aphid
- Rhubarb curculio

GOLDENROD
- Clover leaf weevil

GOURD
- Squash borer
- Squash bug

GROUND CHERRY
- Colorado potato beetle
- Potato stalk borer

HORSE NETTLE
- Colorado potato beetle
- Potato stalk borer

JIMSON WEED
- Colorado potato beetle
- Potato stalk borer

LAMBSQUARTERS
- Clover cutworm
- Garden webworm
- Grasshopper
- Pale striped flea beetle
- Spinach flea beetle
- Spinach leaf miner
- Sugarbeet root aphid

MORNING GLORY
- Tortoise beetle
- Flea beetle

MULLEIN
- Colorado potato beetle

PEPPERGRASS
- Melon aphid
- Black cherry aphid

PIGWEED
- Grasshopper
- Garden webworm
- Pale striped flea beetle
- Spinach flea beetle
- Carrot beetle Harlequin beetle
- Melon aphid

PUNCTURE VINE
  Blister beetle
RAGWEED
  Common stalk borer
  Garden webworm
  Potato aphid
RUSSIAN THISTLE
  Beet webworm
  Diamond-back moth
  Thistle grasshopper
  Beet leaflhopper
  Western corn rootworm
  Sunflower leaf beetle
  Garden webworm
  Turnip aphid
  Potato aphid
  Cabbage aphid
SMARTWEED
  Common stalk borer
  Corn root aphid
SUDAN GRASS
  Chinch bug
VOLUNTEER BARLEY
  Common stalk borer
  True army worm
  Fall army worm
  Cutworm
  Grasshopper
  Aphid
  Chinch bug

Hessian fly
VOLUNTEER SWEET
  CLOVER
  Army worm
  Variegated cutworm
  Grasshopper Pea aphid
VOLUNTEER WHEAT
  True army worm
  Fall army worm
  Army cutworm
  Common stalk borer
  Grasshopper
  Chinch bug
  Wheat strawworm
  Green bug (Toxoptera)
  English grain aphid
  Wheat-stem maggot

WILD ALFALFA
  Wheat white grub

WILD MUSTARD
  Cabbage aphid
  Harlequin cabbage bug
  Pale striped flea beetle
  Turnip aphid

WILD SUNFLOWER
  Variegated cutworm
  Salt marsh caterpillar
  Common stalk borer
  Grasshopper
  Pale striped flea beetle

Conditions that account for weeds, and in turn viral, fungal and bacterial attacks are too complex and interrelated for instant translation. An *Acres U.S.A.* subscriber in what was formerly East Germany, Jurgins Reckin, once sent in the diagram that appears on page 54. It traces out often interrelated conditions that set up the environment for insects and weeds alike. Viruses are only rarely transmitted through seeds. A few carry over in perennials, and some occur in annual weeds when transmitted by insects after visiting diseased plants. Such infected weeds become the source of the inoculum often transferred by insects and the farmer himself to crops of economic value. This is the important thing to remember. The insects which hand-carry viruses to plants feed and multiply on weeds. They not only carry the virus, but also infect the weed host itself.

A case in point. China asters are hard to grow because of aster yellows, a viral disease of wild lettuce (Lactuca genus, several species) and horseweed, *Erigeron canadensis*. Leaf hoppers in turn carry aster yellows from the infested weed to China aster. Much the same mechanism is sometimes invoked to destroy the cucumber crop. Cucumber mosaic is a viral disease that visits eggplant, pepper, celery and cantaloupe. From there the virus is transported to the cucumber vine by plant lice or aphids which visit susceptible, infected weeds such as pokeweed, milkweed, ground cherry, spurge, and velvetleaf. It would be possible to fill a compendium with this information, because many other weeds are on stage center, to act out their role. Typical in transferring viral diseases to economic plants are black nightshade and Jimson weed.

Weeds are less identified with the spread of fungus diseases of plants, and still they act as hosts for the organisms involved. Wild strawberry, for instance, is terribly susceptible to strawberry leaf spot, and is a veritable distribution center for the fungus. Wild barley is famous for harboring the stem rust of wheat, and orchard grass has a reputation for hosting the oat stem rust fungus. Johnson grass is catalogued as furnishing the inoculum for rust of sorghum, and wheat take-all or foot rot can be traced to plants such as buffalo grass, little barley, crested wheatgrass or quackgrass.

A champion in the fungus disease category is ergot. Cattle eat it with serious ailments to follow, death often the consequence. It is spread to rye from wild grasses such as western wheatgrass and several species of wild rye.

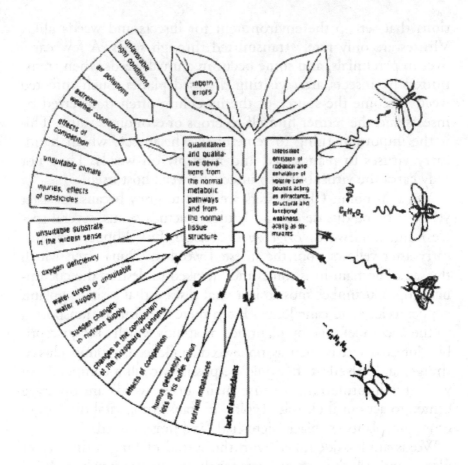

Two years before the Volga Germans brought Turkey red wheat to Kansas, there was an outbreak of hoof-and-mouth disease in the state. Farmers talked about it as recently as the dust storm era. No one liked the idea of hoof-and-mouth disease because of its association with impoverished agriculture, hence the political ploy of calling it gangrenous ergotism. Ergotism, in turn, meant wheat, rye and other grains were infested with *Clavieeps purpurea*. Fed to cattle, the poison constricted the finer capillaries which caused hoofs to be sloughed off, much like hoof-and-mouth disease. The front feet or legs, the ear tip, the tail, even the tongue fell victim to a lack of circulation, thus the term *dry gangrene* was born.

The problem vanished, more or less, except that dallis grass and Argentine bahia grass in the South still bestow the curse. *Claviceps paspali* — another ergot fungus — acts rapidly on the central nervous system, with resultant convulsions. We'll deal with poisonous plants later on, touching everything from selenium poisoning of Custer's horses in Montana to molybdenum toxicity in the San Joaquin Valley of California and the Everglades of Florida.

Here are a few plant diseases common to the Kansas of my youth together with weeds that help perpetuate the disease.

ASTER YELLOWS
Wild lettuce. . . . . *Latuca* genus, several species
Horseweed. . . . . *Erigeron canadensis*

CUCUMBER MOSAIC
Pokeweeed. *Phytolacca decandra*
Milkweed . . . . *Asclepias* genus, several species
Ground cherry. . . . . *Physalis* genus, several species
Spurge. . . . . *Euphorbia hysopifolia, E. preslii*
Velvetleaf. . . . . *Abutilon theophrasti*
Black or garden nightshade . . . . *Solanum nigrum*
Catnip. . . . . *Nepeta cataria*
Pigweed. . . . . *Amaranthus* genus, several species

TOBACCO MOSAIC
Black or garden nightshade . . . . *Solanum nigrum*
Jimson weed . . . . *Datura stramonium*
Ground cherry. . . . . *Physalis* genus, several species

STEM RUST OF WHEAT, OATS AND BARLEY
Western wheatgrass . . . . *Agropyron smithii*
Wild barley . . . . *Hordeum jubatum*
Goatgrass. *Aegilops cylindrica*

TAKE-ALL OF WHEAT
Buffalo grass . . . . *Buchloe dactyloides*
Little barley. . . . . *Hordeum pusillum*

Crested wheatgrass .... *Agropyron cristatum*
Quackgrass .... *Agropyron repens*
Chess........................... *Bromus secalinus*
Slender Fescue................... *Festuca octoflora*
Meadow Fescue.................... *Festuca elatior*
Perennial bristlegrass .... *Setaria geniculata*
ERGOT
Western wheatgrass .... *Agropyron smithii*
Wild rye .... Elymus genus, several species
EARLY BLIGHT OF POTATO
Ground cherry........... Physalis genus, several species
STRAWBERRY LEAF SPOT
Wild strawberry.................. *Fragaria virginiana*

There are others, depending on the area of the country being surveyed. And there are ongoing programs for the purpose of causing one of nature's own to take out an undesirable species, either insect vs. insect, insect vs. weed, or disease vs. both of the above. Internationally, there are well subsidized programs for utilization of exotic vertebrates to control weeds, usually fish species in aquatic situations, which I have ruled out of my outline for want of space. Similarly, organisms have been utilized within their native ranges to control weeds. Often organisms released jump oceans and continents. For instance, a bio-control for lantana, released in 1914 in Australia, Calcomy 3a lantanae, has spread to Papua, New Guinea.

The government agencies of several countries have structured programs to control weeds with insects, fish, organisms, geese, sheep, cattle, goats, and this information is safely anchored in archives and program files. I have not digressed into things like goatweed grazing and weeder geese in the cornfield simply because I wanted to stay decently within the bounds declared by this chapter head.

For now it is enough to note that fertility capable of supporting commercial crops is not generally the type of fertility weeds like. And of course this same fertility can be counted on to short-circuit a great deal of insect proliferation. Partial and imbalanced fertilization always has been and always will be the harbinger of stress, in soils, in plants — and stress is always an open sesame for bacterial, insect and fungal attack — and weeds a'plenty.

More than likely, it will soon be proved to academia's satisfaction that a proper calcium level with magnesium, potassium and phosphates in equilibrium will do more to roll back weed proliferation than all the herbicides in the Dow and Monsanto armamentarium.

Moreover, when costs are subtracted from the poisons bill and punched into the fertility program — with suitable calculations for damage no longer imposed on the soil and the environment — the bottom line suggests arithmetic out of whack during the herbicide theory period now ending. Most mainline farmers have loaded more than their fair share of toxins into the environment during the past fifty years. Few realize that many of those poisons are still out there, the problem being that no one knows exactly where they are. But the weeds seem to know, and they treasure their secret and laugh in silence at man's puny attempts to annihilate their kind with poisons. The final verse in the ode to weeds may well be a paraphrase of Rudyard Kipling's message from Afghanistan —

> At the end of the fight
> Is a tombstone white,
> With the name of the late deceased.
> And the epitaph dr'er,
> A fool lies here,
> Who tried to poison the weeds.

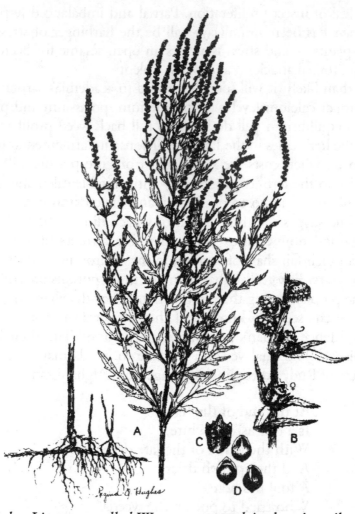

Carolus Linnaeus called Western ragweed Ambrosia psilostachya, *thereby exhibiting a wry sense of humor. Anyone checking out ragweed, and taking the ambrosia term literally, is bound to get a snootful of hayfever pollen. When biological processes in the soil go dormant because of dry weather, release of the right form of potassium comes off in a hard to take colloidally complexed form. This form is just right for ragweed types. The illustration exhibits the plant itself (A); its raceme of male heads and female involucres (B); the achene or one-seeded fruit (C); and seeds (D).*

58   *Weeds, Control Without Poisons*

5

THE SOCRATES SESSIONS

During the late unpleasantness with Germany and Japan, I spent some of my time at a gunnery side camp to the old Las Vegas Army Air Corps Base. It was good duty involving some instruction, lots of KP, and more than ample time to explore the wonders of the desert. During those few weeks I took long walks in the desert. This Nevada desert, I soon discovered, was really a living desert, naked in fewer places than one might imagine. It was spring while I was there, and this meant breathtaking color was in command. Almost out of sight were the remains of Russian thistle from the year before, now submerged by new color and greenery. I didn't know the names of too many desert weeds I encountered then — and I don't know them now — save one, the ubiquitous Russian thistle.

I know I walked over land later used for atomic bomb tests. And I confess that I was not surprised to read in a British science journal that the first growth to return after everything had been incinerated at ground zero was the Russian thistle. It seemed to thrive on radiation the way other weeds thrive on ionized chemicals. I wondered then and I wonder now, what manner of support does this strange weed draw from the cosmos? Years later I found myself digesting the works of Americo Mosca, the chemistry prize winner at the Brussels World Fair.

Mosca made the point that atomic fallout is formed by alpha, beta and gamma rays and neutrons. In the human, animal or vegetable body, a radioactive particle is dangerous only when it disintegrates and discharges its energy. These reactions are determined by the electrons. Atomic fallout and chemicals having free valences in contact with men, animals and plants spontaneously subtract electrons from the hydrogen atoms of amino acids, alter the natural frequency of genetic mutations and afterward form the respective proteinates.

"The damage resulting from nuclear radiation is the same as the damage resulting from the use of toxic genetic chemicals," Mosca wrote. "The use of fungicides of organic synthesis (Zineb, Captan, Phaltan, etc.) annually causes the same damage to present and future generations as atomic fallout from twenty-nine H-bombs of fourteen megatons — or damage equal to fallout of 14,500 atomic bombs, type Hiroshima."

This business of frequency and fallout — and the farm chemical equivalent thereof — was duly noted at the time, but I cannot say that the lesson was applied to the study of weeds. Again, Phil Callahan has come to the rescue.

Those needles, those spines, those special appendages — if that word can be permitted — are like tuning antennas to the cosmos, he said, and ultimately that reality will kick open a new chapter in weed lore. It may explain why the Russian thistle tumbleweed survived and, perhaps, how it drew nourishment after cosmic violence had been loosed on its Nevada homestead acres.

Foxtail is a troublesome weed many schoolmen believed could be vanquished with atrazine, a toxic genetic chemical. Sure enough, the earliest applications mowed down foxtail like tenpins, but the chemical fix seemed as nourishment for a gnarled, many jointed weed called fall panicum. This lower phylum creation seemed to replace foxtail under the atrazine treatment. Before the age of hard chemistry, it was so little known, its appearance sent the experts scrambling to the weed identification manuals.

During its early years, when *Acres U.S.A.* was still refining the rationale for eco-farming, William A. Albrecht, dean emeritus of the Department of Soils, University of Missouri, was good enough to be interested in the project. Until the moment of his death in 1974, I used to have long conversations ("Socrates sessions," we called them) about the great overloads of chemical poisons and herbicides that seemed to produce more weeds than they eliminated. Usually, Albrecht would simply reiterate his life-long observations — that failure of the chemical bandwagon was coming on because we refuse to look into the history of plant domestication. Albrecht pointed out that domestic plants in their virgin condition grew to the climax stage of a clean stand with exclusion of competing weeds. "Growth is possible only through the balance of the several fertility essentials in the soil because better nutrition protects the crop to nearly complete exclusion of all other crops," Albrecht said.

Albrecht and his associates came by this knowledge on the university's test plots called Sanborn Field. There they learned a very simple lesson about nature's answer to the problem of noxious pasture weeds. Two plots had been maintained in continuous grass, namely timothy. One plot had been dressed with barnyard manure at the rate of six tons an acre. The second plot received no treatment. Crops had been removed regularly from both plots.

The untreated plot often became so infested with weeds that plowing and reseeding was required. Accordingly, both plots were similarly treated to plowing and reseeding, regardless of the weed free grass stand on the manured companion plot. The manured plot always delivered a fine sward with early spring and late fall growth of quality hay — two to two and a half tons every summer. The untreated plot exhibited snowy white, wooly tops of broom sedge during seed production time. This attracted a great deal of interest.

Soil samples were collected and sent to B.M. Dugger, one of the research doctors at Lederle Laboratories in New York. These samples made possible the isolation of strain A-377, the source of the antibiotic Aureomycin. Isolation was effected from the weed-infested plot. The same fungus apparently could not be isolated from the manured companion plot, the one that grew excellent timothy hay routinely.

"The important thing to note," said Albrecht, "is that broom sedge failed to invade the nearby plot, yet windborne seed was scattered extensively. Seeds were particularly numerous on the manured plot because winds blew from the west, or from the infested plot." Examination of the forty other plots on Sanborn Field revealed that they, like the manured plot, were immune to infestation by the weed. Broom sedge was a threatening and dangerous weed only to untreated plots and to grass-sod roadways between plots.

It may be that Professor J.W. Sanborn, who laid out those Missouri University plots in 1888, knew what he was talking about when he said, "Fertilize the soil so it will grow grasses which are healthy plants and thereby nutritious feeds, so consequently the troublesome weeds will stay away."

Albrecht scoffed at laws that hoped to prevent machines from carrying noxious weeds from farm to farm. He viewed soils of weakened fertility as the culprits because such soils invite the invader. As for costly weed poisons, they were that: costly. They could not control weeds in the fullness of time. They could only deliver side effects it would take generations to understand fully.

There are some 1,775 plants in the United States that have been characterized as weeds, it being understood that weeds are weeds only in man's eye. Nature has assigned special roles to weeds. Seed producing weeds — especially the annuals — produce a far greater abundance of seeds than so-called cultivated crops. Herein is both a clue and a logic entirely consistent with nature. Few agronomists have picked up either that clue or that logic. Exceptions are people such as Newman Turner, writing in *Fertility Pastures,* and Ehrenfried E. Pfeiffer, writing in *Weeds and What They Tell.*

"Weeds are specialists," wrote Pfeiffer. "Having learned something in the battle for survival they will survive under circumstances where our cultivated plants, softened through centuries of protection and breeding, cannot stand up against nature's caprices." Pfeiffer also noted that weeds "resist conditions which cultivated plants cannot resist, such as drought, acidity of soil, lack of humus, mineral deficiencies, as well as one-sidedness of minerals. They are witness of man's failure to master the soil, and they grow abundantly whenever man has missed the train — they only indicate our errors and nature's corrections."

Pfeiffer saw weeds as a great teacher, "indicating through their mere presence and multiplication what is wrong." And he recited many of the findings C.J. Fenzau and I noted in walking the fields.

There were the weeds that lived on acid soil — the sorrels, docks, and ladysthumb — and in some cases horsetail, hawkweed and knapweed. One group suggested crust formation or hardpan, or both — field mustard, horse nettle, pennycress, morning glory, quackgrass, the camomiles and pineapple weeds. A third group included the weeds of cultivation, or farmers' weed — lambsquarters, plantain, chickweed, buttercup, dandelion, nettle, prostrate knotweed, prickly lettuce, field speedwell, pigweed, common horehound, celandine, mallows and carpetweed.

Pfeiffer's several other classifications were also fairly perceptive. He joined W.E. Brenchley's assessment in *Weeds of Farm Land* in defining the salty soil weeds as shepherd's purse and Russian thistle, to mention a couple. He called attention to weeds brought on by inept fertilization, such as excessive use of salt forms of potash — the wild mustard plants and weeds of the Crucifaerae family, a prolific and troublesome tribe — charlock, Indian mustard, ball mustard, wild radish, the peppergrasses, both common and green flowered, and field peppergrass as well. It is a matter of record that seeds from plants such as charlock and wild radish can lie inert in the soil for up to sixty years. Now and then a farmer will plow up a pasture, forgetting that it was once a grain field. A swift reminder can come on in the form of wild radish, its seed coming to life after several decades in an underground bunker. Also a beneficiary of heavy potassium overload in the soil are the mallows, wormwood, knapweed, fumitory, and the opium poppy. Pfeiffer once pointed out that red clover simply disappears when there is a shortage of potassium, hence its value as an indicator weed plant.

Here are a few more Pfeiffer observations.

Sandy soils often deliver lush growths of goldenrods, arrow leaved wild lettuce, yellow toadflax, onions, partridge pea, Scotch broom, poppies, spurry or corn marigold. Steppe type pastures are often infested with Russian thistle, sage, and loco weed. Alkaline soils of the West deliver a fair complement of ironweed, sagebrush and woody aster under most circumstances.

Limestone soils, such as those along the Missouri River bluffs and the race horse country of Kentucky, identify readily with pennycress, field peppergrass, hare's ear mustard, wormseed, Barnaby's thistle, field madder, and yellow camomile. When lime is absent or perhaps locked up and complexed, yellow or hop clover, rabbit's foot clover, fox glove, wild pansy, sorrel, sundews, white mullein and Scotch broom surface and sour the situation.

Badly drained soils develop quite an inventory of weeds. Other factors figure in just which ones survive and prosper. Generally speaking, the inventory will include smartweed, mild water pepper, hedge bindweed, silverweed, swampy horsetail, white avens, meadow pink, stinking Willie, Canada and narrow leaved goldenrod, Joe-Pye weed and foxtail.

Grain fields are not limited to these, but include them all: wild buckwheat, all the mustards, wild radishes, pennycress, mouse-ear-chickweed, morning glory, purple cockle, bachelor's button, tansy, poppies, chess.

Buttercups, dock, knotweed, all fingerweeds, white avens, grassleaved stickwort, St. Johnswort, pokeweed, milkweed, briar, wild garlic and thistles, all are pasture weeds albeit not limited to that location, other conditions factor into their permission to life.

To put all this in another way, there are reasons why these several weeds tend to grow where observations have placed them. Some weeds announce completely worn out soils, acres so fully deteriorated that they no longer have a living function. Eroded hillsides with a lack of organic matter, and a pattern of nutrients being leached away due to excess rain, both set this stage. Or it may be a case of excess calcium or sodium flowing out of one area and settling into a lower basin area, filling up the catch area with a high sodium content.

For pragmatic observations that did not yet invoke the frequencies imposed by chemicals and the cosmos, C.J. Fenzau was in a class by himself. Here are field notes, yellowed with age, that stand up as well today as when I first set them down while walking his client's acres.

Weeds have a pecking order and can put each other out of business. Both mustard and shepherd's purse collect salt. Grown on a salty marsh and plowed under green, they sweeten the soil and take away the life element of weeds ordinarily growing on salty soil. Much the same is true of rye, which fights chickweed. Wild carrots are moved aside by sweet clover. Quackgrass has a hard time surviving amid soybeans, cowpeas and millet if the land is cultivated and the weather hot and dry. Two successive crops of rye will choke out quackgrass in the cornbelt.

Papaver (poppy) and wild larkspur associate with winter wheat, but dislike barley. Charlock and field mustard prefer oats. Their dormant seeds are awakened when oats are sown, though they do not harm oats. They are very hard on rape and beets.

Lady's thumb (spotted knotweed) can pop up any place where there is slight acidity, not enough surface drainage and lack of air. Cultivation is the best preventive. Seeds are more frequently distributed as impurities in red clover. This one can be recognized by its reed-like stem and lance-shaped leaves, pointed at both ends. Flower spikes are pink or purple. Management of the decay systems with proper levels of calcium is a key in controlling lady's thumb. Cation balance is a better remedy than trying to buy clean clover seeds.

Swamp smartweed indicates standing water. The weed prefers moist pockets, although it grows just about anywhere. Creeping roots are easily broken with cultivation. Continued stress on this weed is the easiest way to elimination.

Sick plants do not have their normal hormone level. As a result they are subject to a lot of insect attacks. Our first thought these days is to find new rescue chemicals and kill the insect instead of going back to the soil and finding the cause of the problem and eliminating it.

Each time I made some farm scene after the above notes were made, some new obvious fact fleshed out previous observations. For instance . . .

• Plowing up and down a hill during the fall when there is no body in the soil can trigger erosion. Under such a circumstance the farmer should not be fall plowing at all. He should be mulching instead. Moreover, machinery systems can be either a plus or a negative, and this can lead to degeneration. The weeds say it all when they tell about a completely deteriorated soil.

• Imbalanced pH soils have no body structure. As a consequence soil particles are subject to wind erosion, leaching or water erosion. These are causes of breakdown in the soil system. All, of course, are related to how a farmer manages his soil. There are weeds that talk about pH character. Soils with a pH in disequilibrium do not have the right structure, body, porosity, or capacity to hold or regulate the release of nutrients. They might have an excess of one cation over another and exhibit a domination effect. Weeds have a lot to say about imbalanced pH — much more, in fact, than the entire lesson on pH in *An Acres U.S.A. Primer*.

• One weed might grow three feet tall under one condition, and grow hardly a foot under another. The same weed may be thick stemmed and have fine leaves in one environment, and it may have a thin stem and a lot of spindly branches in another. Stunted weeds speak of soil limitations and genetic arrangements of the plant itself.

• A lot of weeds point to drainage and how drainage is directly influenced by pH structure. Indeed, pH character makeup — the inner reactions of elements within pH — all have a bearing on function and what it does to change soil structure. pH determines whether the soil drains, whether it holds water tightly, how it aerates, and how it compacts. Soils that clod together invite certain weeds. As respiration continues within a clod, and as organic material ferments, carbon dioxide may be accumulated and trapped within the clod. The presence and concentration of carbon dioxide tends to stimulate a specific group of hormones — the kind that wake up foxtail, nut sedge and watergrass — and weed species dependent on specific hormone-enzyme systems and their presence or absence in the soil seed zone.

• Poor pH structure has a negative effect on water management. As a result poorly drained soils are easily mismanaged. They are often plowed too wet and driven over too early and compacted. Almost all of the weeds on which some farmers use chemicals such as atrazine are of this character. Atrazine is designed to deal with weeds that grow on poorly structured soil. It does absolutely nothing to correct the pH shortfalls in the soil that brought on the weed problem in the first place.

• There are weeds that are related to the direction of decay of organic matter — just as Pfeiffer noted. How residues, roots and crop materials are processed in the soil — and the direction of decay they take — determines whole classes of weeds. Soils that are not balanced properly in terms of cation exchange capacity do not permit the proper decay of organic matter in an undesirable environment. The wrong direction of decay produces alcohols which depress biological processes in the soil. In the absence of biotic activity, hordes of antagonistic hormone processes go into motion, giving farmers buttonweeds, Jimson weeds, in fact all the weeds in that general family. Without exception they are indicators of improper decay of organic matter or, if you will, "soil indigestion." These weeds say the soil is not able to manage decay of organic material into a good, virgin, wholesome, brand new supply of fresh humus, and without this good governor of a living soil system, problem weed types announce the degeneration of soil potential.

• Morning glories and bindweed have rhizomes. Under conditions of improper decay there are no fungi antagonistic to those rhizomes. It takes correction of pH, air capacity and moisture control to set in motion a soil environment that assures the proper decay of organic matter. Under such soil conditions a whole new array of fungal systems can start to break down the rhizome seed stock and eventually correct the soil system for desired crop growth — yet one antagonistic to the bindweed and morning glory. These basic fungal systems can make short work of rhizomes and roots, digest them and remove them.

• Weeds have a lot to say about minerals. Whether there is a mineral imbalance, or whether there is a potential in the soil system to release, complex or simplify minerals held in inventory, all are more important than the actual mineral content of the soil itself. Ragweeds grow behind the grain harvest in very dry soils, or they grow when stretches of dry weather make the soil's surface over-dry. Under dry conditions biological processes are slowed to a snail's pace. Potassium depends on bacterial processes to make it available for utilization. Sluggish bacterial activity in these dry soils causes potassium to be unavailable or available in an improperly processed form, and this is what ragweed is telling the farmer. Ragweed grows late in the season under complexed forms of potassium. It also grows in over-dried soils — or in soils flushed with water, then over-dried again. The sequence of rain — the wilting and drying of soils — determines how nutrients are processed, and this then sets in motion the hormonal environment that stimulates the awakening of various species of weeds. This is the reason weeds come and go. One year may be wet-dry-wet, the next simply wet, the next dry all the way.

• Variables of weather figure because weeds are often the consequence of stress. Fossil fuel-based fertilizers are made water soluble. When the soil dries up, these forms of fertilizers are unavailable and often are totally complexed into the soil base. They change their form and do not remain available for root uptake. This sets the stage for a different plant to function because each weed species often requires a certain form, character and quality of nutrients.

• Weeds almost write a biography about organic matter management on a farm. They tell quite a bit about how residues of previous crops are managed, whether they're plowed under, disced or mulched into the soil and thawing on the theory that hazards of weather will kill pupae and eggs — the latter an asinine proposition. Often the consequences of organic matter mismanagement arrive six months later. Residue left on top of the soil frequently begets a slime mold. This seals off the soil and makes it anaerobic. Over the winter months rain and snow do well to tuck things in and pack down a good residue seal over the soil. And if cattle are allowed to glean crop residue all winter, they are almost certain to be forgotten during a wet stretch. It is then that they do the damage, packing the ground the way a sheepsfoot packer works over a roadbed.

• When water can't pass through the variable density layers of the soil, spring tillage is usually delayed. Most farmers, however, are envious of a neighbor and eager to impress those who have a windshield view of the farming operation. This means they often rush the spring tillage anyway. Tracks beget compaction and compaction begets weeds. Then comes the spring ritual in which farmer bragging reaches an art form — how timely he was in applying a herbicide, modern agriculture's idea of holy water to forgive the sins committed in the name of early soil tillage.

Researchers have worked out the temperatures at which crop seeds come to life. No such list for weed seeds exists. In terms of ballpark figures, it can be noted that many weed seeds germinate at 40-50° F and start to stake out territory immediately. A great deal of commercial crop production runs best when soil temperatures match the optimum temperatures for bacteria, the general range for bacterial activity being between 65° and 70° F. It should be noted, however, that even under lower temperatures, other bacterial and fungal systems continue to function, and each of these systems leaves its mark and eventual effect on the next generation of plant life.

Clean tillage has a nice ring to it, especially in a day and age of toxic chemical worship. The idea hasn't much of a press because TV and magazine ads tout herbicides that last (without carryover, of course) and keep that combine from clogging. The clean tillage side of the fence seemingly has nothing to offer but blood, sweat and tears. Indeed, many weeds are like a Hydra. Cut off one head, and another one appears. Mow down some weeds at the wrong stage of growth, and rather than controlling the pest, it responds with renewed hormonal vigor to quickly replace the flowers and "sneak through" a new crop of seeds. After all, reproduction of the species is the prime function of a plant. Wild carrots, as an example, require fine-tuned mechanical combat. If they are mowed when they begin to blossom there will be two to five new blossoms where mowing removed only one. If they are mowed after seeds are matured, the farmer's activity will serve as a veritable drill, scattering seeds to the soil, and sweeping them under the tractor and mowing machine pass-over.

Some farmers use fire to burn away unwanted weeds. As a consequence, weeds rise like a Phoenix bird from the ashes more suitably fed than ever before. Fire visits destruction on organic balance in the top layer of the soil, coagulates humus colloids, and worsens the situation, but seldom kills the actual seed.

Eradication before and after weeds emerge isn't all that simple either. In theory, frequent mowing and tillage starves roots, taproots and rhizomes of biennials and perennials, the kind of weeds that propagate from root splinters and plant parts. Judgment and insight have to govern the tillage procedure. Harrowing usually does little more than damage rhizomes and taproots and, if the season is wet, the end result will be even more prolific growth. If the soil remains dry, such a frontal attack on biennials and perennials can enjoy a measure of success. Usually deeper working implements are necessary — a spring tooth harrow or duckfoot cultivator. Unless the root is dug up and removed — often an impossibility — there is always a danger of tillage serving to enhance, not inhibit, biennial and perennial weed growth.

Annual weeds, I have pointed out, complete the cycle from seed to seed in a single season. Much like garden crops with small seeds, these weeds germinate very near the surface of the soil. Such weeds are easily disturbed by cultivation. When moisture conditions intervene to prevent reestablishment, annual weed crops falter and die while field crops flourish.

The single point in the question is always the same: *what kind of weed are you dealing with, how does it propagate, and what are the conditions for its growth?* It has been observed that boggy soil is frequently carpeted with willowweed, and that chalk soils exhibit an abundance of chicory, whereas loam likely presents a mixture of weeds with any benchmark species. The conclusion we often draw is that weed flora are determined by the type of soil. Yet mature evaluation of soil types across the country tells us that very few weeds are definitely linked to the soil type. Moreover, a running record of observations suggests that weed communities are more common on different soils than are individual species. So it is only in broad outline that weed communities identify themselves with the character of the soil.

This prompts me to recall an Albrecht dictum, that only fertility can account for a climax crop, the kind that can furnish the auxins needed to cancel out lower phylum plants. Thus I am forced to conclude that many factors interact to announce the weed population for the year. Jurgins Reckin's diagram on page 46 properly suggests that plants, weeds and insects are influenced by wet and dry seasons, light and air, injuries and the effects of pesticides, an unsuitable substrate, a lack of oxygen, water supply or stress, a sudden change in the nutrient supply, changes in the rhizophere organisms, and whether nutrients are confused or complexed. A well-watered lawn, for instance, usually grows a lush stand of grass, and the grass finally crowds out weeds. Let a scorcher of a summer arrive so that the grass becomes stressed, then dormant weeds take over.

In short, there are so many rules they amount to being no rules at all. Often a particular species will be absent from a certain soil in one district, yet both present and abundant elsewhere in the same general area. It seems apparent that weeds will grow anywhere if other conditions are correct. There are exceptions even to this observation. Salt marshes have special plants never to be found inland. Nor can land plants survive the tides or toxins of the sea. Yet when such lands are drained, land plants not only occupy the area, they also oust the marsh plants, which in any case cannot survive without their fix of salt water on a regular basis.

Sorrel and sheep's sorrel are considered acid soil plants, and many agronomists are on record to the effect that these weeds cannot survive when there is a sufficient supply of lime. Yet old Rothamsted test plots have revealed that both of these plants proliferate on well limed soils if there is no competition from other plants. Thus it appears that auxins from competing plants have more to say about sorrel or sheep's sorrel survival than does the acidity of the soil, or the absence of calcium carbonate.

We will probably continue to associate certain arable weeds with soil types, albeit always with certain cautions in tow. We know that few arable weeds can be considered symptomatic of the soil when taken as individuals. But taken as communities, the plot thickens. Sheep's sorrel might suggest acidity and a low nutrient level without defining the soil as heavy or light. But when associated with spurry and annual knawel, the conclusion can be that the soil is very light, sandy and acid. A mixture of, say, black bent, hoary plantain, corn buttercup, coltsfoot and quackgrass suggests a very heavy soil. This concept of communities was given in detail in a book, long out of print, *Weeds of Farm Land*, that came to me from the library of the late William A. Albrecht. Some of these passages are abstracted in depth from that source and combined with my own field observations, those of C.J. Fenzau and Carey Reams, and a hundred others who have contributed to the pages of *Acres U.S.A.* over the decades.

As an opener, there are weeds that must be considered "of general occurrence." Sometimes it seems these weeds are quite indifferent about their habitat, but this observation is simplistic in the extreme. For instance, the appearance of scabious on chalky land is equally as characteristic as that of wild mignonette, the latter being virtually confined to that environment. The point here is that individual plants can serve as indicator plants only rarely and, except for groupings, it would be impossible to link weeds with different soil types.

It may well be that the sheep's sorrel survives in acid soil because other weeds don't, and it isn't so much a case of that weed disliking a more hospitable clime as other weeds spilling out auxins that sheep's sorrel can't stand. Moreover, some weeds — knotgrass for instance — can have wiry stems, and it can be almost succulent with large broad leaves two inches long. Are these differences sub-species? In many cases we do not know because we have never asked the question.

It has become difficult for most university-trained farmers to ask the right questions because of the atmosphere of intimidation under which most classroom fare is ladled out. Old timers with an observer's link to nature are more likely to wonder why fertilization systems govern weed proliferation more than soil types.

Thus some weeds seem ubiquitous, growing everywhere and anywhere. Except for the fact that mouse-ear-chickweed, creeping thistle, petty spurge, corn cockle, forget-me-not, ribwort plantain, wild radish, shepherd's needle, field madder and field speedwell fail to grow in peat, this list can be considered valid for England, Canada and the United States.

Bent grass . . . . Agrostis genus, several species
Shepherd's purse . . . . *Capsella bursa-pastoris*
Mouse-ear-chickweed . . . . *Cerastium vulgatum*
Lambsquarters. . . . . *Chenopodium album*
Creeping thistle. . . . . *Cirsium arvense*

Petty spurge. . . . . *Euphorbia peplus*
Corn cockle. . . . . *Lychnis githago*
Field forget-me-not . . . . *Myosotis arvensis*
Ribwort plantain. . . . . *Plantago lanceolata*
Knotgrass . . . . *Polygonum aviculare*
Black bindweed . . . . *Polygonum convolvulus*
Silverweed. . . . . *Potentilla anserina*
Creeping buttercup. . . . . *Ranunculus repens*
Wild radish. . . . . *Raphanus raphanistrum*
Curled dock . . . . *Rumex crispus*
Shepherd's needle . . . . *Scandix pecten*
Groundsel . . . . *Senecio vulgaris*
Field madder . . . . *Sheradia arvensis*
Chickweed . . . . *Stellaria media*
Field speedwell . . . . *Veronica agrestis*

This tells part of the story, but not all. The worst of the weeds — thistle, lambsquarters, knotgrass, black bindweed — all take hold and simply won't let go. Creeping thistle may be the worst. It takes good compost and the introduction of microorganisms that can rot out the rhizomes of these plants to effect suitable control. Poisons are worse than useless. Curled dock runs rampant, whereas ribwort plantain and shepherd's needle are usually not abundant, and often quite local in distribution.

Farmers are not too concerned with scarce weeds, namely the types of plants chiefly of interest to schoolmen. The following belong to this category.

Bulbous buttercup. . . . . *Ranunculus bulbosus*
Daisy. . . . . *Bellis perennis*
Dog daisy . . . . *Chrysanthemum leucanthemum*
Hedge mustard . . . . *Sisymbrium officinale*
Red champion. . . . . *Lychnis dioica*
Selfheal . . . . *Prunella vulgaris*
Yarrow. . . . . *Achillea millefolium*

On other pages of this volume, I will examine important farm weeds, sometimes one at a time, which is the way the farmer thinks of them and often encounters them. But first let me reproduce a table that codifies findings from as far back as Buckman in 1855, Long in 1910, and Brenchley, who did his work near the turn of the century. These weeds are generally associated with peat.

Quackgrass	*Agropyron repens*
Bent grass	Agrostis genus, several species
Lady's mantle	*Alchemilla arvensis*
Black bent	*Alopecurus agrestis*
Scarlet pimpernel	*Anagallis arvensis*
Corn camomile	*Anthemis arvensis*
Stinking mayweed	*Anthemis cotula*
Thyme-leaved sandwort	*Arenaria serpyllifolia*
Orache	*Atriplex patula*
Red bartsia	*Bartsia odontites*
White mustard	*Brassica alba*
Charlock	*Brassica sinapis*
Shepherd's purse	*Capsella bursa-pastoris*
Musk thistle	*Carduus nutans*
Hardhead	*Centaurea nigra*
Greater knapweed	*Centaurea scabiosa*
Mouse-ear-chickweed	*Cerastium vulgatum*
Lambsquarters	*Chenopodium album*
Corn marigold	*Chrysanthemum segetum*
Creeping thistle	*Cirsium arvense*
Bindweed	*Convolvulus arvensis*
Wild carrot	*Daucus carota*
Horsetail	*Equisetum arvense*
Dwarf spurge	*Euphorbia exigua*
Sun spurge	*Euphorbia helioscopia*
Petty spurge	*Euphorbia peplus*
Cudweed	*Filago germanica*
Fumitory	*Fumaria officinalis*
Cleavers	*Galium aparine*
Cut-leaved geranium	*Geranium dissectum*
Soft crane's bill	*Geranium molle*

Small crane's bill . . . . *Geranium pusillum*
Marsh cudweed. . . . . *Gnaphalium uliginosum*
Hogweed. . . . . *Heracleum sphondylium*
Henbit . . . . *Lamium amplexicaule*
Red deadnettle . . . . *Lamium purpureum*
Nipplewort . . . . *Lapsana communis*
Corn campanula . . . . *Legousia hybrida*
Round-leaved toadflax . . . . *Linaria spuria*
Yellow toadflax . . . . *Linaria vulgaris*
Corn gromwell . . . . *Lithospermum arvense*
Corn cockle . . . . *Lychnis githago*
White campion . . . . *Lychnis vespertina*
Field alkanet . . . . *Lycopsis arvensis*
Wild camomile . . . . *Matricaria chamomilla*
Scentless mayweed . . . . *Matricaria inodora*
Corn mint. . . . . *Mentha arvensis*
Field forget-me-not . . . . *Myosotis arvensis*
Pale poppy . . . . *Papaver argemone*
Red poppy. . . . . *Papaver rhoeas*
Ribwort plantain. *Plantago lancelota*
Greater plantain . . . . *Plantago major*
Hoary plantain . . . . *Plantago media*
Annual meadowgrass . . . . *Poa annua*
Knotgrass . . . . *Polygonum aviculare*
Black bindweed. . . . . *Polygonum convolvulus*
Willowweed . . . . *Polygonum persecaria*
Silverweed. . . . . *Potentilla anserina*
Tall buttercup. . . . . *Ranunculus acris*
Corn buttercup . . . . *Ranunculus arvensis*
Creeping buttercup . . . . *Ranunculus repens*
Wild radish. *Raphanus raphanistrum*
Wild mignonette . . . . *Reseda lutea*
Sheep's sorrel. . . . . *Rumex acetosella*
Curled dock . . . . *Rumex crispus*
Broad dock . . . . *Rumex obtusifolius*
Field scabious . . . . *Scabiosa arvensis*
Shepherd's needle . . . . *Scandix pecten*
Annual knawel . . . . *Scleranthus annuus*

Swinecress	*Senebiera coronopus*
Groundsel	*Senecio vulgaris*
Field madder	*Sheradia arvensis*
Bladder campion	*Silene inflata*
Corn sowthistle	*Sonchus arvensis*
Spurry	*Spergula arvensis*
Chickweed	*Stellaria media*
Dandelion	*Taraxacum vulgare*
Coltsfoot	*Tussilago farfara*
Small nettle	*Urtica urens*
Lamb's lettuce	*Valerianella olitoria*
Field speedwell	*Veronica agrestis*
Wall speedwell	*Veronica arvensis*
Ivy-leaved speedwell	*Veronica hederaefolia*
Thyme-leaved speedwell	*Veronica serpyllifolia*
Large field speedwell	*Veronica tournefortii*
Field pansy	*Viola tricolor*

The problem with assigning habitat status to weeds according to soil types as generally classified should be at once apparent. The presence or absence of other weeds figures, as does the use of chemicals of organic synthesis and salt fertilizers. The above-ground struggle for light may be as important as auxins from competitive growth in defining the scope and power of any weed crop. And, as nature would have it, there are weeds that seem to thrive amidst a smothering crop — the geranium, campion and field madder for instance. But how do commercial crops themselves deal with the intruders? This is a question not often asked in an age that sees manmade molecules of poisons as high science. But now, since we have asked the questions, we will stay on for some answers. In order to do so, it now becomes necessary to introduce a grammar and lessons not available to those who are governed by approved science, the conventional wisdom, and legislated botany. Our starting point will be a rare treatise published in 1923 by a scientist who was to flee Germany under the Nazi regime. The name of that scientist is Albert Einstein, and his perception of relativity has everything to do with the weed connection.

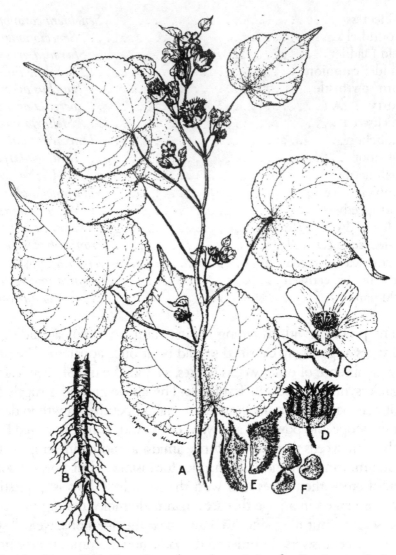

Velvetleaf is called Abutilon theophrasti *in the Latinate. It is actually fertilized — in a manner of speaking — by Lasso and 2,4-D, herbicides which raise the general vitality of velvetleaf. On the other hand, high calcium lime makes it difficult for the weed to thrive. Shown here is Abutilon theophrasti (A); its rootstock (B); flower (C); capsule (D); carpels, or female portions of the flower (E); and the seeds (F).*

6

THE LORE OF WEEDS

In *The Miracle Worker*, which is the story of Helen Keller, there is a closing scene in which the blind and deaf girl makes the connection between things and language. Touch signs from her teacher and the liquid from a pump come together in the child's mind, and for the first time she finds use for her vocal cords and exclaims, "Water!" The precocious child had mastered that one word at six months of age before an illness resulted in her becoming blind and deaf.

Teachers do not often hear the cry of *water* come through so loud and clear. The fondest expressions and the most transparently obvious proofs often miss their mark. I hope this will not be the case by the time these lessons run their course.

While working with Dan Skow on *Mainline Farming for Century 21*, the thought came to me from *Genesis* 1:3, "Let there be light." And there was light, moving at a speed of 186,280 miles per second. This light is an undulating, vibrational creation based on photons, electrons, atoms. The full extension of this conceptionalization says that:

Two or more photons make an electron.

Two or more electrons make an atom.

Two or more atoms make an element.

Two or more elements make a compound.

Two or more compounds make a substance.

Two or more substances make a cell.

Two or more cells make an organ.

Two or more organs make a system.

Two or more systems make up bodies — human, animal or plant.

And behold, the weed — a member of the plant king-dom — was born. Some say God rolled dice, and that the development of each weed was left to chance. Albert Einstein didn't think so. He reasoned that matter was energy and that rapid release of this energy was possible, hence the theory — then the reality — of the atomic bomb. I have used the above equations to prove that all energy comes from the sun and that all economic profits for a system are really free revenue from the sun — that source of photons used to construct the electron that becomes the basis for the atom, etc. Thus the primacy of raw materials in the operation of an economy. No, the Creator didn't roll dice. Everything in nature suggests an ordered universe. Weeds are a part of that order, and they have a reason for being.

There is more lore to weeds than there is to cash crops. Even that statement requires modification, for weeds as cash crops for some few specialists make wheat and oats and corn pale into insignificance. There was a time when the advisers to farmers had three "official" methods for dealing with, say, bindweed: cultivation, including the smother crop, sodium chlorate, and plain table salt, sodium chloride. Sudan grass and forage varieties of sorghum were used to smother out the weed, most of planting to take place between June 15 and July 1, with variations for latitude. Smother crops, however, were counseled after intensive cultivation from spring to the hour annointed for seeding, with eradication of bindweed sometimes taking up to four years diligent attack. Nor was cultivation as a control tool windshield stuff. Successful bindweed eradication depended upon a run through the field each two weeks, duckfoots or sloping blades set three to five inches deep. The sodium chlorate chemical system was reserved for patches too small to cultivate. On roadbeds and railway tracks, common table salt was used.

We learned soon enough that orchard weeds changed with the age of trees. Just about any farm youngster learned to expect pigweed, horsetail, wild lettuce and chess grass in young fruit tree groves. Young trees simply did not shade them out, Dad used to point out. The remedy was hand *unkraut* removal, and the hard work of hoeing. Once the trees were large enough to provide the prayed for shade, then another menace struck — perennial grasses and other weeds too numerous to mention. We didn't worry much about the grasses. Dad kept them mowed with a sickle mower often used to trim the county ditches. It was not until I attended one of the Carey Reams courses that the sickle mower was blessed as a tool of choice because it laid down the grass in nice mats so that decay could operate and vital juices soak into the soil. Withal, we knew that weeds had to go because they harbored insects and had truck with disease.

Dad always kept his pastures clean, so the business of toxic weeds taking a toll on milk cows (we never liked to spell it the German milch) was never a problem. They were gone before they had time to peep above the short prairie grass, either juiced out of business by unfriendly auxins, or slammed to death with a grub hoe. Yet no art of man could protect milk from an off-taste imparted by peppergrass and pennycress. Later, in another part of Kansas, we had the same problem with wild onion and garlic. There were others, and they were identified one at a time, although they all didn't show up in any one season.

Wild onion, garlic, leek, chives . . . . .Allium genus, several species
Bitterweed, narrow-leaved sneezeweed . . . . *Helenium tenuifolium*
Mayweed or dog fennel . . . .*Anthemis cotula*
Ragweed . . . .*Ambrosia elatior*
Giant ragweed . . . .*Ambrosia trifida*
Shepherd's purse . . . .*Capsella bursapastoris*
Wild lettuce. . . . . Lactuca genus, several species
Boneset . . . .*Eupatorium perfoliatum*
Tansy. . . . .*Tanacetum vulgare*

Pennycress, French weed . . . . *Thlaspi arvense*
Peppergrasses . . . . *Lepidium genus, several species*

We had a plum grove near the farm pond on our Ness County, Kansas farm, and we also had a flock of free roaming chickens, Mother's cleanup crew. Chickens consume vast quantities of weed seeds, eating even the poisonous corn cockle with impunity. Small chicks were not allowed to roam, and so we never suffered losses. I don't think anyone on the farm knew that corn cockle contained saponin, a poison that dissolves red blood corpuscles. Either our grown-up chooks didn't eat enough, or they had constitutions as tough as hammered iron. In any case, the gizzard grinding machine is a natural wonder. Not many weed seeds can endure this treatment, pass through the digestive tract, and still germinate.

We didn't use much *store boughten* poultry feed in those days, but even if stray weed seeds arrived they couldn't make it past that avian police force.

Weeds, to our way of thinking, were plants one cursed *soto voce* when thinking of a specific crop. Thus charlock meant trouble in the wheat and oat field, and field bindweed was something that took over a weak barley stand or land left fallow. Creeping thistle — you could find it anywhere except in wheat and oat fields because these crops seemed to have a secret weapon against the tribe.

Charlock, shepherd's purse, curled dock and field speedwell shower the earth with enormous quantities of seeds. Not all of them germinate at once, to be sure. Some go into a holding pattern, as if to provide backup forces for when the farmer succeeds in eliminating the shock troops of frustration via clean tillage. Creeping thistle and bindweed have runners and underground stems capable of growing under almost all circumstances. It takes special microorganisms to annihilate these entrenched invaders, usually those available in well made compost. Corn sowthistle and groundsel have a plumed fruit. Seeds survive in the soil from one year to the next, with a fresh supply arriving by wind throughout the year in the case of groundsel, in late summer and early autumn in the case of corn sowthistle.

Root crops often have a powerful apothecary kept on-scene for weed control. That is why you often read those tiresome lines about such and such a weed grows only in ditches, waste areas, along fences — charges that are somewhat true and somewhat false. The red poppy with a colorful Latinate name is a good example. It may proliferate in an area, yet is usually absent among root crops in the same area. The soil may be loaded with seeds, but under conditions of cultivation nothing happens. White mustard behaves much the same way. Coltsfoot seems to occupy a halfway house position. It fights for its position among root crops, sometimes winning, sometimes losing.

There are weeds generally associated with temporary grass and clover seeds or with seeds and wheat crops. Such seeds form a smother crop. Sown thickly they immediately spread out and cover the soil. Weeds usually do not stand much of a chance among such seeds, unless the soil system is completely out of whack and cultivation is obnoxious to such weeds.

There are weeds that are definitely discouraged by seed crops. Included are weeds that are absolutely indifferent to the nature of the soil in which they can establish themselves.

Annual meadow grass	*Poa annua*
Bent grass	*Agrostis* genus, several species
Black bindweed	*Polygonum convolvulus*
Chickweed	*Stellaria media*
Corn mint	*Mentha arvensis*
Quackgrass	*Agropyron repens*
Lambsquarters	*Chenopodium album*
Goosegrass	*Galium aparine*
Horsetail	*Equisetum arvense*
Ivy-leaved speedwell	*Veronica hederaefolia*
Knotgrass	*Polygonum aviculare*
Large field speedwell	*Veronica tournefortii*
Orache	*Atriplex patula*
Red deadnettle	*Lamium purpureum*
Spurry	*Spergula arvensis*
Willowweed	*Polygonum persecaria*

All these weeds are seriously handicapped when required to grow in the vicinity of seeds crops, some being more affected than others. Bent grass, horsetail, goosegrass, corn mint, and large field speedwell are less influenced by seeds crops than most. Orache, knotgrass, willowweed, and ivy-leaved speedwell are more seriously affected. Orache, goosegrass red deadnettle, corn mint, willow-weed, chickweed, quackgrass and ivy-leaved speedwell seem never to dominate here, even though they rate attention as the chief weed among other crops. There are weeds discouraged by peas and beans. They are:

Bladder campion . . . . *Silene inflata*
Dandelion . . . . *Taraxacum vulgare*
Field scabious. . . . . *Scabiosa arvensis*
Fumatory . . . . *Fumaria officinalis*
Hardhead. . . . . *Centaurea nigra*
Silverweed . . . . *Potentilla answerina*
Sun spurge . . . . *Euphorbia helioscopia*

Why don't some weeds make it among certain crops? I hinted at many of the answers in chapter two and chapter five. I could hint again, but for now it seems sufficient to rate the losers for what they are, unequal contestants for air, nutrients and water when commercial crops are managed with attention to the principles of eco-agriculture.

Weeds that make it in the wheat field, but fail more often when they appear among barley are as follows:

Annual meadow-grass. . . . . *Poa annua*
Bent grass. . . . . Agrostis genus, several species
Corn buttercup . . . . *Ranunculus arvensis*
Field forget-me-not . . . . *Myosotis arvensis*
Lady's Mantle. . . . . *Alchemiella arvensis*
Mouse-ear chickweed . . . . *cerastium vulgatum*
Red bartsia . . . . *Bartsia odontites*
Wall speedwell . . . . *Veronica arvensis*

The following weeds are more likely problems in the wheat field: black bent, thyme-leaved sandwort and goosegrass. On the other hand, you find lambsquarters and spurry less frequently among wheat than among all other cereals.

Lambsquarters, sun spurge and bladder campion are frequent invaders in the barley field, but quackgrass, scentless Mayweed and field madder are less frequent. Oats are more likely to give room and board to sheep's sorrel and spurry, less frequently dove's foot and wall speedwell.

The crude chemistry used to deal with weeds between the 1870s and up to WWII — sodium chlorate and sodium chloride — has now graduated a sophisticated killer tribe of agents that threatens the entire planet. It seems incredible that the issue of weeds, and their control, has been used as an excuse to poison the world's water supplies, assault human chromosomes and loose upon earth a new black death that has graduated from polio to AIDS, with some new and more deadly syndrome slightly visible on the horizon — all because of weeds.

Arden Andersen, the author of *The Anatomy of Life and Energy in Agriculture,* and *Science in Agriculture,* has considered the insanity afloat and projected new thinking. Anderson is one of the bright young men in agriculture who dares think for himself.

Farmers are well aware of the fact that corn is fertilized quite differently than potatoes, and potatoes in turn are nourished differently than grapes. The nutrient ration suitable for ocean sea plants is deadly to a fresh water plant or alfalfa. Andersen deserves quotation in depth.

Farmers experience these differences every day and acknowledge them as common understandings, [Andersen said in words designed for inclusion in this book]. Why then is it so difficult for people to grasp the principle that healthy soil does not support weeds and crops equally well. By prevailing logic asparagus, blueberries, and alfalfa should all grow well in the same soil. They don't. It is also a common belief that insect pests are ravenous, undiscriminating eaters of our food and fiber crops. They are not.

Both of these beliefs are fundamentally and logically incorrect. It has been shown time and again that insect pests are correlated to nutritional balance of the crop and are readily curtailed or eliminated by raising the nutrient density and refractometer reading of the crop. Insect pests are essentially nature's "sanitation engineers."

Weeds also have a "sanitation engineering" role. Velvetleaf, for example, works at cleaning up excess methane in the soil. More often, however, weeds seem to fill the role of "construction engineer" and lighthouse. They can play an important role in altering soil structure, tilth, and composition. They signal the position of the soil health profile. The belief that healthy soil grows weeds equally well as the desired crop is based upon the misconception that the soil in question is healthy. Evaluating the refractometer reading of the plants — both weeds and crops — growing in the same soil tells the observer whether the soil is truly healthy. In this case one will find that the refractometer reading of both the crop and the weeds are about the same, probably in the four to eight range. Neither the crop nor the weeds are balanced nutritionally at these brix levels, but the conventional soil test and nutrient standard may say that this is a "healthy" soil. In any event, it is not.

Some people will contend that the refractometer is not a valid indicator of plant or soil health. In every case that I have evaluated where the consultant, farmer, or fertilizer dealer has made such a statement, it is a case where he is unable to get the refractometer of the crop to increase and, therefore, contends that the refractometer concept, in plant and soil health, is invalid. This is merely a convenient deception.

Very basically, as Dr. Carey Reams instructed, sour grass weeds such as quackgrass are indicative of calcium deficiencies, qualitatively if not quantitatively. Broadleaf weeds are indicative of an improper phosphate to potash ratio. Using the LaMotte soil testing method, this ratio should be two pounds of phosphate to one pound of potash for row crops and four pounds of phosphate to one pound of potash for alfalfa and grass crops. Succulent type plants such as purslane are indicative of soils deficient in biologically active carbons.

Here are grasses that are commonly a problem to row crop producers:

Balloonvile . . . . *Cardiospermum halicacabum*
Beggartick . . . . *Bidens frondosa*
Black nightshade . . . . *Solanum nigrum*
Bristly starbur . . . . *Acanthospermum hispidum*
Buffalo bur. . . . . *Solanum rostratum*
Burgherkin. . . . . *Cucumis anguria*
Canada thistle . . . . *Cirsium arvense*
Carpetweed . . . . *Mollugo verticillata*
Citron . . . . *Citrullus vulgaris*
Climbing milkweed . . . . *Sarcostemma cyanchoides*
Cocklebur, heartleaf . . . . *Xanthium strumarium*
Cocklebur, common . . . . *Xanthium pennsylvanicum*
Cocklebur . . . . *Xanthium strumarium*
Coffee Senna . . . . *Cassia occidentalis*
Common purslane . . . . *Portulaca oleracea*
Common dandelion . . . . *Taraxacum officinale*
Common milkweed . . . . *Asclepias syriaca*
Common ragweed . . . . *Ambrosia artemisifolia*
Common lambsquarters. . . . . *Chenopodium album*
Crotalaria, showy . . . . *Crotalaria spectabilis*
Dayflower . . . . Commelina species
Devilsclaw . . . . *Probiscidea louisianica*
Eastern black nightshade . . . . *Solanum ptycanthum*
Field pennycress . . . . *Thlaspi arvense*
Field bindweed . . . . *Convolvulus arvensis*
Florida beggarweed . . . . *Desmodium tortuosum*
Galinsoga . . . . Galinsoga species
Giant ragweed . . . . *Ambrosia trifida*
Ground cherry, cutleaf . . . . *Physalis angulata*
Ground cherry, lanceleaf . . . . *Physalis laceifolia*
Hairy Indigo . . . . *Indigofera hirsuta*
Hedge bindweed . . . . *Convolvulus sepium*
Hophornbean copperleaf . . . . *Acalypha ostryaefolia*
Jimsonweed . . . . *Datura stramonium*

Ladysthumb .... *Polygonum persicaria*
Mare's tail .... *Hippuris vulgaris*
Mexicanweed .... *Caperonia palustris*
Morning glory, smallflower .... *Jaquemontia tamnifolia*
Morning glory, cypressvine .... *Ipomoea quamoclit*
Morning glory, annual .... Ipomoea species
Northern jointvetch .... *Aeschynomene virginica*
Palmer amaranth .... *Amaranthus palmeri*
Pennsylvania smartweed .... *Polygonum pensylvanicum*
Poorjoe .... *Diodia teres*
Prickly lettuce .... *Lactuca serriola*
Prickly sida or Teaweed .... *Sida spinosa*
Prostrate pigweed .... *Amaranthus blitoides*
Prostrate spurge .... *Euphorbia supina*
Redroot pigweed .... *Amaranthus retroflexus*
Redvine .... *Brunnichia cirrhosa*
Redweed .... *Melochia corchorifolia*
Sesbania, Hemp .... *Sesbania exaltata*
Shepherd's purse .... *Capsella bursa-pastoris*
Sickle pod .... *Cassia obtusifolia*
Smellmelon .... *Cucumis melo*
Smooth pigweed .... *Amaranthus hybridis*
Spiny amaranth .... *Amaranthus spinosus*
Spotted spurge .... *Euphorbia maculata*
Spurred anoda .... *Anoda cristata*
Tall waterhemp .... *Amaranthus ruberculatos*
Texas Gourd .... *Cucurbita texana*
Tropic croton .... *Croton glandulosus*
Trumpetcreeper .... *Campsis radicans*
Velvetleaf .... *Abutilon theophrasti*
Venice mallow .... *Hibiscus trionum*
Virginia copperleaf .... *Acalypha virginica*
Volunteer cowpea .... *Vigna sinensis*
Wild sunflower .... *Helianthus annuus*
Wild spiney cucumber .... *Cucumis dipsaceus*
Wild mustard .... *Sinapis arvensis*
Wild buckwheat .... *Polygonum convolvulus*
Woolly croton .... *Croton capitatus*

Yellow nutsedge . . . . *Cyperus esculentus*
Yellow rocket . . . .*Barbarea vulgaris*

Weeds characterized as broadleafs command a great deal of attention from the poison vendors. However, a quick look at the inventory styled "Cast of Characters" in Chapter 13 will reveal answers well removed from the alchemy now touted as conventional agriculture.

Suffice it to say that specific varieties of weeds within the three categories — broadleafs, grasses, and succulents — are indicative of specific nutrient conditions beyond the general group meaning.

Ragweed, for example, is generally indicative of a phosphate-potash imbalance, but more specifically it indicates a copper problem. Copper is important in the utilization of manganese and iron as well as being important in the many metabolic reactions. Copper also seems to be important in the control of fungal disorders. Many people have allergic reactions to ragweed pollen. This seems to be more related to a copper deficiency in their mucous. Eventually this weed would reduce the calcium deficiency and loosen the soil as a result. This might take nature decades or even centuries to do, but the conceptualized result is nonetheless valid.

The other mechanism under which weeds operate is to actually deposit nutrients into the soil. This is another difficult concept that stretches many people too far. How can a plant possibly deposit nutrients into the soil? Where are the weeds getting their nutrients?

Plants — weeds as well as crops — actually get about 80% of their nutrition from the air. Most of this nutrition is taken from carbon dioxide and water, but it also includes cosmic and solar energy and airborne nutrients. The effectiveness of this direction of nutrient flow is totally dependent upon two conditions: the inherent integrity of the plant and/or seed and the health of the soil.

The soil-plant relationship can be thought of as a radio apparatus. The soil contains the electrical ground and the receiver-tuner, whereas the plant is the antenna. If the antenna (plant) or the receiver-tuner, or the electrical ground (soil) are faulty or malfunctioning, the entire system is moot, and there is no plant growth. If there is only a slight fault or malfunctioning, then there is poor quality music obtained, or just static.

If there is a nutrient deficiency in the plant which started with seed quality, then there will be increased resistance in the antenna and it will not function at its designed intention. If the nutrient deficiency is great enough, a short circuit occurs and the antenna, the plant, will not function at all. In the case of weeds, they are designed according to their genes to collect specific nutrients and energy spectra from the air, convert them to specific nutrients or metabolites and, subsequently, deposit them into the soil.

If there is a deficiency in the soil, then there will be a poor electric ground, creating increased resistance resulting in increased heat and depletion of the soil, and also poor antenna functioning. Additionally, the deficiency reduces the effectiveness of the receiver-tuner. If this mechanism cannot function properly, then what energy and nutrition that does make its way into the soil is not utilized and processed as efficiently as it should be resulting in further malfunctioning of the system, or at least lowered quality.

The entire system is designed to be an alternating current system in which flow of energy and nutrients occurs in both directions. Unfortunately, we almost always observe only a direct current system with energy and nutrients flowing only in one direction. In this case it is an extractive process resulting in soil depletion. Weeds are and have differently designed antennas. These are intended to reestablish the alternating current system. Read and evaluated properly, weeds can be extremely helpful in deciding what steps the farmer needs to take to reestablish this alternating current system for his commercial crop.

We would do well to back up in our thinking to when man found himself on a planet with nothing more than raw materials, weeds included. Then we would realize that exchanges and funny money and tricks of the trade came only after someone climbed up a tree to knock down some fruit, or tilled the soil to harvest a crop. Later the farm and the factory delivered production for exchange, fair exchange being the norm, not some wild-eyed abstraction.

A few farmers now compute the atoms of hydrogen in a drop of water before fertilizing a field. Most prefer to operate by the seat of their pants.

Farmers who rely on herbicides to control weeds are chemical amateurs who have never made the connection between energy from the sun and the energy requirements of plants according to genus and species.

We know that weed control without poisons requires farmers to alter fertilizer practices in such a way as to change the nutrient status of the soil. Conventionally, we add a given quantity of a particular nutrient if it is said to be deficient, often giving no thought or consideration to its side effects, biological compatibility, or actual need. The most important concept to understand is that the soil is, ideally, a living system. The life of this system is dependent upon the status of the uncountable numbers of microorganisms inhabiting the soil. The key to this is the specific groups of microorganisms that are in the majority. Ideally, we would have a majority of aerobic microbes *vs.* anaerobic microbes. The desirable microbes are ultimately responsible for the availability of all nutrients in the soil. As a result, any and every fertilizer material used must be compatible with these microbes. Since microbes are ultimately responsible for nutrient availability, the real crop is the microbe. He is the guy who really needs feeding. If the microbe is happy, he will take care of nutrient availabiltiy to the plant. This means that the farmer often may add materials to the soil different than what he perceives as deficient in the plant or unavailable to the plant.

Weeds are the lighthouses, in this case, to aid the farmer in making these decisions. Often times these can be difficult to interpret, so the use of other tools becomes valuable in determining the most appropriate material to add to the soil.

With this much background considered, let's remember that there seem to be no absolutes, including this one. But there is always a need for a connection, a realization that everything is related to everything else.

Jimson weed, Datura stramonium, *is narcotic and poisonous, and not the good cowfeed Gene Autry's song suggests. Jimson weed is a nemesis to soybean growers. It wakes up when decay has gone wrong, producing ethane. Such decay releases too much cobalt. An improved calcium level in colloidal position, a regulated pH, and proper field decay of organic matter together provide control for this weed without poisons. Illustrated is the upper part of the plant (A); the cauline leaf (B); a ripe capsule (C); and seeds (D).*

7
THE BE & CEC CONCEPT

"I am not in favor of herbicides for the killing of grasses and plants," said the late Carey Reams in one of his lectures. "If you will supply your plant with plenty of the kinds of nutrients it needs, you will not have to be bothered with pesty weeds. The crop will quench them out."

Reams came by his conclusion quite naturally. As a farm consultant — he liked to say "engineer" — for thirty-eight years, he handled not only crop acres, but golf courses as well. "We fertilized the specific variety of grass they wanted, and it grew so quick it quenched out the rest." It was the observation William A. Albrecht and C.J. Fenzau had made — that certain grasses required certain energy levels of nutrients, and that without the appropriate fertility levels, the crop would falter and weeds would stake out their claim.

From pragmatic observations, scientific research and great insight has emerged a principle that needs only to be fleshed out in understandable terms so that farmers can control weeds without poisons.

Albrecht and his followers relied on the base exchange and cation exchange capacity soil testing system. Almost all commercial soil testing laboratories make use of readouts similar to the ones designed by Albrecht, the objective being to stimulate the production of a climax crop, meaning one capable of defending itself against bacterial, fungal and insect attack — and weed proliferation. The basics for this concept have been detailed in *An Acres U.S.A. Primer.*

Plants are not mobile, and they do not have a stomach. Indeed, the soil system has to provide the anchor and the digestive apparatus for the entire crop, and earth the nutrient overload as well. The soil system is the stomach. And into it are fed nutrients — whether as canal mud or manure or factory fertilizer — and these must be digested and made ready for plant use. It is the conceptualization of laboratory scientists that these nutrients must become ions, cations if they are charged positively, anions if they are negatively charged acid elements. They are perceived to enter plant roots the way electricity flows, so to speak, in chemical equivalents. This has been compared to the action one gets when positive and negative poles of a battery are connected. Interactions of cations and anions dovetail with the sun's energy to sustain plant life.

The first order of business for the soil colloid, then, is to hold nutrients — nutrients that can be traded off as the roots of a plant demand them. Thus the first index from the laboratory — the energy in the clay and the humus. Let's consider this entry on the soil audit sheet.

Soils Sample No.	ACTUAL	MAX	LOW
Total Exchange Capacity (M.E.)	24	30	37.5
pH of Soil Sample	7.5	7.0	7.0

Almost all laboratories report cation exchange capacity, and they do this in terms of milliequivalents, or ME. If it helps, you can think of an electrician measuring in terms of volts and amperes, or a physicist measuring magnetic energy in terms of ergs and joules. The soil laboratory has its own lexicon. It measures colloidal energy in terms of milliequivalents of a total exchange capacity, since soil colloids — composed of clay and organic matter — are negatively charged particles. Negative attracts positive. Cation nutrients are attracted and held on the soil colloids. Since anions are not attracted by the negative soil colloids, they remain free to move in the soil solution or water.

A milliequivalent is the exchange capacity of 100 grams of oven-dry soil involved with 1/1000 of a gram of hydrogen (hence the prefix *milli*). This is laboratory talk. What this means is that the ME figure on a soil audit report will tell the farmer the pedigree of his soil, just the way horsepower rating of a tractor spells out the machine's power, or the way the cup, pint or quart defines the volume capacity of a vessel. Some soils have no great capacity for holding plant nutrients, and accordingly they can do very little to deliver the goodies when a hungry root arrives. Cation exchange capacity of a soil depends on the type of clay and the amount of humus. These can vary widely. There are CEC figures as low as one and as high as 80. The clays themselves vary, kaolinite in the South often measuring 10-20, montmorillonite in the West measuring 40-80. CEC values for organic matter are higher yet — 100-200 ME being common. Obviously, pure sand gravel would have a CEC near zero. But the moment sand or gravel starts accumulating colloidal clay and humus, its CEC can go up dramatically.

ME represents the amount of colloidal energy needed to absorb and hold to the soil's colloid in the top seven inches of one acre of soil 400 pounds of calcium, or 240 pounds of magnesium, or 780 pounds of potassium, or simply 20 pounds of exchangeable hydrogen.

The upper portion of the earth's solid crust, to a depth of a few miles, has been estimated to consist of only eight chemical elements to the tune of 98.3%. They are in the order of their decreasing abundance, oxygen, silicon, aluminum and iron; calcium, magnesium, potassium and sodium.

Of the 98.3%, oxygen comprises 47%; silicon 27%; aluminum 8% and iron 5%. These first four elements are either acidic or weakly alkaline in character. The last four — calcium, magnesium, potassium and sodium — comprise 11.3% of this 98.3%, and they are all four strongly alkaline in character. They are also positively charged elements, meaning their atoms bear positive rather than negative electrical charges. The remaining 84 known elements are contained in the remaining 1.7% of the earth's crust. Remember *calcium, magnesium, potassium* and *sodium*. Those four nutrient elements have a lot to do with pH management, maintenance of balanced hormone and enzyme systems, healthy plants, protection against insect, bacterial and fungal attack, weed control, and the business called eco-agriculture.

In any sample audit readout, it will be noted that sandy soil has a lower CEC in terms of ME than silty loam, clay loam or rich muck. The CEC then is an index of what the soil complex can take or will require if a farmer tries to effect balance. Let's move on.

...._..ange Capacity (M.E.)..	..-	5.	..-
pH of Soil Sample	7.5	7.9	7.8
Organic Matter Percent	2 1/0	~ 2~	8.30

Soil laboratories deal with pH values, often on the basis of premises eco-farmers find wanting. Formally stated, the pH figure is the logarithm of the concentration of the active hydrogen or ions, not molecules. Distilled water has one millionth of a gram (.000001, or ten to the minus seven grams) of active hydrogen per liter, said to be pH 7. Such water tastes flat. With a bit more acidity or ionized hydrogen (.000001, or ten to the minus six grams) or more acidity at a pH of 6.0, taste takes on character. Thus as the pH value is smaller, the degree of acidity is higher because there are more active hydrogen ions per unit volume as the ion concentration is higher. In eco-agriculture, an acid soil is viewed as a deficient soil. Calcium may be in short supply, but this may also be true of magnesium, sodium and potassium. The acid condition of the soil means very little if not related to the availability or absence of these major cation nutrients. In fact, we will not deal with pH as such. By bringing calcium, magnesium, sodium and potassium into equilibrium, we will automatically adjust pH in a soil system suitable for plant growth. In the meantime, pH provides a clue, albeit one that can be easily misread if fundamentals of soil balance are not kept in mind.

The clay-humus complex can exist in two fairly distinct physical states. Everyone is familiar with the colloid called gelatin. This substance can exist as a mobile fluid or a flexible solid, the agency for determining the difference being temperature. Much the same is true in a soil system, although acidity, not temperature, determines the state. In a neutral medium (high pH), soil colloids tend to be stable (gel). Under conditions of acidity (low pH), a more mobile (sol) state is achieved. Obviously when molecules of clay and humus become mobile in response to acidity, there is more chemical action in the soil. More nutrients are etched from the parent material. It is not possible, for instance, to farm without factory acidulated fertilizers if pH is kept too high, or neutral. Natural farming in any form requires mild acidity in the soil, more specifically, ideal acidity of the *colloidal portions* within the soil.

Much the same is true of organic matter. Almost all soil audits state organic matter in terms of percent.

Organic Matter, Percent	2.40	2.30	8.30

The road from organic matter in the soil to humus, punctuated with bacteria, dressed with earthworm castings at times, is long and delicate, but in the end it is the balancewheel of the clay-humus complex. From the chair of soil fertility and structure, clay particles resemble humus molecules more than they do the fragments of silt and sand, which are considered inert chemically. The clay-humus complex is chemically active. Molecules and humus not only link to each other, they also have spare valences with which to trap mineral elements and hold them available for plant use. When this active complex is not operative in a soil system, a rain shower washes the soluble salts of potassium, magnesium and ammonium down and away. In other words, it takes the clay-humus complex to make salt fertilizers work, and yet when the clay-humus complex is maintained at peak performance, salt forms of fertilizer are no longer necessary.

Much as a good physician might read signs and symptoms and treat a patient accordingly, some few farmers and agronomists read what the plants have to say and take the saving action in time. Most farmers, however, tooled into compliance with theory-period instruction, would do best to take inventory, to draw appropriate conclusions, and to act accordingly.

The next section of the soil audit has to do with anions, the negatively charged nutrients. Since the soil colloid — composed of humus and clay — is negative in electrical charge, anions cannot attach themselves. Negative repels negative just as positive repels positive. That is why anion elements are held in the soil solution. Plants absorb them through root hairs.

Nitrogen:	lbs/acre		62	59	111
Sulfates:	lbs/acre		1714	2171	3345
Phosphates:	Desired Value		253	275	315
as (P$_2$O$_5$)	Value Found		524	617	403
lbs/acre	Deficit				

The conceptualization of chemistry puts it this way. Phosphorus, sulfur, chloride, boron and molybdenum as plant nutrients must be converted by the soil's refining process to each element's anion phase. Microorganisms handle this chore. Using their bodies as a chelating apparatus, microorganisms convert nitrogen to a nitrate form, phosphorus to a phosphate, sulfur to sulfate, chlorine to chloride, boron to borate, molybdenum to molybdate. Of the anions, phosphorus is the most difficult to comprehend. The country is full of farms with several thousands of pounds P_2O_5 per acre, and crops on those farms are still suffering a phosphorus deficiency. Usually release is the limiting factor, and release is governed by the physical and biological condition of the soil. The soil audit simply states P_2O_5 in pounds per acre. But this is a laboratory chemical judgment and must relate to other plant food elements, how they are related to the values found in the exchange capacity, conditions of temperature and moisture. By itself a laboratory reading means very little then, unless it is understood by the farmer in terms of the grand mosaic of the whole.

Much the same is true of sulfur in a sulfate form. The soil audit states values found by chemical evaluation in terms of pounds per acre.

Ditto for nitrogen. Even though the atmosphere is 78% nitrogen, it has to become fixed with one or more elements in the soil before it can be of use to plant life. Rain does a little fixing, but not much, perhaps only five pounds per acre per year. Soil bacteria and microorganisms fix nitrogen in their bodies. Some of these little fellows are symbiotic and some are non-symbiotic, the former being associated with legumes, the latter living independently. A natural nitrogen cycle depends on healthy living soil. This is the reason nitrogen costs become a farmer's ball and chain as soils go dead. In any case, this is what figures say, but what they really mean is so interdependent that we must defer explanation until a few more facets of the soil profile can be brought into the arena.

Remember the figure at the top of the soil readout exhibited in this chapter. It said CEC (cation exchange capacity). This is the part of the soil readout that catches most attention. It is that part scientific eco-farmers use to adjust pH as a starter. It is the part that is the linchpin in achieving balance and bringing the anion nutrients into the ballpark as well.

Exchangeable Cations					
	Calcium:	Desired Value	6048	7200	9000
	lbs/acre	Value Found	6240	8224	6768
		Deficit			2232
	Magnesium:	Desired Value	980	1440	1800
	lbs/acre	Value Found	1040	1480	2880
		Deficit			
	Potassium:	Desired Value	749	796	850
	lbs/acre	Value Found	2336	1648	4800
		Deficit			
	Sodium:	lbs/acre	84	62	470

As explained earlier, soil colloids, both clay and humus, have a holding capacity for plant nutrients. They operate more like a catchpen. They determine the pedigree of the soil, its potential, its possibilities in crop management. Some soils have no great capacity for holding plant nutrients and accordingly they can do very little to deliver the goodies when hungry roots arrive. CEC qualifies what you have and what you can expect if you take certain actions.

These concepts are not as difficult to handle as first inspection might suggest. Let's forget the laboratory for a minute and think in terms of something we all "think" we understand, your pickup truck, tractor or automobile. All have batteries, each with a positive pole and a negative pole. A flick of a switch will cause movement from one pole to the other — electrical energy! This energy starts the vehicle, operates the lights, permits you to broadcast "breaker, breaker" on the CB radio. The flow of current or energy is always positive to negative.

Nature is inclined to like electrical balance. Therefore a natural movement is an example. Lightning, a product of thunderstorms, not only balances energy in the heavens, it serves as a great producer of nitrogen. An activity that runs counterclockwise to natural balanced energy is the explosion of an atomic bomb.

Farmers of course deal with soil systems, not laboratory experiments or nuclear theory. They look to soil structure, tilth, biotic activity and nutrient uptake for healthy plant construction.

Soil colloids are negatively charged. That is why there is an attraction between the soil colloid for base or cation elements — the old business of positive to negative. This attraction is called colloid adsorption. The capacity to exchange base elements from soil colloids is called cation exchange capacity, or CEC. When negative colloids are neutralized by an accumulation of positive base elements, the system is said to have achieved 100% base saturation.

In your soil audit, the base elements are calcium, magnesium, potassium, sodium and the base trace elements. A soil should be saturated with usable cation nutrients up to 85 or 90% of its capacity. This leaves 10 to 15% for hydrogen, a non-fertilizer.

This is an oversimplification, but hopefully it will provide a fair insight into the scope of soil chemistry. This base element adsorption is called chemical binding. Cation exchange capacity — to put it plainly — means the ability of a soil to act as a source of supply for the exchange base so it can give up nutrient elements to plants in exchange for hydrogen, another base. This means that loading nutrients over to the soil colloid, not feeding the plant, is the name of the soil fertilization game, and in this sense the term plant food is a misnomer. Once an eco-farmer gets this straight he's well on the way to making it happen with nature.

A paragraph or two ago we related that it would take four hundred pounds of calcium to fully load the top seven inches of an acre of one ME soil. Therefore it would take 4,000 pounds per acre for a ten ME tested soil. Needless to say, no farmer would want to go whole hog on one nutrient and neglect the rest. Obviously an audit tells only about cation inventory, not the objective. There are differing theories, and there are sub-schools of thought within each group as to what target figures ought to be. Among eco-farmers, the Albrecht formula is both gaining strength and rolling up millions of acres of proof as well. It works to a remarkable degree.

It was Professor William A. Albrecht, working at the University of Missouri, who found that for best crop production, the soil's colloid had to be loaded with 65-70% calcium, only 15% magnesium, and that potassium had to be in the 2-4% range. Sodium was never much of a problem since it was normally satisfied under the other bases. These values, Albrecht held, were saturation figures when nature was at her finest balance and capable of producing healthy crops and canceling out weeds.

Take calcium for a 12 CEC soil. If such a soil were fully loaded with calcium, the equation would read 400 x 12 = 4,800 (400 pounds for each ME in the top seven inches of an acre). Calcium should take up perhaps 65% of the CEC. Thus the computation should read:

$$12 \ \times \ 400 \ = \ 4,800 \text{ pounds}$$
$$\underline{\times \ \ 65\%}$$
$$3,120$$

Since this is the value found in the soil audit for this CEC soil, the calcium part would appear to be in perfect harmony.

Computations can be made this way for each of the cations. In the case of magnesium, multiplication would read:

$$12 \ \times \ 240 \ = \ 2,880$$
$$\underline{\times \ \ 15\%}$$
$$432$$

Here, again, if this is the value actually found, magnesium should be no problem in this soil. But let's follow the arithmetic all the way on CEC 12 soil, taking potassium.

$$12 \ \times \ 780 \ = \ 9,360$$
$$\underline{\times \ \ 3\%}$$
$$280$$
$$\underline{-312}$$
$$-32$$

The negative thirty-two is not far off target, and probably this soil requires no treatment in terms of potassium.

The next section of a sample soil audit ought to come clear at this point.

Base Saturation Percent				
Calcium (60 to 70%) ⎫ 80%		64.97	68.60	45.34
Magnesium (10 to 20%) ⎭		17.83	20.32	31.75
Potassium (2 to 5%)		12.45	7.04	16.48
Sodium (.5 to 3%)		.75	.43	2.73
Other Bases (Variable)		4.00	3.61	3.71

These data merely represent the extensions simple arithmetic would duly account for. Each of the soil types has a saturation percentage once computations are completed. Note how the first soil is relatively in cation balance. The second soil is fair also. The third needs repair.

As each of the equations for each of the chief cation elements fall into place, a principle of eco-farming becomes transparently clear. pH becomes self-adjusting when calcium, magnesium, potassium and sodium are in proper equilibrium. To answer low pH with lime regardless of the character of that lime rates attention as frustration agronomy.

pH means acidity to some people, but to eco-farmers it means a shortage of fertility elements, the same fertility elements named in the paragraph above. Professor C.E. Marshall of the University of Missouri once designed electrodes and membranes to measure ionic activity of calcium and potassium in the same way hydrogen ions are measured to determine pH. Marshall's pK and pCa illustrated clearly that ionic activities of a mixture of elements were not independent of each other. Taking calcium and potassium in combination, he discovered that potassium gained ascendency in relative activity as cations become narrower. Magnesium, pound for pound, could raise pH up to 1.4

times higher than calcium. A soil high in magnesium and low in calcium could test pH 6.5 and still be entirely inadequate for the growth of alfalfa and superb for certain types of weed production. Any of the major cations — calcium, magnesium, potassium and sodium — in excess can push pH up, and any one of them in lower amounts can take pH down. They have to be in balance or the pH reading is likely to be meaningless. An equilibrium of pH at 6.2 or 6.3 for farm crops (based on these four elements in balance) will prompt plants to grow well and produce bins and bushels in tune with both the pedigree of the seed and the character of the soil. Weeds, in turn, will be pushed back.

As the reader might suspect, the equation presented here represents pure theory — theory that has been proved to a great extent — yet one missing on a few cylinders. C.J. Fenzau for years found that the plants were saying something not evident in those fine-tuned soil reports. The laboratory measured availability, but it failed to tell whether nutrients were in colloidal position, or floating around somewhere else, feeding the readout, albeit not the plant. Plant growth seemed to say nutrients were remaining water soluble. Some obviously hadn't been loaded over to the colloid — the humus/clay complex. Yet usual laboratory readouts handled them as one and the same.

This prompted C.J. Fenzau to design a new soil readout form, one that accounted for this discrepancy. A good laboratory has the capability of giving the colloidal position answer, but before C.J. came along, no one had ever asked the question.

Looking at almost any of the hundreds of research efforts on his plots, the thesis and its proof becomes at once apparent. Fenzau's usual procedure was to divide a plot, using a full NPK fertilizer program on one section, pH modifiers plus a ton of compost on the other. pH modifiers are blends of calcium, magnesium and potassium (or sulfur) deionized and prepared for field application in solution form. Rate of application is usually 10-20 pounds per acre, each spray treatment being worth three to four pounds calcium in perfect form. Next, the crop was planted. A sample was taken July 24, another in November, one during a growth season, one during a dormant season. The procedure was followed year after year. One can only marvel at the readout changes that took place according to plot.

In each case CEC was adjusted upward on the eco-plot. Organic matter improved dramatically. pH moved in the desired direction toward 6.0 and 6.2, often in as little as seven months. As though they were trained circus performers, calcium, magnesium, potassium and sodium moved toward and reached their equilibrium.

If, say, 17% of 500 pounds of calcium is water soluble, it will still measure *available* via the laboratory test, but there will be a shortage on the colloid. Ditto for the other traditional cations. If, on the other hand, a system of humus is working properly etching out nutrients from locked-up positions that aren't even measured, the working colloidal system remains close to constant, a dinner table set for full meals as commercial plants require them.

Complexed supplies mean very little to a farming system that relies on bagged N, P and K year after year because the organic matter complex and the humus supply will be low and poorly functional. In any soil there is a tremendous amount of calcium, aluminum, magnesium, silica, iron and zinc, all a part of the permanent base. At any given point they will not show on the colloidal position or on the soluble position. But they are there. If a good humus system is working, they can be etched out every day they are needed, leaving the level unchanged.

Unfortunately there is no commercial test that will give a farmer a readout of nutrients in a soil in all their forms. This would be too costly. Yet it is known that many soils carry from 40,000 to 80,000 pounds of P_2O_5 per acre in the top seven inches. The farmer does not want that much for a crop year. But if he can figure out how to etch it out — take it out of the bank account, so to speak — then it makes poor economic sense to buy the bagged product and pour it on the soil only to have it join more phosphorus already in the lockup.

As for sampling, the optimum date should make little difference if governing principles are kept in mind, and if enough records exist to explain the variation. Warm soils release more phosphate. A sample taken in February will be different from the one taken in May. This does not mean either is wrong. If a sample is taken in the middle of winter, it is only logical to expect the potassium to be lower than in July.

By managing organic matter, water, air, and temperature properly, the farmer can diminish the amount of N, P and K he has to use. Indeed, the actual yield potential is determined by these other principles to a greater extent than by N, P and K. Nearly 95% of the nutritional factors are related to carbon dioxide, sunlight and water — photosynthesis, in short — together with temperature.

Simplistic N, P and K fertilization, without sound CEC principles in tow, amounts to seat-of-the-pants fertility management and therefore seat-of-the-pants weed control. Laboratories seem incapable of arriving at the same answers for the same soil samples. It leads me to believe that we have exhausted what we can learn from pragmatic observations and official lock-stepped science, and that the time has come to introduce a few new dimensions in making our weed connection.

The late Carey Reams refused to accept the proposition that outside of wet chemistry, calcium was a cation. Dry, and sans contamination, it did not carry electrical current, and was therefore an anion — and with that conceptualization he put his Biological Theory of Ionization at loggersheads with much of base exchange and cation exchange capacity thinking. Reams found weed control best effected in maintaining plant nutrient levels as follows, stated in terms of pounds per acre: calcium, 2,000; phosphate, 400; potassium, 200; sulfate, 200; nitrate nitrogen, 40; ammonical nitrogen, 40; iron, 40.

No one can argue with the success of the Reams conceptualization, both in producing crops and managing weeds without poisons. Mistakes and bad farming are not the issue. Residue fermentation instead of decay, soil degeneration, poverty soils, marked imbalances, low calcium, high magnesium — all have been mentioned as precursors for weed proliferation.

There are lots of laboratories and lots of tests, and farmers sometimes complain that different labs will return different test results based on the same sample. I once confirmed this problem when the same samples were sent to four different laboratories. When recommendations came back, drastic disagreement surfaced on at least one sample, and general inconsistencies laced the entire set of readouts. One lab recommended five and one half tons of lime, and another recommended one ton, both basing their recommendations on the same sample. If the five and one half ton people were right, then one ton would be a waste of time and money. If one ton was right, then five and one half tons meant wasted money and a soil system oversaturated with calcium. Neither was specific as to the quality of the lime in any case. A single ton of fine $CaCO_3$ would be of more value than five tons of coarse-ground 20% $CaCO_3$ as lime. Laboratories often do not know the calcium or calcium-magnesium content of ag lime, nor do they know the coarseness or its availability.

Ag courses use a manual of approved procedures for testing soils, and not all labs have the same equipment or use the same procedure. The results should nevertheless be close, but sometimes they aren't. Some laboratories avoid this dilemma by reporting in terms of high, low, medium for certain cations, and expressing pH, organic matter and humus in the same approximate terms.

And still the above formula fails to explain why and how certain fertility products support weeds and distress crops, or vice versa. Thus our venture into a twilight zone of science in the pages that follow begins.

Canada thistle, or Cirsium arvense, *likes low iron, low calcium and a poor organic matter structure in the soil. When calcium is inadequate to govern trace mineral release, and the colloidal pH is improperly positioned, some metals are released in excess. Canada thistle also means low phosphate or complexed phosphate because of low humus. Cirsium arvense is illustrated above together with its root profile (A); its head (B); flower (C); and dry indehiscent one-seeded fruit (D). Anhydrous ammonia helps Canada thistles proliferate.*

8
FERTILIZING THE WEEDS

There was a time not too many years ago when scientists referred to a single living cell as a "simple cell." But that was before James Watson, Francis Crick and George Palade and DNA, RNA and endoplasmic reticulum entered everyday vocabulary. All three have been described as complicated, beautiful and significant, the last because they have caused a conceit of modern science to crumble. That conceit is the idea that molecules simply banged around in jelly-like protoplasm to create cells, all according to the laws of chance. Now scientists such as Lewis Thomas, M.D., in *The Lives of a Cell*, tell us that a single cell is more complex than a city. It has more systems in operation — energy generators, invasion guards, transports, food factories, barriers, waste disposal and communication links than Chicago. We conceive it thus:

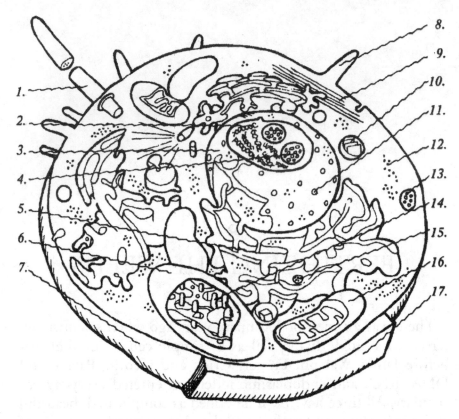

1. Cilia (locomotion); 2. Chromosome (contains DNA); 3. Nucleus (heredity bearing core); 4. Nucleolus (center of synthetic activity and storage); 5. Endoplasmic reticulum (pathway to nucleus, bears ribosomes); 6. Chloroplast (photosynthesis center of cell); 7. Cell membrane; 8. Microvilli (promote absorption); 9. Microfilaments (maintain cell shape); 10. Lysosome (scavenger organelle); 11. Pore (allows diffusion to and from nucleus); 12. Ribosomes (contain RNA); 13. Food storage gland; 14. Chlorophyll; 15. Secretion gland; 16. Mitochondria (regulates cellular activity); 17. Plasma membrane.

The surface membrane of this cell controls the entry and exit of everything for the unit. For all the world it suggests a chemical sense of taste and smell. When the right molecule floats by, its membrane creates an appendage of sorts to reach out and secure the needed nutrient. Chemical enzymes function as a sort of communications system, regulating business traffic with other cells and the outside world.

The RNA that Watson told about in *The Double Helix* is the messenger in the city called the cell. It has some of the earmarks of the DNA with this exception — it has permission to leave the nucleus, code and deliver the message, and in effect hold the larger organism together.

How all this happens has been a wonderment ever since science set about the task of asking the right questions. Some of the right questions were asked when atomic bombs were tested hard on the heels of WWII. The survival of the ubiquitous Russian thistle at ground zero was not the only item of scientific interest. It was known, of course, that x-ray radiation increased the mutation rate of genes, and that farm chemicals did the same. It was therefore a matter for concern at the Atomic Energy Commission that test proliferation would increase radiation, and this in turn would have an effect on human gene mutation. Accordingly, genetics research became "immediate attention" stuff.

The Atomic Energy Commission did what government agencies always do. It threw money at the problem. Some of it took root at the University of Indiana, where James Watson and Francis Crick unraveled the molecular structure of the DNA. This was Nobel Prize stuff, but it wasn't the first time scientists had investigated the fine-tuned apparatus called the cell.

In *The Phenomena of Life*, George Crile noted that electrical energy plays a fundamental part in the organization, growth and function of protoplasm. Like Georges Lakhovsky, Crile held that living cells were electrical cells functioning like a system of generators, inductance lines and insulators, and that the role played by radiation and electricity — low-level energy, in short — was no more mysterious in man, animals and plants than in batteries and dynamos.

Philip S. Callahan, the author of *Tuning In To Nature*, has concluded that the key to life is low-level energy. A few agronomists have written about energy from the cosmos, notably Rudolf Steiner and Ehrenfried Pfeiffer, but their insightful suggestions have been consigned to intellectual underworld status.

Before I continue and then terminate these lessons on weeds, some few notes on low-level energy seem appropriate.

From a schoolman's point of view, what I have to offer now may look like so much arcane knowledge. And except for Callahan's dictum, I might leave it out. But if low-level energy in fact rules life, should we not attempt the connection that explains weeds and suggests non-toxic control?

The Kybalion deals with certain insights entertained by philosophers in ancient Egypt and Greece. There were seven principles as follows:

1. *The principle of mentalism.* It said that the *all* is mind, that the universe is mental.

2. *The principle of correspondence.* This principle embodies the truth that there is always a correspondence between the laws and phenomena of the various planes of being and life.

3. *The principle of vibration.* It states that nothing rests; everything moves; everything vibrates.

4. *The principle of polarity.* Everything is dual. Everything has poles. Everything has its pair of opposites. Like and unlike are the same, opposites are identical in nature, but different in degree. Extremes meet. All truths are but half-truths. Paradoxes may be reconciled.

5. *The principle of rhythm.* Everything flows, out and in. Everything has its tides. All things rise and fall. The pendulum swing manifests itself in everything. The measure of the swing to the right is the measure of the swing to the left. Rhythm compensates.

6. *The principle of cause and effect.* Every cause has its effect. Every effect has its cause. Everything happens according to law. Chance is but the name for law not recognized. There are many phases of causation, but nothing escapes law.

7. *The principle of gender.* Gender is in everything. Everything has its masculine and feminine principles. Gender manifests on all planes.

Heraclitus said it all, that everything is in motion, and he meant everything, down to the smallest cell.

Our bodies contain approximately two hundred quintillion cells. In this fabulous number there are hardly two cells vibrating with the same frequency, this being partly due to the incessant activity taking place within the cells, and partly to the specific characteristics of different tissues, plus other factors. From a biological point of view, it would be impossible to find at any given time two individual cells exactly alike in every respect. Every cell of every individual tissue of any particular species — plant, animal or man — is characterized by its own oscillatory shock. In disequilibrated cells, it would be necessary to generate as many wavelengths for correction as there are different cells in any given system. The problem would thus seem to be insoluble. With remarkable imaginative insight Georges Lakhovsky evolved a solution. He designed a new type of radioelectrical apparatus, the multiple-wave oscillator, capable of generating a field in resonance. The practical results he obtained in various hospitals soon confirmed the validity of his theory. His agricultural experiments were equally impressive, and have been detailed in *The Secret of Life*.

This has been one key a number of hard knocks inventors have relied on to rediscover the multiple-wave oscillator, and harness it to field situations. Galen Hieronymus pursued the low-level energy principle in the 1930s, standing on the shoulders of Albert Abrams, Ruth Drown, G.W. Delawarr and others from a century or less earlier.

The term *radiesthesia* is not well known by the general public. It covers sensitivity to radiation, and this includes all the low-level energies. Fertilizers are packed with energy, none of which will turn a motor or move the needle demanded by laboratory science. Radionics is an instrumental form of radiesthesia. Its most significant agricultural use is diagnostic.

The term *scan* is often misunderstood. A computer can scan a piece of writing. This means it rapidly examines each word, each comma, each period, either searching for some word, or to identify the correctness of every word, such as in spell checking.

A fast reader often skims a book, usually to get the gist of the presentation without actually reading all of it. No one would suggest that skim reading delivers total comprehension. Scan reading does in terms of its objective. This distinction has prompted many users of the radionics device to call it a scanner.

It would take a short course or two to explain the scanner. The basic premise of the scanner is that each body — animal, human, plant — each organism or chemical — absorbs energy via a wave field with unique radiation-type characteristics. The most complex material has the most complex wave form. William A. Tiller is the granddaddy of making complicated things appear simple. His *Radionics, Radiesthesia and Physics* paper has a diagram which is redrawn here. It illustrates how the fundamental carrier wave "is thought to be polarized with a rotating polarization vector."

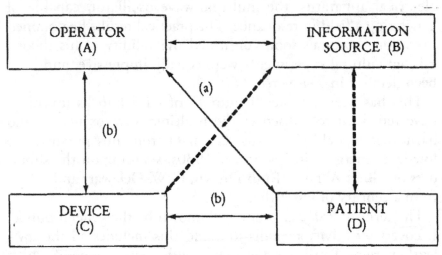

Pat Flanagan, the scientist author of *Pyramid Power*, has noted, "When an operator's mind and emanations from the tuner are on the same wavelength, a type of resonance is established, and the detector indicates this mode. The Hieronymus detector is simply a sheet of bakelite or plexiglass under which is placed a flat spirally wound coil, connected to the output of the amplifier and the ground. When resonance is established, there is a change of tactile characteristic in the top of the detector. The change of characteristic is detected by lightly running the fingertips on the surface of the detector plate while turning the vernier dial of the prism. Hieronymus established numbers which correlate with the known chemical elements and combinations . . . Although the Hieronymus machine cannot be explained by modern physics, it does have merit by the fact that the results can be duplicated."

Pat Flanagan came by his insight quite naturally. At age 15 he invented a neurophone for the deaf because he realized that the human brain was not hard-wired, as neurologists and anatomists had believed. This concept suggested direct nerve connections, say, from ear to certain brain areas associated with hearing, from eyes to visual areas, and so on. Flanagan believed the brain to be holographic, meaning that many areas of the brain are capable of performing multiple functions. The neurophone relied on this concept, and used the skin to set up a new hearing organ.

In addition to the hearing described above, there are such things as eyeless sight, called dermoptical activity, clairaudience telepathy, dowsing, and so on. The radiations associated with the senses are well known. Briefly, radionics enables one to work with and direct a minute amount of energy because everything in the universe emanates an energy. It is radiating that energy and that energy is on a specific frequency. If you have a dozen radios you could have each one of those radios tuned to a different station. In other words, you could be listening to Bach over here, Beethoven over there, a ball game over here, rock-n-roll over there, and the news elsewhere, each one of them tuned to a different frequency. That is what many farmers work with in radionics using a scanner. They work with specific frequencies to produce a specific effect. So, let's say you have a milk cow with mastitis. Mastitis resonates at a specific frequency. So the modulation of that energy has a specific sign wave. A seed has its reading, and so does a soil.

The directed application of the mind is a key to developing an ability to use special instruments like the scanner and tune in on an information source not now considered state of the art. A few people like to think of the scanner as tomorrow's physics. Some of their ideas may be found wanting at some future date, but for now they seem to stand up to all reasoned attacks. It is beyond the purview of this text to either explain or defend the scanner. But since scanner findings are the premise for many fertilization recommendations, it has its reason for being.

Hieronymus told me something about how Abrams became interested in low-level energies. "Abrams was a student at Heidelberg and one of his professors, a Herr Doktor DeSauer was a gardener. He grew onion plants in a flat. Before the frost was over for the season, he had them growing, say, eight or ten inches high. When it was time to transplant them, he pulled up a number of these plants and transplanted them, but he had a few left over. So he brought these back into the house and laid them on the table alongside the flat with the growing plants. After a few days he noticed that there was some effect from the apparently dead plants on the growing plants in the end of the box. And that was the beginning of his observation that some sort of irradiation was coming from the roots of those plants. He smeared some yeast cells on microscope slides, put them near those roots, and the cells were destroyed. Abrams, being one of DeSauer's prize pupils, became very interested in that. And that's how Abrams got started with the idea that there was something emanating from those plants. He carried the idea farther, and I take off all of my hats to Albert Abrams for having pioneered the idea of emanations coming from things. In my research I found that each isotope of each element emanates an energy at a specific frequency for that particular material, and no matter what shape or form of combination you find it in, you'll get that emanation. For instance, sodium chloride has not only the sodium emanations and the chlorine emanations, but also that molecular combination which you called salt."

The world now knows that Albert Abrams evolved a theory and began the experiments that led to the first radionics instru-

ments — the Abrams Oscilloclast and the Abrams Reflexo-
phone — and he taught physicians and chiropractors how to use
them.

The late Galen Hieronymus and his wife Sarah, used Abrams'
principles to control weeds without poisons. After many years of
research, the two Georgia scientists brought to the farm scene
the Cosmic Pipe. Its function was to broadcast intensified sun
energy into the soil, much as the experiments of DeSauer and
Abrams suggested. Three outstanding and unlooked for results
became a consequence. Hieronymus defined these as follows:

1. Concentrated sunlight energy brought from the energy col-
lector head down wires to the center of the pipe — where it was
modulated by the positive energies of the energized reagents in
the well — acted as a purifying power to remove chemical toxins
from the affected land.

2. Experiments in Georgia, Missouri, Arkansas, and North
Dakota revealed musk thistles diminished in size from a bristly
six to seven feet tall down to a two-foot-tall plant. Wild lettuce
became dwarfed. Before the season of pipe energy, the cows
could not get through the forest of tall thistles with their big
purple blooms. After the pipe energy had been broadcast for several seasons, musk thistles grew two to two and a half feet tall,
no more, and had a shorter tap root. Cows ate the seed pods off
the top. Wild lettuce plants in wheat fields in North Dakota
were also dwarfed after a season of Cosmic Pipe energy had been
broadcast. The plants grew hardly six inches to two feet, and not
the usual four feet.

3. Another anomaly produced by the Cosmic Pipe was the
elimination of chemical poisons from the soil.

Galen Hieronymus named the energy he had on tap *eloptic*
energy. As regulated by the Cosmic Pipe, it "creates a balanced
soil and harmonious conditions in which the elemental forces of
nature can pour their energies of growth and power into the soil
and plants," became an explanation Sarah Hieronymus used in a
communication to *Acres U.S.A.* The general concept was mentioned by Rudolf Steiner in his book, *Spiritual Forces.*

The Energy Law of Similars has a long and distinguished biography. It was referenced by Hippocrates, the Father of Medicine; by the physician Paracelsus in the 15th century; by the oracle of Delphi; and by Shakespeare during the reign of Queen Elizabeth. Homeopathic medicine, of course, is based on the Law of Similars.

The theory as used by Hieronymus and associates to eliminate weeds without poisons may be considered fringe science by those who have never spent 100 hours study eloptic energy, but it works.

Musk thistle leaves picked from the parent plant will weaken and die in the well of the instrument. This debilitating status can be broadcast to the same weeds in the field. The result is lower energy, weakness, and even death for the invader. "Sometimes we take weed specimens sent to us by farmers and transfer their dying energy into vials of water," explained Sarah Hieronymus. "This can be broadcast to fields by putting the vials into the Cosmic Pipe and treating it with the weed's diminishing and faltering energy using an Hieronymus Analyzer Treatment Unit.

These researchers have also obtained good results in weed elimination by transferring burned weed seed energy to a vial of neutralized oil, and leaving the vial in the Cosmic Pipe through the winter.

As mentioned earlier, it takes short course training to use properly an Analyzer Treatment Unit. For those who are familiar with eloptic energy and radionics, here are the instrument settings that will reveal the general vitality of a weed, hence its efficacy in projecting negative or dying energy to the same weed standing in the field.

Weeds	Rate
Wild alfalfa, *Psoralea floribunda*	63.25 - 49.25
Hedge bindweed, *Convolvulus sepium*	21.5 - 7.75
Bristly star bur, *Acanthospermum hispidum*	30.75 - 73
Broom sedge, *Andropogon virginicus*	16.5 - 14
Bull thistle, *Cirsium vulgare*	23.25 - 68.25
Buttonweed, *Diodia teres*	22.25 - 27
Canada thistle, *Cirsium arvense*	7.5 - 19.5
Cheat, *Bromus secalinus*	37.5 - 57.5
Chickweed, *Stellaria media*	24.2 - 53

Pasture thistle, *Cirsium altissimum*	4.5	- 21.25
Cocklebur, *Xanthium pennsylvanicum*	61.25	- 82
Common burdock, *Arctium minus*	73.5	- 37
Corn gromwell, *Veronica persica*	59	- 37.5
Dandelion, *Taraxacum officinale*	65	- 71.75
Facelis, *Panicum dichotomiflerum*	18	- 26.5
Fall panicum, *Panicum dichotomiflorum*	36	- 41.25
Horsetail, *Equisetum arvense*	38.5	- 41.5
Fleabane, Erigeron genus, several species	8	- 25.75
Florida beggarweed, *Desmodum tortuosum*	24.5	- 10.75
Foxtail barley, *Hordeum jubatum*	36	- 23.25
Golden rod, *Solidago canadensis*	12.25	- 21.25
Giant foxtail, *Setaria faberi*	16.5	- 14
Barnyard grass, *Echinochloa crusgalli*	88.5	- 41
Crabgrass, *Digitaria sanguinalis*	19.25	- 23.25
Johnsongrass, *Sorghum halepense*	20.75	- 70
Lovegrass, see stinkgrass	19.25	- 22
Quackgrass, *Agropyron repens*	23.25	- 27.75
Sage grass, *Artemisia fugida*	14.5	- 21
Stinkgrass, *Eragrostis cilianensis*	15.75	- 14.5
Venus looking glass, *Specularia perfoliata*	18.5	- 9
Horseweed, *Erigeron canadensis*	53	- 69
Japanese hedge parsley, *Aethusa cynapium*	9.25	- 22.25
Jimson weed, *Datura stramonium*	32.25	- 40.5
Knotweed, *Centaurea nigra*	20	- 30
Lambsquarters, *Chenopodium album*	40.5	- 36
Mayweed, *Anthemis cotula*	47.5	- 65.5
Milkweed, Asclepias genus, several species	16.5	- 45.25
Morning glory, Ipomoea genus, several species	72.5	- 58
Mustard sedge, *Cyperus rotundus*	42.25	- 57.75
Nutshade, *Cyperus esculentus*	30	- 42
Joe-Pye weed, *Eupatorium purpureum*	9.5	- 22
Purslane speedwell, *Veronica peregrina*	41.25	- 52
Ragweed, Ambrosia genus, several species	46.25	- 51
Redroot pigweed, *Amaranthus retroflexus*	24.25	- 49.5
Red sorrel, *Rumex acetosella*	22.75	- 24.75
Russian thistle, *Salsola kali*	13.25	- 18
Sicklepod, *Ajuga replans*	11.75	- 7

Smartweed, *Polygonum pensylvanicum*	45	-	44
Sowthistle, Sonchus genus, several species	65.5	-	68.25
St. Augustine, *Paspartum distichum*	13.75	-	52.75
Stinging Nettle, Urtica genus, several species	88.5	-	48.5
Sulfur cinquefoil, *Potentilla recta*	11.75	-	25.25
Smooth sumac, *Rhus glabra*	4	-	18.5
Teaweed, *Chenopodium ambrosioides*	71	-	28.5
Trumpet creeper, Ipomoea genus, several species	23	-	44
Western ragweed, *Ambrosia coronopifolia*	11.25	-	13
Wild grape, *Vitus lambrusca*	43.75	-	32.5
Wild lettuce, Lactuca genus, several species	19.25	-	47
Wild mustard, *Brassica kaber*	82	-	42.5
Wild oats, *Avena fatua*	31	-	3.5
Winter vetch, *Uicia villosa*	27.75	-	52.75
Yellow nutsedge, *Cyperus esculentus*	95.25	-	94
Fleabane, Erigeron genus, several species	8	-	25.75
Prostrate knotweed, *Polygonum aviculare*	20	-	31
Foxtail, Setaria genus, several species	8.75	-	42.75
Sage, *Artemisia vulgaris*	14.5	-	21
Toadflax, *Linaria vulgaris*	14.25	-	27.5
Sorrel, *Rumex acetosella*	22.75	-	24.75
Cinquefoil, Potentilla genus, several species	11.75	-	25.25
Pigweed, Amanranthus genus, several species	41	-	33.5

These weed and weed seed energy rates were obtained in the laboratory of Advanced Sciences Research and Development Corporation by scanning actual weed samples with Hieronymus instruments. They are offered here as an aid to farmers who need help with weed problems. These rates, much like those in the Advanced Sciences Health and Cosmiculture Manuals, apply only to the firm's own instruments. Some good results occasionally may be obtained with other instruments, but not on a consistent basis. These rate settings may be charged into vials of distilled water, and used to treat or eliminate weed infestations. Advanced Sciences makes reagents for elimination of special types of weeds. A specimen of the weed from the person who needs the reagent for treating this type of weed is required.

Hieronymus explained, "Conventional science has certain tools, most of which are electrically operated. This is not electricity. It is not in the electromagnetic spectrum as now understood. Most of our scientists deal with the electromagnetic spectrum and the instruments and devices used to measure the activities in the electromagnetic spectrum."

It is this ability to diagnose that has earned the scanner a role in non-toxic weed management. In dealing with weeds, the scanner has proved itself by furnishing answers to sometimes unasked questions.

Some few years ago, when I started writing this book, the late Jerry Fridenstine of Energy Refractors helped me design a worksheet for the purpose of finding scanner answers to weed problems. Our objective was to scan both soil samples and weeds to see what conclusions would flow from the evidence.

Two findings emerged soon enough. First, *general vitality* seemed to be in command. When a general vitality reading for weeds raced ahead of the same reading for the crop, then weed proliferation would be an accomplished fact. Moreover, concentration of nutrients in weeds usually means a shortage of the same nutrients in the soil and crops.

The idea emerged to find a combination of fertilizers that drop the weed's energy value to zero, then take a sample of the crop involved and make certain that the fertilizer does not drop the crop's energy value to zero. Let's say you have a corn plant in one tube and a foxtail in the other. Most of the time you will discover that calcium will make the foxtail rather ill, and the corn plant well. If calcium doesn't do the job, one of the liquid humates with calcium will. I have seen farmers use the scanner to eliminate weeds in most parts of the country. One grower with wild oats in his barley stand appealed to a consultant for help. The foxtail remedy worked on wild oats. Generally, reports Dan Skow, as you bring the phosphorous-potassium ratio in line there are less weeds. Better aeration and more microbial life figure. The broad-spectrum remedies and fine-tuning approaches both work, even though neither have made it into Weed Society thinking.

The scanner evidence that shook the ground, in my opinion, was composed of readings for fertilizers. Certain fertilizers actually "fertilized" weeds. Jay McCaman pointed this out as early as 1985 in his monograph, *Weeds! Why?* He noted that velvetleaf developed a GV readout of 470 on the scanner. Application of muriate of potash (0-0-60) increased the GV to 740, and this provided an assist to the production of velvetleaf. The application of high calcium lime, McCaman said, reduced the GV number to zero. Based on this finding, it is reasonable to expect high calcium lime to create a soil condition antagonistic to the proliferation of velvetleaf, which is exactly what more conventional approaches have confirmed.

McCaman's little monogram in effect said "bingo" all the way. It said that if velvetleaf is a problem, then Lasso or 2,4-D cannot be considered for weed control because "both raise the GV of velvetleaf."

Jay McCaman operates McCaman Farms at Sand Lake, Michigan. His construction of a fertilizer, toxic chemicals, weed index followed quite naturally once the doors to the closets housing radionics had been kicked open. I think *Acres U.S.A.* had a role in this. There are some 300 farm magazines in the United States. Only *Acres U.S.A.* has been willing to examine the radionics instrument. Some radionics people claim they can zap insects and cure everything from shingles to the heartbreak of psoriasis. I do not know whether these claims are true or not. The scientific establishment so far has succeeded only in driving to an early grave men with credentials and standing who even entertained investigating low-level energy. Thus it has come down to farmers and fearless uninstitutionalized scientists to probe for answers.

McCaman wrote, "Basic fertilizers . . . usually contain more than one mineral or material. Muriate of potash (0-0-60) consists of both potassium and chlorine. Sulfate of potash consists of both potassium and the sulfate form of sulfur. Soft rock phosphate has over 60 minerals but no nitrogen. Many times GV readings may be in response to the combination of minerals contained within the product and not to just one mineral. For instance, black nightshade responds the same to both muriate of potash and sulfate of potash. It can be assumed therefore, that this pesty weed prefers the potassium. Velvetleaf appears to respond to the soil-destroying influence of the chlorine in the muriate of potash more than to sulfate of potash. Also the energy released by the sulfate may be causing a change in some other minerals of soil conditions which the velvetleaf prefers to avoid."

McCaman has identified some 800 weeds in the United States and accomplished the scanner work needed to identify how fertilizers and chemicals of organic synthesis — as well as other materials such as Basic H, and other proprietary products — help or hinder weed production.

Many salt fertilizers actually fertilize weeds, 0-0-50 and 0-0-60 leading the way. Anhydrous is certain to give quackgrass, foxtail, field bindweed, prostrate knotweed, Canada thistle, ragweed and many others a shot in the hip. Parenthetically, it will also give corn borers, corn earworm, corn smut, Colorado potato beetles, alfalfa weevil and a roster of insect and fungal agents too long to detail, a signal to deliver damage. In fact, it might be stated fairly that anhydrous is an insurance policy for the sale of great overloads of pesticides.

Soft rock phosphate, on the other hand, sucks energy out of quackgrass and all other weeds, depriving them of healthy life. High calcium lime is even more effective in making life tough on weeds.

In order to make use of scanner technology, weed seeds should be collected in the fall and, failing that, weed heads should be collected in the spring. Some farmers go through the entire regents set to find fertility combinations that lower the vitality of each weed and enhance the vitality of crops. Only a few practitioners handle the scanner chore commercially. Jay McCaman furnishes scanner results for a small fee, identifying weeds and soil applied products that will lower the general vitality of each weed tested. A contact point is Jay McCaman, Box 22, Sand Lake, Michigan 49343.

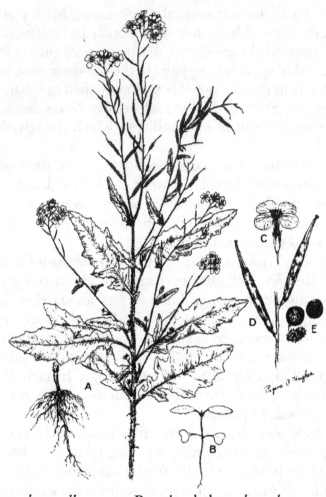

Wild mustard usually means Brassica kaber, *but there are many mustards — charlock,* Brassica arvensis; *Indian mustard,* Brassica juncea; *ball mustard,* Neslia paniculata. *Wild mustard is usually related to a field planted to small grains and the development of slime molds. The weed grows best in areas stressed due to poor drainage and poor structure. Control comes down to applying good compost or nitrogen to get the decay process moving properly. Above, an artist's conception of pinnatifida variety (A); the seedling (B); a flower (C); siliques, an elongated fruit divided by a partition between the two carpels in two sections (D); and seeds (E).*

9

POVERTY PASTURES,
POVERTY WEEDS

I do not think it likely that very many farmers will come to understand either pastures or weeds that torment these swards without reading and mastering Andre Voisin's fantastic statement, *Grass Productivity*. Equally important is *Holistic Resource Management*, by Allan Savory, a provocative book that addresses the question of why — in spite of all efforts to halt desertification — land, air and water resources continue to deteriorate. The life and times of weeds are not the focal points of these texts, yet somehow I have a feeling the many details on weeds presented here will make little impression if the bigger picture is not understood and preserved.

On more than one trip to Minnesota, I have seen wild mustard moving in and taking whole fields of soybeans. I have seen where weeds were taking over pastures and corn rows were being choked to death by weeds. Later I presented my field notes to William A. Albrecht at the University of Missouri to see if rhyme or reason could be made out of what was happening. Albrecht's usual response was that toxic technology was a sunset operation, that the anatomy of weed control was to be seated in fertility management.

Biodynamics is a study in itself, the basics being outside the purview of this little book. Countless texts and even more short courses here and abroad train farmers in the biodynamic art, the objective being a totally sustainable agriculture that builds soils, crops and people. In what may well be one of the most profound books on agriculture ever written, *Bio-Dynamic Agriculture Introductory Lectures, Volume I*, Alexander Podolinsky set down a few *Podolinsky-isms*.

• Plants not allowed seasonally optimum growth on top will gradually also shorten roots, and sod-bound shallow roots result.

• Microbial and worm activity ceases below root levels.

• The need for any soil ripping is a result of bad farming. Mechanical ripping is costly and will only temporarily relieve the compacted conditions.

• Ripping wettish clay only causes cutting smearing of soil pores where cut, thus inhibiting air penetration.

• The biological equivalent to European winter for Australian soils is the state of soil hardness and inactivity of extreme dryness.

• Soil, when it is truly biologically active, alone can account for produce with natural quality.

• When there is an immediate requirement for major or minor nutrients, judicious biodynamic procedures would get these major or minor elements out of fertilizer bags in the conventional way — relying on a sheet composting action through preparation 500 in the soil — rather than running the risk of introducing concentrations of undesirable chemicals into the soil, via dubious, so-called "organic" manures, city refuse, etc.

• The important thing about a humus colloid is that the soluble elements in it are at all times available to the plant, and yet they will neither evaporate not leach out. Humus will hold 75% of its own volume in water.

• A plant actually grows from the leaves downward as well as upward from the roots.

• Artificial fertilizers are not poisons . . . but they actually become available in a form which is outside the organization of nature. That, of course, is rather dangerous.

• In most cases, so-called organic manures are of highly dubious value, and these include chicken, feedlot out of the oceans is full of heavy metals and pesticide residues. These materials are invariably applied in a form that permits water solubility and do not constitute real compost in the sense of Preparation 500, where a total has developed. There is as much danger in water solubility problems from these organic manures as there is from factory acidulated salt fertilizers.

• Bloat does not occur at all on Bio-Dynamic farms. Neither does sterility, acetonemia, etc.

• We are farming within a vast cosmological and earthly environment. After all, our earth is also a cosmic body, and we must not forget that fact. We are a little bit too tied down to the fact that this is a material earth, and everything seems solid. We are inclined to think that something even as important as sunlight is a bit mystical, because it comes from far away. It is not at all. We are, in conjunction with other cosmic bodies, one huge cosmic ecology. If we work within that vast environment, then we are working within the organization of nature, and that would be true biological farming, not just using organic manures or green manures.

• At first when you sow down clover, you are not going to build up nitrogen, you are going to lose nitrogen in the soil. If peas and beans and vetchs and many other legumes have been sown, and have been allowed to grow just beyond flowering stage, even if they have not formed a decent pod yet, they will be found to have used more nitrogen than they leave, if they are mown down or plowed in at that stage.

In other words, Alex Podolinsky represents first rate science. And those who view biodynamics as some sort of mysticism are merely codifying their ignorance. Few would characterize Einstein as a clairvoyant. Instead, he is seen as a scientist who could conceptualize a part of the Creator's plan. Similarly, when Rudolf Steiner conceptualized the foundation principles that led to biodynamic agriculture, he discovered realms of nature others would not comprehend for decades. All the biodynamic preparations — starting with 500 — are the end products of reasoned science dovetailed together with experiments and practice. We can sketch a few details, but in the final analysis there can be no substitute for reading Podolinsky's book, or Hugh Lovel's treatise on the same subject. Without clear understanding and obedience to nature's ruler, reliance on a preparation is useless.

It will be noted that no mention of weeds was made in these *Podolinsky-isms*. Yet his experiences with a million and a half acres (some his own, more belonging to clients) have proved that healthy grass is anathema to weeds.

Biodynamic preparation 500 was conceived by Rudolf Steiner. It is made under rules that appear esoteric to the uninitiated, but in fact comply with the cosmic nature of farming. Briefly, preparation 500 is made by burying fresh manure from cows in a cow horn over the winter, when microbial activity is dormant. Harvested and stored correctly, this "developed" material is introduced into water stirred a prescribed number of times one direction, then reversed, each achieved vortex rising and falling. The solution is sprayed on pasture grass during evening hours when the temperature is optimum. The object is to cause pasture grass to recast the makeup of the soil so that a climax crop can follow. And as Albrecht pointed out, a climax crop is its own insurance policy against weed infestation. I have seen clay soil so hard it could be and was diced and used for bricks to build a clubhouse for the Tasmanian Organic Growers Association, adobe style. That same soil, after preparation 500 treatment, became so mellow, it was possible to run an arm in too near the elbow.

Weeds no longer figured, and growers could figure on having no weeds — all because of the primacy of a system.

Weed control from a biodynamic point of view requires a new focus. The plants we think of as weeds have their own functions in the overall scheme of things. "When we do not know what the weed's function and purpose is, how can we tell whether the plant is beneficial or not?" asked Hugh Lovel.

Hugh Lovel has worked with *Acres U.S.A.* for so long now, it seems appropriate to let him speak on the subject of weed control in terms of biodynamics regardless of how the term is capitalized or hyphenated.

Two of the most virulent weeds in the Southeast, [writes Lovel], are kudzu and water hyacinth. The former curtails erosion by growing rampantly on our acid-clay soils. In time it leaves them rich and mellow. The latter filters the waterways along the coast, cleaning the waters while it obstructs boat traffic. Both put a lot of biomass into the ecosystem. We need good sources of biomass in the Southeast since our soils tend to degrade rapidly. Such biological potential should be appreciated. These weeds could be put to use instead of warred against.

This points up the fact that weed *elimination* does not equal *weed control*. Let us examine what control means. Take a car. To control it we must be able to start, guide and stop it. If any one of these three is beyond our ability, we do not control the car. The same with weeds. We need to know how to get a weed started in an area, change the way it grows and make it cease growing there — all three, before we can say that we control it.

If I plant garlic in October and I get a good cover of chickweed in it over the winter, it virtually eliminates other weeds and I will not have to cultivate again until I dig my garlic. My loss in yield is slight and my gain is in ecological diversity and fertility. I must know how to get chickweed started in my garlic just as much as I must know how to eliminate the Jerusalem artichoke from my cornfield.

Getting a weed started in a field may require planting it under favorable conditions. But, what are favorable conditions? Commonly, what is ideal for one plant is inimical to another. I once had problems with spiny amaranth, Jimson weed and smartweed because I was fertilizing with raw manure. Certainly these weeds love raw manure. When I changed over to composting manures, the weeds that predominated were lambsquarters, redroot pigweed and galinsoga, for these weeds preferred compost. Before I restocked my soil pantry with granite dust from the local gravel quarry and raised my pH close to 7, I used to have broom sedge, a poverty weed that requires an acid and degenerating soil. Now I have fescue and red clover, which require more neutral conditions. Many of the worst weed problems occur where the soils are not suitable for the crops being grown there, but are instead favorable for weeds. Some knowledge of weeds and the conditions they prefer provides a seven-league stride toward controlling them.

Almost all farmers have weed tales to tell. One may get rid of his thistles by spraying blackstrap molasses. Another may phase out his coastal bermuda by alternating between winter rye and summer soybeans. Another may move his weeds from field to field by taking their seeds up in fodder crops and spreading them again in recycled manure, thus ensuring a healthy diversity in the field. The list might as well be endless. Each weed is different, reflects a different aspect of the heavens, relies on different soil conditions, has a different function and purpose. Patience, observation and experiment will yield all manner of insights.

For control of weeds, biodynamic agriculture looks to the manipulation of all the forces at work. If a certain weed is beneficial in the rotation, the farm may be managed in such a way as to bring the seeds of that weed to each field at the right time. Fertilization, cultivation and rotation may all be used to start, change and stop the weed. One wants just the right amount of chamomile in wheat, chicory in corn, or wild geranium in the hay. Achieving these optimum results, especially since nature is ever changing, is a challenge to even the most organized, perceptive and creative biodynamic farmers.

Some weeds are very difficult to control, even by the biodynamic expert. They may be easy to get started, yet nearly impossible to keep in check or eliminate. Their seeds are numerous. They overwhelm crops, contaminate harvests and ruin use of the land. And the extremes of clean cultivation may be nearly as bad as the use of herbicides. In lecture six of *Agriculture*, Rudolf Steiner — who gave biodynamic agriculture its start — outlines a remedy is what biodynamic growers call "making a weed pepper."

The year a weed grows too prolifically it might as well be accepted. But, seed from it should be gathered. If the weed is not propagated by seeds, those parts of the plant that reproduce it should be gathered. These should be burned to ash, preferably in a wood fire, and the ash saved. If there is enough ash it may be ground to uniform fineness with a mortar and pestle and homeopathically diluted and potentized for spraying so that a very strong effect is obtained from only a small amount of material. This homeopathic potency process may be done as follows.

Using a one-ounce bottle, place one-tenth of an ounce of ash in it and add nine-tenths ounces of rainwater (or other pure water). Succuss the contents by rhythmical, intensive shaking for a set period of time, such as three minutes. This is the 1X or D1, potency, depending on which school of nomenclature is followed. One-tenth of this ounce of D1 weed pepper is then added to another one-ounce bottle and nine-tenths ounces of water is added. This bottle is succussed to to produce the D2 potency. This process is repeated for the third, fourth, fifth potentcies, ad infinitum, for as far as is desired. I usually go no farther than the tenth potency. Usually the eighth potency is the most effective for my uses. Since some potencies may eliminate the weed whereas others may actually stimulate the weed to grow and proliferate, choosing the right potency is important.

Two concepts figure in how I choose a potency. First, I "pendulum dowse" down the list of potencies, asking for the potency most effective in eliminating the weed. For me a strong clockwise swing is the right indication. Then I check on this with a specimen of the weed in my radionic scanner. I measure the general vitality of the weed (its 9-49) and then measure what each potency does to this general vitality reading. The potency that shows the greatest reduction in the general vitality is the one I use. Presumably, if I did not get a large enough reduction in the weed's vitality with any of the first ten potencies, I might have to go to higher potencies.

To make enough spray to cover an acre or less, I go back to an earlier potency. For instance, I can take a tenth of an ounce of my D5 to nine-tenths water and make a full ounce of D6. After succussing it, I can take this ounce of D6 and add it to nine ounces of water in a quart jar. After succussion I can add this ten ounces of D7 to ninety ounces of water in a gallon jug and succuss for one-hundred ounces of D8 weed pepper. This is at the limit of what can conveniently be potentized by succussion. Usually this is all I need for the areas I deal with in my market garden, and I can apply it with my gallon-sized pump sprayer.

Each person has his or her own way of doing things. One farmer may add a touch of hydrogen peroxide to the water. I have seen some evidence that small amounts of hydrogen peroxide may make stronger homeopathic potencies. Another may need to cover large acreages and may make up 80 gallons or even 800 gallons. He may go back to the D4 or the D3 potencies and once he reaches the 1,000-ounce size he may use his BD prep stirring machine to potentize, and his spray rig for application. Another may put a sample of the appropriate potency in his cosmic pipe (a passive radionic field unit) because it keeps hammering the remedy home. Some may find it easier to derive a rate for the potency they intend to apply, and use their radionic equipment to imprint this rate on a spray tank of water. Whatever works, go for it.

Rudolf Steiner explains that it can take up to four years to completely eliminate a given species. I have been afraid to test this because the diversity of species is the key to the fertility of my farming operation. A diverse ecology is generally a balanced and healthy ecology, and I do not want to get rid of something completely when I do not fully understand why it is there and what it does.

My method has been to gather a broad spectrum of weeds and make a pepper out of the whole collection, spray it on the worst spots and put the potency in my cosmic pipe. I did that for two years running and the result was far fewer of most of the weeds in the collection. A few of them increased rather than diminishing, and I do not know for certain why. Perhaps that particular weed needed a different potency or needed to be burned in a certain constellation of the moon. I simply report this so that others might watch for it. The third year I was afraid I might go too far and not have enough weeds, most of which are beneficial in small quantities. So I made no pepper the third year. In the fourth year I had a resurgence of weeds. This meant a return to weed pepper the fourth year.

I make my weed peppers without regard for which constellation the moon is in. Presumably I could pendulum dowse for which constellation to burn each type of weed seed in. I also make my weed peppers from seeds collected on my own farm. I do not know how specific each weed pepper is and whether making a pepper from one generic strain will affect other relatives. For instance, will a pepper from our annual bindweed in Georgia get rid of the perennial bindweed found in Kansas? Likewise, if a radionic researcher derives a rate for my bindweed pepper, will this be the appropriate rate for bindweeds found elsewhere? These questions cannot be answered because, so far, they have not been asked in any meaningful way.

The biodynamic approach to controlling weeds is not only cheap and ecologically sound, it avoids harm that herbicides and too much clean cultivation deliver. The treatment for elimination of a weed is designed to affect only the species treated. But, because it is so effective it should be used with care. When there are a lot of dandelions, wild garlic, purslane, or St. John'swort in a field, and these weeds are doing no real harm, my suggestion is to study them. Let them perform their function and fulfill their purpose. Just observe them and learn them. There is a good chance here weeds are beneficial in the overall scheme of things. Do not go out there giving them a dose of D8 once a month for four years and wipe the field clean of it. Use good sense. If your fields are healthier with a few weeds, you can laugh right back at the ridicule of your neighbors. Go ahead and tweak their noses. If your fields are balanced, healthy and fertile you can afford it.

So advised Georgia farmer Hugh Lovel while this book was in preparation.

Prairie land and grass swards are more than nature's benediction. The grass crop is seldom a monoculture, but rather a community of plants at least originally native to the soil. Unlike crops grown on arable land, it matters very little what particular species make up the herbage as long as they do not injure the crop or poison the feeding value for livestock. In the pasture more than most places, the distinction between grassland weeds is sharply drawn — yet a species of value in one situation may be considered a pest at best, noxious at worst. From the farmer's point of view, the feeding value of the plant makes the difference. David C. McCoy, an *Acres U.S.A.* writer from Ohio, once suggested cutting foxtail and putting it up in bales for its feed value. In Dust Bowl days in western Kansas, even the Russian thistle tumbleweed became cow feed in the spring, although the season for such use was short. Cattle ate it because they had to, and also — I suppose — because the Russian thistle contained alkaline salts. People in the Middle East used to burn Russian thistle to make salty ash that could be mixed with oil to make soap. Only a few of the Volga Germans in western Kansas used the Russian thistle that way.

Bent grass, quackgrass, dandelion, hardhead, sheep's sorrel, silverweed, sorrel and Yorkshire fog — so called in England and Canada, its Latinized name being *Holcus lanatus* — have some feed value if they do not whole-hog the growing area and grow too luxuriantly. The problem with pasture weeds is that they tend to grow rank and coarse under dry conditions. There is little reason to consider thistles, nettles, chervil and docks as anything other than unwanted weeds in less than climax pastures. Much the same is true of running plants, such as crabgrass, creeping buttercup, bindweed and bent grass. These cover great areas and anchor down their vast systems of stems and roots. Mouse-ear hawkweed simply suffocates everything in reach. Neither the farmer nor the pasture can endure it. Well digested compost and other biological means must be invoked to attack the root systems and rot them out. Commercial poisons seldom serve, except to further destroy the life in the soil.

I have discussed several poisonous or injurious plants in another chapter. Suffice it to note that purging flax, hemlock and garlic cannot be tolerated very well. Some other plants can be tolerated, but barely. It may be that they have medicinal value at times, as is the case with horsetail, but on balance the following have to be considered weeds under pasture circumstances: autumn crocus, bindweed, buttercup, horsetail, huffcaps, purging flax, tansy ragwort, ramsons and wild barley.

Damp meadows have weed guests all their own, especially when peaty soils are involved. Ragged robin, meadowsweet, creeping jenny, mint, sedge and bedstraw being typical. If the water stays on for long periods of time, water and marsh plants make their debut — marigold, arrowhead, lady's smock, watercress, pennywort and the rushes.

Now drain the pasture and develop high grassland. The grasses no longer grow belly high to a pony. Instead they stay short and fine, and if weeds are seen, they will be things like the dog daisy, yellow rattle, pignut, sorrel, and the rough brome, depending on geography. Poor pastures on dryland often are

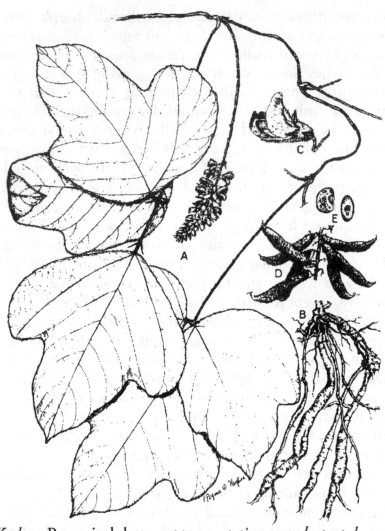

Kudzu, Pueraria lobata, *appears at times ready to take over the countryside. Yet it curtails erosion by growing rapidly on acid-clay soils. Kudzu has spawned a cult of sorts, replete with a bible, The* Book of Kudzu — A Culinary and Healing Guide. *Kudzu is rich in calcium and contains more N, P, and K than red clover. Acccording to our index of nature's formula, this means the soils in which it grows best are short in these areas. Illustrated here is* Pueraria lobata *(A); its root (B); flower (C); legumes (D); and seeds (E).*

infested by milkwort, hardhead, beaked hawksbeard, thyme, lady's mantle and tansy ragwort. Really worthless grasses such as soft brome, *Brachypodium pinnatum* and *Brachypodium sylvaticum* and false brome, *Bromus mollis*, will probably confer on graziers the curse of Sisyphus.

Depending on the part of North America in which one farms, it is correct to consider any of the following as reason for concern because they deteriorate the quality of the pasture — cat's ear, chervil, dog daisy, docks, hogweed, nettles, restharrow, scabious, thistles, wild carrot and yarrow. Or perhaps it would be more correct to say the pasture deteriorates for whatever reasons, giving permission for life to these weeds. There are moments when the thistles, nettles and hogweed have nutritive value for livestock. Some types of livestock will even eat them after they are cut and dried, but acceptability starts getting pretty thin.

False brome, soft brome, quackgrass and sedge have low feeding values. In fact they are poverty weeds for poverty soils. Manure for sheet composting helps this situation a bit, but for a more rapid comeback the manure should be composted with a good inoculant.

Parasitic weeds have been discussed before. The point here is that they do not exempt pastures, especially dodder, eyebright, lousewort and yellow rattle.

In all cases, it is best to identify the weed, refer to the Latinized name, and get the lay of the land. The weeds always provide their own biography, just as animals and humans provide their own *biochemical photograph*, to use Andre Voisin's term.

There are lower forms of plant life often classed as weeds, namely mosses and fungi. Mosses, of course, suggest poor drainage. They march across the landscape with a rapid pace, setting up competition with grass, thereby making the herbage that survives less valuable. Fungi in turn infest grassland in damp weather, leaving a fingerprint called fairy rings. These rings make the pasture shoot up in tufts of uneven growth. On close examination white threads of hyphae can be seen. These form a mycelium which spreads. At intervals, fructifications called toadstools two to four inches, sometimes larger, appear. Usually a ring manures the growth area for spreading growth the following season and with a resultant growth of very luxuriant dark grass. Eventually the grass fades back to be in harmony with the rest of the pasture. Yarrow and ribgrass sometimes make their appearance in the thick grass of the ring. Sometimes the weed is cocksfoot or hogweed. Other weeds — ryegrass, cocksfoot, sorrel — have been found in these rings. All indicate a certain poverty soil.

The best remedy is compost with its billions of unpaid microbial workers.

Many of the experiment stations have hit the weed problem a glancing blow. Almost all of their booklets are little more than sales pieces for the makers of chemicals of organic synthesis. In the process weeds are designated by style, annual, perennial, biennials — and there is usually a bow to where the weeds can be found. One can read fields, waste places, dryland, wetland, high ground, low ground, prairies, open woods, thickets, gardens, alluvial areas, fencerows, blowsand areas, to a point of absolute weariness, yet most of these treatises do not point out that in almost all cases there are exceptions.

Why can't farmers see the variables that cause the several exceptions? The obvious answer is, "because they are invisible."

Moreover, we know so little about biological time or the arithmetic of weeds. Only fragments of Pythagorean onomastics have survived. Pythagoras had his numbers game, descended from Orpheus, and practiced the oracular use of digits. Ignorance always takes refuge in decrees and definitions. Thus Arabic numbers were perceived to be the work of the devil at one time. In fact the great invention of zero to ten came to Europe by way of India, where Hindu priests indeed made oracular use of numbers. Arab mathematicians merely borrowed the device and gave it their name, and imposed some alterations, of course. In *Nature's Harmonic Unity*, author Samuel Coleman illustrated — with a great deal of analysis — how the triangle, the square, the pentagon and pentagram, the hexagon and hexagram, the octagon and the circle are the determining geometrical elements of tiny plants and the physical world. He might have added the double helix. This was long before the DNA was discovered and long after the judgment was made that some plants — in their growth — obey the cadence of Fibinocci's series —

$$1, 1, 2, 3, 5, 8, 13, 21, \text{etc.}$$

— each number being the sum of the previous two numbers — or the square of numbers. It has been argued that the angles and lines of the plant kingdom are the precise lines used in the construction of the Parthenon and the Great Pyramid. If true, the case is strengthened that sound, light and color follow the laws of form, much as Dinshah Ghadiali suggested in the 1930s.

In 1796 Sam Hahnemann declared, *Similar similibus curatur,* or *like cures like*. He meant that diseases are cured by drugs which produce similar symptoms. The hostility of allopathic medicine became so intense, Hahnemann was forced to leave Leipzig and finally flee to Paris. We can expect no less when we declare that fertility to the crop is anathema to the weed, and vice versa.

Many of the fertilizer materials used on pasture lands in fact feed weeds and destroy grass. As the kids might say, these fertilizer materials have bad vibes.

Heraclitus said, *everything is in motion*, everything moves, and he might as well have said everything vibrates.

If the thoughts expressed so far are correct, it will become obvious to all who wish to see that weed control without poisons rests, ultimately, on a sensitivity to radiations, and instruments that can detect them.

Curly dock, Rumex crispus, *is often a hardpan weed. It prospers when soil moisture is high, either because the spring has been wet, or hardpan has prevented normal insoak of water. In this complexed environment, improper decay is the general rule. Rumex crispus is illustrated (A); with fruit surrounded by an outer set of sterile floral leaves with valves (B); and a one-seeded closed fruit (C).*

10
A CUP OF HEMLOCK

When I was a youngster of Boy Scout age, I had the high ambition of being a cowboy. Mother wondered if the priesthood might not be better. She preferred *Leyende der Helligen* over *The Saga of Billy the Kid*, and routinely provided analysis of Henry VIII's life and sins rather than discuss Fred Sutton's claim to fame.

Fred Sutton and A.B. MacDonald had written *Hands Up* about the year I was born, a library copy of which I studied more than the Bible. In it Sutton said he saved the life of Billy the Kid in a Dodge City dance hall. Our old Ness County home was only a county or two removed from Dodge City, and Fred Sutton had bumped shoulders with two of my Kansas City cousins. The last was probably apocryphal. But he lived in the same town, that was certain. Such a connection was stuff for history, I argued. Mother fairly chortled. "You better learn to do your arithmetic," she said. It took me a week to crowd out of her what she meant, during which time I found out more about Henry VIII and Oliver Cromwell than I cared to know at the time. Apparently some people were boiled in oil in those days, but Mother made it sound as if it happened two weeks ago last

Wednesday. Finally I got my answer, and somehow it led me to an appreciation of weeds.

The arithmetic was simple enough. There had been stories about famous outlaws in one of the German-language newspapers. Billy the Kid was buried on July 15, 1881, "neatly and properly dressed," in the old military cemetery at Fort Sumner, New Mexico. This meant Fred Sutton — accepting the date of his birth in *A Handbook of Oklahoma Writers* as correct — could only have been three years old when he saved the life of Billy the Kid.

Sutton knew them all — Wild Bill Hickok, Pat Garret, Bat Masterson, Wyatt Earp, Belle Star, Jesse James. The problem, I discovered soon enough, was that he had this problem with the truth, and almost everything he wrote proved to be a falsehood. "Do your arithmetic," Mother reminded, much to my chagrin. It was a blow from which my youthful ambition to be a cowboy never recovered.

I salvaged a little of my self esteem when a kinsman — a marathon liar — claimed Grandpa sold hay for Custer's horses when Yellow Hair was in command at Fort Hays. This was a highly unlikely story. Custer and his men died at the Battle of the Little Big Horn in Montana on June 25, 1876, about four months before the arrival of the Volga German immigrants. I used this inventory of information to annihilate my kinsman's lie at a funeral dinner one day, and I have never heard it since. But the kinsman was a Custer man to the hilt. *Those dastardly Sioux would never have licked Custer except that all the Indians in the world — at least 40,000 — rode down on a few brave men*, he said. Mother's reprimand still rang in my ears . . . *do your arithmetic!*

The battle involving Custer actually was fought on very few acres, each acre being made up of 7,840 square yards. By putting an optimum number of Indians and horses on each acre, I concluded that there could only have been about 3,000-3,500 Indians at the battle, no more, perhaps less.

There was another enemy, and it may have had more to do with Custer's demise than Sitting Bull's leadership or the bravado of Rain-in-the-Face. Western stockmen have been afraid of selenium poisoning since 1857, when cavalry horses at Fort Randall, South Dakota became sick while grazing pastures near the post. Animals die when they ingest too much selenium through forage and grain. Blind staggers is an advanced form of poisoning, and it cut into the fitness of the horse supply on the frontier during the dry summers of the Indian campaigns. Less than one-fifth of an ounce in a ton of hay prevents nutritional deficiencies in livestock, a deficiency causing degeneration of the liver, pancreas, heart or muscle tissue. But selenium is also highly toxic. Ranchers call selenium poisoning alkali disease because soils that produce range vegetation with selenium are common in some fifteen western states. Approximately fifteen species of Astragalus accumulate selenium. Ranchers generally refer to the offending plants as poison vetch. When selenium accumulators thrive on tilled acres, their leaves and other plant parts end up plowed or disced into the soil. In some cases this poisoning kills forage grain crops, and sometimes the soluble toxins are taken up by normally harmless plants. Animals on the receiving end of such plants often suffer emaciation, hoof deformity and lameness, plus other maladies already mentioned.

Wild mustard imported from Pakistan will remove selenium from the soil. Five mustard crops in a row will pick up 50% of the soluble selenium in the top twelve inches of soil, according to USDA researchers.

Scientists in the business of defending man-made molecules of toxic chemistry never tire of pointing out that nature has her own apothecary of dangerous toxins. Their point seems to be that being natural doesn't mean a thing, and I would have to agree. I had a dead walnut tree on my acres at one time that propped up a superb poison ivy vine. My son Fred cut down the walnut tree and in the process covered himself with ivy sawdust wherever skin was exposed. We didn't realize it then, but we appreciate now the fact that poison ivy, poison oak and poison sumac all contain a chemical similar to lacquer. It is an allergen molecule that can cause dermatitis, which is a polite way of saying a bruised ivy plant exacts total vengeance. Burning any of the ivy plants and staying on to inhale the smoke may be more dangerous than wallowing in ivy sawdust. This last sent my son Fred to the clinic, puffed up like a doughnut head to toe.

Of all the weeds I have encountered — from Weed, California, to Everglade City, Florida — the ivy plants seem hardest to recognize, they are that variable, especially poison ivy and poison oak. They'll turn up as ground vines, climbing vines or shrubs, with distribution in both likely and unlikely places. Leaves vary in texture, size and in cutting. Poison sumac can be characterized as either a tall shrub or a small tree. Each leaf is made up from seven to eleven leaflets juxtaposed along a red central axis, a single leaf at the tip whether the poison sumac dice roll seven or eleven, or in between, the leaves will not have the sharply pointed edges often confused with nonpoisonous relations.

Physicians and botanists conversant with poisonous plants point out a difference between poison ivy, poison oak and poison sumac and other plants, many of them found growing in the tropics, that seem to affect human beings and animals in a similar way. It is the difference between allergy and true poisoning. Allergy depends on target sensitivity; genuine poisoning of the skin does not. Leafy spurge, sun spurge, caper spurge, spotted spurge, snow-on-the-mountain and other spurges have a sap that burns like acid. John M. Kingsley, in his *Poisonous Plants of the United States and Canada*, says snow-on-the-mountain sap has been used by Texas cattlemen in place of a branding iron. I have never known anyone who did this, but I have no doubt that the burn would produce a brand. Florida has enough botany to keep a siege of herons busy surveying the scene. Snowbirds who descend on Florida in the winter sometimes encounter troublesome rare plants, the manchineel tree south of Fort Myers and Palm Beach, for instance. Many of these plants can blind and burn, and have been therefore largely eradicated. I have been shown some of these specimens, but I don't think I could recognize them any longer. It seems that dangerous plants continue to be a threat only when they make the transition from natives in the wild to being ornamental for sale at the grocery store or flower shop. Snow-on-the-mountain plants are often sold to families with children, and kids do eat the leaves. This causes gastric distress and sometimes death.

The poinsettia, crown-of-thorns candelabra cactus, pencil tree and cypress spurge are of the same ilk. Wild spurges are more anonymous than the rest because they are so hard to recognize. They have a white, milky sap which is dangerous, but then many other plants have a white milky sap, notably the harmless dandelion. The flowers of a flowering spurge plant hold a clue to recognition. Actually the flower is not a flower at all, but a whorl of four to five colored leaves with male flowers, each a single stamen. The exact center has one female pistil. You have to go to color manuals to get the picture, and to the field to find the real thing. Later, in a chapter on poisons, I will try to nail down the difference between natural poisons and man-made poisons. For now, let me settle for a quick run-through on the most troublesome poisonous plants farmers are likely to encounter.

Such an outline will leave out a lot of exotic plants which are interesting in a trivial pursuit sort of way, but are of little interest to the producers of corn, soybeans, milo, and wheat.

A great deal of discovery work on agriculture weeds was done by the United States Department of Agriculture as early as the 1870s, when the army appealed to the newly-formed USDA for help in keeping the cavalry in horses. Loco poisoning was even more of a problem than blind staggers. Two species were indicated soon enough, Astralagus and Oxytropis genus. It would take a list of 300 species to flesh out the roster of Astralagus. In the worst cases final paralysis damaged the brain.

Although there is a toxic principle in hundreds of weeds and herbs, there is a medicinal principle in equally as many. Many are rare around the farmstead. Agave, for instance, contains steroidal sapogenins and a photosensitizing pigment. Yohimbe contains the alkaloid yohimbine, sometimes known as quebrachine, aphrodine and corynine. It is a harmine analog and therefore a mild hallucinogen. Between A and Z in almost any compendium are exotic plants with toxic or medicinal properties, but few of these plants invade the cornfield or trouble the soybean producer. Readers enchanted by herbal medications might be interested in a book by that name — *Herbal Medications* — by David G. Spoerke, M.D., which is kept in print by Woodbridge Press, Santa Barbara, California.

Regardless of where poisons from plants are warehoused and how they are delivered, these errant compounds have the community up from its chairs faster if the human population is involved. Milk sickness via white snakeroot and lactating animals is such a malady. Human victims frequently exhibit symptoms before the cow trembles, the indicator symptom that white snakeroot ingestion has taken place. The bovine has to eat the herbaceous perennial for several days before poisoning is evident since trembles arrive slowly.

White snakeroot became etched in history because it was identified with the death of Nancy Hanks, the mother of Abraham Lincoln. From time to time since the American Revolution, snakeroot poisoning, or milk sickness, has reached epidemic proportions delivering weakness, nausea and prostration to whole communities. These epidemics subsided with recognition of the guilty weed and greater efforts at control as well as fencing cattle away from the weed — a stiff affair, sometimes branched, sometimes unbranched, usually three to four feet tall with heart-shaped leaves on the long stem. There are three main veins on the under surface. Very tiny flowers form up a flowering mass at the tips of branches, lacy, airy, delicate. USDA scientists identified the toxic principle as tremetol, a molecule that is soluble in fats. This explains its affinity for milk and butter. The mechanism for mischief is about the same as burning ether instead of gasoline in an automobile. Food is burned too fast, and this forms acetone-like compounds, hence the odor associated with milk sickness in humans, acetonemia in cattle.

White snakeroot has relatives, one of which must be unique to weed nomenclature. It is *Eupatorium wrightii,* and it is distinctive because it has no common name. It is toxic, but the toxic principle is not tremetol of white snakeroot fame.

Milkweeds are generally toxic, some slightly toxic, some dangerously so, with species that grow in the West the most dangerous of all. Milkweeds are not a problem to human beings, possibly because no one has taste buds numb enough to permit consumption. Hungry cattle will eat the plant, however, with resultant losses heavy.

Cocklebur has a toxic seed in a hard spiney bur. This is a bonus arranged for both man and animals, since the bur protects the seed until long after it germinates, often in mud along pond edges. Seedlings retain a measure of toxicity during early stages of growth, and this makes them dangerous. New mud usually means new seedlings, and so the dangerous stage of the life cycle repeats itself. The poison here is called hydroquinone. It acts on the digestive system first. General weakness follows, then prostration and paralysis. Administration of fats and oils such as lard, butter, and linseed oil are indicated when seedlings have been consumed.

Larkspur is another weed with seasonal toxicity, its season for mischief being early growth. As seeds form, toxicity migrates in that direction from foliage. This toxicity is a complicated alkaloid that attacks the nervous system. Cattle go down and can't regain their feet when poisoned by larkspur. Often there is respiratory paralysis. Rumen gas sometimes is trapped with bloat and a ruptured rumen the result. This bloat is often the consequence of intestines pressuring the rumen in a way that makes belching impossible. I have seen my Dad save cows by inserting a knife into the bloat area, and I have also seen death result from this do-it-yourself operation.

For a reason not at once apparent, larkspur alkaloids literally annihilate cattle, but not sheep. Apparently sheep have enough sense to not eat too much, for USDA investigators have been able to bring on in sheep symptoms cattle experience by feeding large doses.

There is a veritable apothecary of toxicity in nature, to be sure, and apologists for man-made molecules of poison never tire of making comparisons, the implication being that the world would be just as toxic had the chemists never learned how to synthesize poisons. This is a Hitler-sized lie. The poisonous plants identified here are often rare, and rarely of concern to careful husbandmen. In many cases nature has a safety valve. Toxins in the precatory bean and castor bean are activated by heat. There are lethal concentrations of cyanide in the cassava tubers I and other *Acres U.S.A.* subscribers saw near Sãu Paulo, Brazil, but the station agronomist was quick to point out that soaking, mashing and heating made the tubers safe.

Rape seed is not so easily made safe. It isn't even understood, except that cattle pastured on this plant suffer having their digestive system go off duty and develop pulmonary emphysema. No one would dare call it a weed. But this plant delivers anemia, jaundice and blood in the urine, nitrate poisoning — and even blindness and disorientation — with the best of the poisonous *unkraut* types.

Pharmacologists take credit for many laboratory inventions, but the fact remains that solanine, as in nightshade and potato toxicity, was invented by plants. It is so complex that experts consider it a glycoside, an alkaloid, a saponin and a steroid at the same time. False hellebore and death camas contain alkaloids. Western false hellebore on the high mountain ranges of the West acts as a teratogen, and causes monkey face disease. Groundsel, crotalarea, poppy — all harness the alkaloid principle to deliver mischief. Horsetail and bracken have been known to kill horses, and the bracken fern has killed cattle. The toxic principle remains unknown, but the results speak out — the white blood cells count simply goes down until there is no defense against infection, much like the syndrome called AIDS in humans sans HIV virus.

Most readers will be familiar with the glycoside principle. It was the cyanide producing glycoside of almond pits that gave the health food movement amygdalin, a cancer remedy. Amygdalin acts only when the molecule is broken down at the tumor site. Many plants, including members of the rose family, contain glycosides. Digitilis is simply a poisonous glycoside called ranuculin.

Saponins, as the name suggests, cause soap-like froth, but the exact toxic principle remains unknown. Bouncing bet and corn cockle are trouble makers, not only in pastures and grain fields, but also when ground into flour.

There are many more weeds that could rate entry space in this chapter. St. Johnswort and buckwheat, lechugiulla, sacahuiste, puncture vine, latana, all are responsible for photosensitization and liver injury. Horsebush rates attention as the most dangerous of the above as far as livestock are concerned. Sacahuiste will not trigger photo sensitization unless chlorophyll is also consumed, and there is no chlorophyll in buds, blooms or fruits of the sacahuiste plant.

I don't know how much these baseball scores and player observations contribute to the study of weeds. I do know that every cell has chromosomes intertwined like a strand of intestines in its nucleus. These strands are the DNA. In our time we like to compare this information bank to a computer program, and it is accepted that the genes preside over the complexities of life. And though we search for meaning in a confused world of nutrition and soil management, in the final analysis I am compelled to realize that the DNA is largely in charge, meaning scientific knowledge is puny enough. "There is something fascinating about science," wrote Mark Twain in *Life on the Mississippi*. "One gets such wholesale returns of conjecture out of such a trifling investment of facts." Science promises all the

Tansy ragwort, Senecio jacobaea, *bespeaks soil limitations and poverty pastures. It is generally confined to the coastal areas of northern California, Oregon and Maine to Rhode Island. It is toxic to livestock. Its alkaloids are not destroyed by drying or during silage fermentation. Illustrated is the tansy ragwort plant (A); the flower head (B); the ray flower (C); disc flower (D); achenes, ray flower (E); and the achenes disc flower (F).*

answers, but this has been impossible when it comes to weeds, for it has never asked all the questions.

I tried to ask as many questions as possible when 86 rare horses on the Spanish Barb Reserve Foundation Ranch, Birkenfield, Oregon, perished, poisoned by 2,4-D and 2,4,5-T. The animals were Barb, Spanish Barb and Cayuse Indian ponies, all authenticated by their bones, blood, physical characteristics and genetic size. It had taken Wes and Jackie Strasburger 20 years to prove the purity of their animals.

Tansy ragwort is a biennial or short-lived perennial herb introduced from Europe. A weed that grows in marginal pastures, tansy ragwort is toxic to livestock, particularly cattle and horses. Poisoning can result from consumption of small quantities over many days. Dried foliage is equally toxic because alkaloids are not destroyed on drying or during silage fermentation. Tansy ragwort generally flowers from July to September. The weed is not well- known in most parts of the country.

This much stated, the story can continue, for there entered — from some corner of the stage — officials from USDA, Washington, D.C., and schoolmen from the University of Washington-Pullman. They had in tow one of those monuments to the stupidity of man — an eradication program based on 2,4-D and 2,4,5-T, or Agent Orange. At first the Strasburgers refused to use the spray, relying on the grub hoe and other tools. Then the couple were ordered to spray or the Department of Agriculture would do it for them and hand them the bill.

On the premise that official damn fools had to be obeyed, the Strasburgers sprayed, and by October the horses started dying. When Jackie Strasburger asked the veterinarian if the spray might not be the problem, the vet closed his bag without a word, issued a bill, and left. And thus surfaced one of the problems with man-made poisons — a genuine lack of information and mendacity among officials from top to bottom. No one seemed willing to lay it out in spades.

The herbicide 2,4,5-T will kill the broad leaf plants, not the narrow leaf plants. But it will cause a change in the molecular structure of the narrow leaf plant which becomes high in nitrates. Animals that eat these plants become poisoned, and when the nitrate turns to nitrite the blood comes under attack and loses its ability to carry oxygen. It takes on a reddish brown color. This is one of the clues to nitrate poisoning. The liver tries to clean up the blood and is soon saturated and ineffective. When it can no longer do the job, the kidney and the rest of the vital organs fail. Eventually the sick animal dies painfully and horribly.

Under auspices of the Environmental Protection Agency, a horse was taken to the University of Oregon at Corvallis, Oregon and examined. The necropsy examination revealed the horse had died of malnutrition and a severe case of worms. This is true since in the final couple of months the animal is so run down and weak that the worms do take over. However, if you worm the horse you kill it, and if you don't, the worms kill the horse. Worms are only a *symptom*. The real problem is and remains the initial contamination of the pasture by 2,4-D and 2,4,5-T. No diseases were found in the horses other than worms.

Tansy ragwort is generally confined to the coastal area of extreme northern California, Washington and Oregon and along the Atlantic coast from Maine to Rhode Island. It grows in moist, badly drained soil and bespeaks limitations in the soil, apparently concentrating potassium via luxury consumption. Spraying for eradication is a useless procedure. Usually animals will eat tansy ragwort only when desperate for feed, a situation keepers of prize animals would not allow in any case.

I ran the story of the Barbs and Cayuse ponies in *Acres U.S.A.* with a picture that caused some readers to cry. It showed a rare horse that died of 2,4-D and 2,4,5-T poisoning. It was a salmon gaited horse, one of only two in the United States. The horse had a smooth gait. As it went through its paces, its back end would wiggle like a fish in water. This was the movement for which it was named the salmon gaited horse.

Search as I might, I have not been able to turn up many serious cases of livestock poisoning by natural agents. But chemicals of organic synthesis used to control weeds, they have left a trail of carnage equal to the day after the battle when Genghis Kahn came through.

In ancient Greece, officials gave Socrates his cup of hemlock, probably *Conium maculatum*, for departing from official doctrine when teaching the youth of Athens. It was an accepted form of execution. Alkaloids and nicotine in the hemlock conspired to cause muscle paralysis until breathing stopped.

Unfortunately, officials are still ordering up their cups of hemlock, only now the entire population is involved. In our time the church has become politicized and the state has become sanctified. That is why, perhaps the people stand still for a technology that delivers infants with undeveloped limbs and retarded minds — human sacrifices, just as in the days of Ur, to the gods of the Netherworld, the dollars of high finance.

And the weeds live on.

Common burdock, Arctium minus, *may be a weed, but it is also a cash crop. It is a good phosphate feeder. When common burdock shows up, it is a signal that the soil is dominated by iron and is badly in need of calcium. Often a surplus of released aluminum is involved. When calcium levels are low, aluminum is flushed out easily, as is iron. That is why burdock proliferates in environments that kill off commercial crops. Illustrated is the giant leaf of common burdock as well as the root, leaf and upper raceme of heads (A); the flower phyllaries (B); and the dry one-seeded fruit, or achene (C).*

11
WEEDS AS A CASH CROP

I had it in mind at one time — before the editorial pencil took command of my time and life — to grow for profit the fabled youth root. Flavus Josephus, the Jewish historian, called it amomum, but long before Josephus there was the *Epic of Gilgamesh*.

Let me uncover for you, Gilgamesh, a secret thing.
A secret of the Gods let me tell you.
There is a plant. Its roots go deep, like the boxthorn;
its spike will prick your hand like a bramble.
If you get your hands on this plant,
you'll have everlasting life.

I will carry it to Uruk of the Sheepfold; I will
give it to the elders to eat;
They will divide the plant among them.
Its name is The Old-Man-Will-Be-Made-Young
I too will eat it, and I will return to
what I was in my youth.

So runs the John Gardener and John Maier translation, *Gilgamesh*, published by the Alfred A. Knopf company in 1984. The plant's name is *sibu issahir amelu*, meaning "a return to a man in his prime."

This one got lost in the horse latitudes, so to speak. *Viola odorata* has been described as having a violet flower, but some scholars think orrisroot or köku was the youth root in Gilgamesh. Orrisroot comes from the European iris, the underground parts of which have a faint violet odor. Accordingly this root is used to make sachets and tooth powder. Some 500,000 pounds are imported into the United States each year from a production industry centered in Florence, Italy. I figure all of this could be produced in the United States, but I am not certain orrisroot is amomum, the weed that Uknapishtim gave to the Babylonian Noah. There is a weed that proliferates on the site and in the vicinity of where Noah's Ark was discovered on Mount Mahser Dagi, Doomsday Mountain, near Ararat, in the mid 1980s.

Much like my enchantment with Wyatt Earp and Wild Bill Hickok, such an interest was bound to pass, leaving in its wake a deeper perspective — in my case, an appreciation of weeds as a cash crop.

While I was in the process of publishing *The Potential of Herbs as a Cash Crop*, I asked author Richard A. Miller to provide me with a list of profitable weeds that could be harvested from wilderness acres with little or no expenditure of cash, and a normal amount of labor. Miller complied, sending me a list by regions, and he assured me he had customers for nature's free products. Not all of the entries could qualify as weeds, but all of them had products that could make a cash register ring. The list follows.

NORTHEAST UNITED STATES

Elder	*Sambucus* genus, several species
Forest tree cones	
Forest tree seeds	
Mandrake	*Mandragora officanarum*
Nettle	*Urtica* genus, several species
Pokeweed	*Phytolacca americana*
Sassafras rootbark	*Sassafras albidum*

St. Johnswort . . . . *Hypericum perforatum*
Wild cherry . . . . *Prunus serotina*

SOUTH UNITED STATES
Black cohosh . . . . *Cimicifuga racemosa*
Bloodroot. *Sanguinaria canadensis*
Ginseng . . . .*Panax quinquefolium*
Goldenseal . . . . .Hydrastis genus, several species
Passion flower. . . . . *Passiflora caerulea*
Prince's pine . . . . *Chimaphila umbellate*
Saw palmetto berries . . . . *Serenoa repens*
Slippery elm. . . . .*Ulmus fulva*
White oak . . . . Querus genus, several species
Wintergreen. . . . . *Gaultheria procumbens*

MIDWEST UNITED STATES
Black haw. *Viburnum prunifolia*
Burdock. . . . .*Arctium lappa*
Catnip . . . .*Nepeta cataria*
Echinacea. *Echinacea angustifolia*
Horsetail . . . . .Equisetum genus, several species
Lobelia. . . . .*Lobelia inflata*
Pods
Pussywillow pods . . . .*Salix nigra*
Scotch broom. . . . . *Cytisus scoparius*
Wild indigo . . . .*Baptisia tinctoria*

NORTHWEST UNITED STATES
Bay laurel. . . . . *Umbellularia californicia*
Cascara segrada . . . .*Rhamnus purshiana*
Devil's club. . . . . *Oplopanax horridum*
Eucalyptus . . . . *Eucalyptus globulus*
False hellebore . . . . *Veratrum viride*
Huckleberry foliage . . . .*Vaccinium ovatum*
Mosses
Oregon grape. . . . . *Berberis acquifolium*
Sword fern . . . . Polystichum genus, several species
Wild ginger . . . . Zingiber genus, several species

SOUTHWEST UNITED STATES

Baby's breath . . . . *Gypsophila paniculata*
Chaparral . . . .*Larrea divaricata*
Chicory . . . . *Cichorium intybus*
Dandelion . . . . *Taraxacum officinale*
Mormon tea . . . . *Ephedra nevadensis*
Mullein . . . . *Verbascum thapsiforme*
Wildflowers
Yarrow . . . .*Achillea millefolium*
Yellow dock . . . . *Rumex crispus*
Yerba santa . . . .*Ermodictyon californicum*

The weed components on this roster are not generally trouble-some to farmers, and all have standing in manuals dealing with medicinal herbs and pharmaceutical products. They were catalogued and used in the medicinal, cosmetics and food industries long before anyone even conceptualized the DNA and RNA. I doubt there are enough computers in the world to unscramble the genetic codes that make these several plants concentrate minerals, create chemicals, fabricate dyes and otherwise deal chemists a hard day's work unraveling their botanical make-up for economic gain. The point here is that many farmers could find useful employment for themselves collecting plants or plant parts for markets that already exist. The lore of medicinal plants is rich. For generations these denizens of the wilderness doctored the nation, perhaps more successfully than is now possible with coal-tar derivative drugs. Pharmaceutical products, in any case, are generally discovered in plants. Once identified, the industry tries to synthesize the active weed and herb product cheaply, often missing unidentified factors. Criticism of synthetics coupled with higher prices for the barrel of oil from which so many products are synthesized has forced a partial return to botanicals. Many weeds and forest products are purchased in substantial quantities ranging from a few tons to more than 2,000 tons annually, according to Miller and Northwest Botanicals, Grants Pass, Oregon.

Among the common weeds utilized by the pharmaceutical industry are popular wild flowers. Included are mullein, thistle, baby's breath and straw flowers.

Feverweed is an old Indian remedy for open sores and internal distress. Also known as Joe-Pye weed, this plant grows in damp thickets, and invites foraging. I do not believe it is grown commercially.

The lore of uncommon weeds becomes a narrative stranger than fiction, and often orders up a knowledge of mythology for literate comprehension. Horse elder, for instance, has the Latinate name of *Inula helenium*. Anything with "Helen" in it harks back to Helen of Troy. Her tears, it will be remembered, fell to the earth in a regular squall when she was captured and brought to Troy. Those same tears became a plant with a thick yellow taproot, a camphor odor, and the products helenin and insulin. These are carbohydrates that are slowly digested, making them valuable in preparations for diabetics. The plant products also treat catarrh of the lungs and heaves in horses. Further, a medicinal wine — alout wine — based on Helen's tear plant entered the classical literature and stomach by way of Plinius, who gave extracts of the plant his blessing for Roman women so they could preserve their beauty.

One weed — tansy or parsley fern — has a bitter and aromatic odor. No matter, for the Greeks considered it an immortality plant because it never wilted. An extract of the plant was used to deal with oxyuri intestinal worms. The Volga Germans used it to protect meat from flies and mosquitoes. Ehrenfried Pfeiffer suggests that the extract will chase fleas off the backs of dogs.

It would take an entire book to describe the various forest and weed products now marketed, including such items as floral greens, cones for seed and decoration, mushrooms, and a variety of mosses. A number of major drug plants also are harvested for export. Examples are Cascara segrada bark from the West Coast, and sassafras root bark from the East Coast.

Although many of these products possess no real medicinal properties, their collection continues to be important because of established markets. Mullein and echinacea are typical examples. They contain chemistries associated with their use. Products which do contain specific chemistries have become cash crops in their regions of harvest. Another major market is that of the wholesale florist and decorative market. Dried flowers and unusual herb and spice byproducts are a very large business.

Europeans have made use of weed and wildflower resources for centuries. Several wholesale houses have been in business for more than 250 years, all family-owned. Many of those wholesale houses are currently exporting botanicals to North America. The irony of this situation is that these products were originally harvested in North America, but collection was stopped due to World War I and World War II. During World War II, major pharmaceutical houses had their sources of supply cut off, and had to reorient their production to *synthesis* technologies, abandoning the traditional *extraction* processes natural plants permit.

Almost 80% of the currently used weed and herb raw materials are imports. There are some botanicals, however, which have been exported for over 100 years. Such things as goldenseal root and wild ginseng are typical products for the South, whereas *Cascara segrada* bark has been an export laxative for more than 40 years from the Pacific northwest. Other types of foraged products include mushrooms, sold to Japan, and picked fern, sold to Germany.

Many new markets are now available again, due in part, to the revived extraction direction of the pharmaceutical houses and the health food boom since the 1970s. The domestic potential is open again in the weed category, since most are now imported into the United States and Canada. It is up to the forager to consider creative ways of utilizing unproductive lands and recognizing resources which they offer.

There is also a growing market for plants in the biochemical industry. This market is especially valid for the small farmer who is either not fully employed, or has a farm operation which does not require his full-time attention. Many so-called noxious weeds have good market potentials. Although these crops vary from one community to another, their harvest considerations are quite similar. Once natural resources have been recognized and markets identified, they can provide meaningful self-employment.

The concept of foraging is well suited to those who have chosen a rural style of living, but must augment sources of income until other farming plans are realized. Foraging cooperatives, organized along the line of the old Grange, present an excellent way for the local community to develop rural jobs. A number of foraged products are also suited to the cottage industry concept.

To illustrate, take the case of mullein, *Verbascum thapsus*. This herb is considered a noxious weed. It grows abundantly throughout the country. It is also an import from Yugoslavia. During a recent year, more than 50 tons were imported by only one brokerage house. Yet this product is treated as a waste disposal problem. It can be conditioned and laid into a windrow, and then baled when dry with relative ease. Most processors will pay almost a $1,000 a ton for it. If it is cut into a "chip" form and sacked, it brings several hundred dollars more per ton.

A few years ago, a feasibility study for harvesting mullein was made in a forest district in southern Oregon. That district had endured a major forest fire. Reseeding programs proved almost futile in the poor, pumice soil. After a sixth reseeding the trees were invaded by solid stands of mullein. Herbicides had been banned several years earlier. The forest district people assumed that they were going to lose their plantation. Mullein grows to six feet, whereas the new trees were only twelve inches tall.

A number of members from a cooperative went in and cut the mullein with machetes. The herb was then trucked to lower fields for drying and baling. Not only did the forest district save the new plantation, it actually made a small amount of money from the brush permits issued. And, most important, a number of rural jobs were created, producing a product that was previously imported. It also provided a strong argument for alternative methods in weed control.

Dandelion, Taraxacum officinale, *seems to offend the mind and psyche of mankind. It is an index of sedimentation, root webbing and organic matter forever in place. For a quick remedy, soil has to be treated six to seven inches deep with high calcium lime. Shown here are the plant parts in total (A); the flower (B); the one seeded fruit (C); and the fruit with pappus.*

The future of foraging as a supplement to rural income lies with the ability to recognize natural resources. Each region of North America contains similar potentials. A forest can become more than a source for timber. It can also be utilized as farm ground since it is perfectly suited for specific botanicals with existing markets. As one silvaculturist once said about foraging: "For the first time, I now can see a way I can do what I went to college to study: *forest management rather than timber management!*"

Here are native plants of commercial importance for various regions of the country.

In the Northeast

Bloodroot, *Sanguinaria canadensis*. The root is used in dental creams to prevent gum bleeding and as an anti-tumor agent.

Mayapple, *Podopyllum peltatum*. The root is used mainly to treat venereal warts, and sometimes as a laxative ingredient.

Lobelia, *Lobelia inflata*. The herb is used extensively in cough preparations, and in some anti-smoking mixtures.

Sassafras, *Sassafras albidum*. The inner rootbark was formerly used to flavor root beer. Now it is mostly used to make herb teas.

Sweet birch, *Betula lenta*. The oil from the bark is now used to produce a wintergreen (or root beer) flavor in most all foods.

In the South

Goldenseal, *Hydrastis canadensis*. The root is used in stopping uterine hemorrhage and in relieving menstrual pain. It has also been used in eyewashes.

Saw palmetto, *Serenoa serrulata*. The berries are used to treat chronic cystitis and serving as a mucous membrane stimulant to the genitourinary tract.

Slippery elm, *Ulmus fulva*. The bark has a tradition of use as a demulcent and emollient, while the powdered bark was used as a soothing poultice.

Pokeweed, *Phytolacca americana*. A classic root used to ease the pain of chronic rheumatism, and also used in creams for fungal infections.

Wild cherry, *Prunus avium*. The bark is used as a flavoring agent for a number of cold and cough preparations, including herbal tea blends.

In the Midwest

Maypop, *Passiflora incarnata*. The vine is used as an ingredient in some sedative preparations, as well as a flavoring component in alcoholic beverages.

Black haw, *Viburnum prunifolium*. The bark has uterine antispasmodic properties, and is used as uterine sedative and in antidiarrheal preparations.

Wild indigo, *Baptisia tinctoria*. The root forms the well-known indigo blue dye for jeans and other clothing.

Coneflower, *Echinacea angustifolia*. The roots are used by herbalists to enhance the immune system, and is used extensively in herbal preparations.

Ginseng, *Panax quinquefolium*. The root is the king of tonics. Used extensively to tone the body, has been called a "biocatalyzer."

In the Northwest

Cascara segrada, *Rhamnus purshiana*. The root is used extensively in laxative preparations, and some limited use in sun-screens.

Oregon grape, *Berberis aquifolium*. The root has similar chemistries as goldenseal, although its use is more limited.

Bay laurel, *Umbellularia californica*. The leaf is a major cooking spice, and is preferred over the Turkish bay leaf.

Eucalyptus, *Eucalyptus globulus*. The leaf is used in numerous cold and cough preparations, including cough drops.

Hellebore, *Veratrum viride*. The root contains alkaloids which drastically depress the action of the heart and reduce blood pressure.

In the Southwest

Mormon tea, *Ephedra nevadenses*. The herb is used as a bronchial dialator and blood-flow stimulant in several pharmaceutical preparations.

Yerba santa, *Eriodictyon californicum*. The leaf is used to flavor pharmaceutical preparations, especially those containing bitter drugs such as quinine.

Chaparral, *Larrea tridentata*. The leaf is now used in several anti-tumor preparations, and in the treatment of specific cancers.

Burdock, *Arctium lappa*. The root is used in some cosmetic and toiletry preparations for its skin-cleansing properties. It is also used as a food.

Yellow dock, *Rumex crispus*. The root is used as a red dye for wool, and is also used as an abrasive detrifrice in several toothpastes.

Withal, these few notes are offered more as an aside, and possibly as a hint to send readers scampering to Miller's *The Potential of Herbs as a Cash Crop*. Whether some of these cash crop plants are weeds or not becomes a moot point, the final arbiter being the "cash" designation.

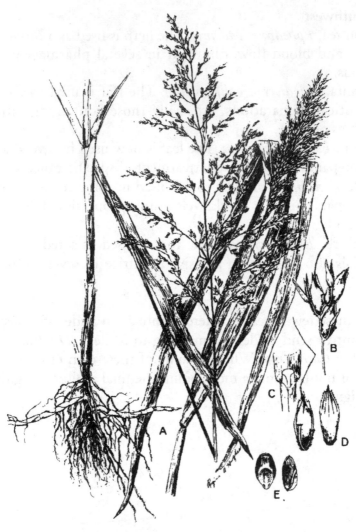

Johnson grass, Sorghum halepense, *is a perennial with both seed and rhizome reproduction. It is of the same family as quackgrass, but cannot — much like many human beings — live in the same space with a family member. Both weeds are related to the iron to manganese ratio as released by other soil factors. If iron to manganese are kept in equilibrium, the environment for almost all rhizome-type weeds is removed. Shown here is the plant in general (A); the spikelet (B); ligule (C); florets (D) and seed (E).*

12
THE DEVIL'S PANTRY

Two systems of weed control are before the world. One looks to annihilation of species and varieties with killer technology. The other suggests a natural balance, with energized crops protecting themselves against uneconomic weed competition. One accepts a byproduct of instant death, lingering illness and a cancerous legacy for the human, animal and plant population. The other seeks to enforce weed control before the fact of competition and costly crop loss without the obscene presence of toxic chemistry. One system delivers to farmers pauperism, ignorance, depopulation and barbarism. The other increases wealth, intelligence and civilization.

"For the first time in the history of the world," wrote Rachel Carson in *Silent Spring,* "today every human creature comes in contact with poisonous chemical substances from the moment of conception till death." She went on to accuse the chemical industry of poisoning humanity with the consent of scientists whose knowledge and concept of toxicity dates back to the Stone Age, and she charged that we have become victims of "cancer, nerve paralysis, genetic mutations and . . . are now in no better situation than Borgia's guests."

I have deferred to this late chapter a fuller discussion on how not to control weeds for reasons at once apparent in both the preceding and following pages. And I have to admit that — once upon a time — I fell for the sales pitch of the chemical shills. Anyone who develops blisters pulling *unkraut* out of potato patches and corn fields tends to get pretty primitive, and annihilation of the weed tribe seems something devoutly to be wished.

Then came a moment of truth. I was working with the National Park Service one summer in the late 1940s. Each morning our trail crew climbed Battle Mountain in Rocky Mountain National Park for the noble purpose of eradicating blister rust on white pine. The method of attack had a propriety name — Weedone — which was really 2,4-D as a brand. The idea was to scarify the roots of the ribe bush, and apply 2,4-D to the known residence of the organism that offended the white pine. Many of the workers carelessly washed their hands in Weedone, and some ended up sick near to death. Something was wrong here and I, in effect, started my life's work.

There were detours, best represented by some of my books — *Angry Testament, Holding Action, Unforgiven* — but *Salsola kali*, variety tenuifolia, was never far from my mind. Nor was the vehemence with which western Kansas farmers fought the Russian thistle and other weeds. I knew more about the tumbleweed than I did about the sickening stuff we used on the ribe bush, having watched mules relish *Salsola kali*, and sparrows feed on its many seeds — as did the goldfinch, horned lark, lark bunting, Oregon junco and slate colored junco. From the first, manufacturers and users of 2,4-D and 2,4,5-T asserted that these were merely harmless weed killers, but in fact many members of nature's community, especially women and children, were endangered and victimized by its use.

2,4,5-T (2,4,5-tetrachlorophenoxyacetic acid) and 2,4-D (2,4-dichlorophenoxyacetic acid) are chlorinated hydrocarbons and have the effect of hormones on plants, stimulating their growth until veins and bark burst open, causing death and rapid decay. Applied by helicopter as a spray to be absorbed through the leaves, or injected directly into tree trunks, these defoliants were commonly used in the United States for weed and brush control and to clear cattle pastures. They were also sprayed directly on food crops: apples, rice, oranges, pears, grapefruit, peaches, sorghum, lettuce, cabbage, beans, beets, potatoes, mustard, wheat, soybeans, corn, barley, alfalfa, oats and hay. Users were warned by a long list of precautions not to inhale the fumes or spill the chemicals on their skin, not to spray near lakes, streams or dwellings, not to plant crops until three months after treatment, or until the chemical has disappeared from the soil.

The Bionetics Research Study by the National Cancer Institute was motivated by the widespread use of 2,4,5-T and 2,4-D in Vietnam. It revealed that "all dosages, routes, and strains resulted in increased incidence of abnormal fetuses" in laboratory rats and mice. Fetuses miscarried with no eyes, faulty eyes, cystic kidneys, cleft palates, enlarged livers, damage to the heart, liver, skeletal musculature, lungs and reproductive organs.

In Vietnam, a generation of deformed children was born to women who drank contaminated water in areas heavily sprayed with Agent Orange (a mixture of 2,4,5-T and 2,4-D). In Arizona, ten- and twelve-year-old females suffered premenstrual hemorrhaging, necessitating hysterectomies, and women over 65 years of age suffered swelling, rashes, and postmenopausal bleeding when the Tonto National Forest was sprayed. In Arkansas, a field was sprayed above a spring supplying water to twenty people. Six out of eight babies conceived in that watershed resulted in miscarriages, one severely deformed with a cleft head and no legs.

Dow Chemical Company, the major manufacturer of 2,4,5-T, asserted that the teratogenic (birth defect producing) agent was not 2,4,5-T itself, but rather dioxin, a "contaminant" of 2,4,5-T. Dioxin is ever-present in 2,4,5-T, inseparable from it, and even produced by "pure" 2,4,5-T under specific conditions of heat and light. Jacqueline Verrett, a supervisory chemist for the U.S. Food and Drug Administration, said "Dioxin is one hundred to one million times as dangerous in producing birth defects as the notorious thalidomide."

In 1971, President Richard Nixon, upon advice from the scientific community, banned the use of 2,4,5-T for the military, and the Environmental Protection Agency severely limited its domestic uses. Dow Chemical Company, however, appealed the EPA ruling and continued to distribute 2,4,5-T despite hazards to the public. Manufacturers and users of 2,4,5-T enjoyed considerable economic gain from chemically-induced unnatural rapid growth. Application of 2,4,5-T was an inexpensive way to clear land for cattle pasture; to increase food crop yields for greater agribusiness profits; to transform national forests into timber farms, replacing natural hardwoods with faster growing, higher profit producing pines — a treatment at the expense of not only every living thing in the rudely disrupted woodlands, but at great expense to the American taxpayers who lost their national forests while a few businessmen capitalized on the lumber. 2,4,5-T meant lower costs, higher profits to business with the financial means to legally manipulate government controls.

In addition to domestic exploitation, the U.S. State Department became involved in schemes to dispose of the 2.5 million gallons of "Agent Orange" (outlawed Vietnam stock) by remerchandising the rusting drums for sale to South America military forces for development of the people's land without their consent. Both at home and abroad, 2,4,5-T propaganda was designed to deceive the people that it is a safe idea to use their poison "to control unwanted vegetation."

With this deadly game afloat, it is more than tragic to note that decision making — more often than not — imposes no more intelligence than can be found amid the bickering of office boys. Boards ignore information in order to look for more information, the "latest" being somewhat magic. At one of Iowa's prestige colleges, emissaries from commerce were not-so-subtly told, "For $100,000 we will prove anything," an admission of sophistry at best, scientific gangsterism at worst.

There is an old saying in newspapering that the earliest version of a story of shocking import is usually the most accurate. Within hours after the first story hits the wires, details get shaded, pressures find their mark, and those offended find ways of softening the blow.

The Bionetics Study indeed illustrated the point. In 1969, there was a big furor because 2,4,5-T was being used in Vietnam, causing birth deformities. Abnormalities noted in 2,4,5-T test animals included eye abnormalities like macropthalmia, or bulged eyes; anopthalmia, or absence of eyes; microphthalmia, or small eyes; as well as other defects including ectopic intestines, hydrocepholus, club foot, and encephalocele. Since this is not the kind of stuff chemical shills like to believe, the usual response is to call for more research. If twenty years of seeking the truth is good, then forty years must be better, this logic seems to run.

All this would be tragic enough. What is even more tragic is the fact that these boards, commissions and other obfuscating agencies singled out only 2,4,5-T, allowing a sister deadly (2,4-D) a clean sweep of the sales field. This became the ploy from the moment phenoxy herbicides first drew critical fire. Hold hearings on 2,4,5-T, which is teratogenic (albeit not generally available for food crops), and let it draw the fire so that 2,4-D (which also produces tumors) can be used on millions of acres of food crops. Should eco-freaks make a breakthrough by some miracle, then only 2,4,5-T would be banned. This leaves 2,4-D in command of the field. After all, some thirty times more 2,4-D was sold than 2,4,5-T.

Yet the newsman had it right in the first version. "Not since the Romans salted the land after destroying Carthage has a nation taken such pains to visit the war upon future generations," the wire report on Operation Hades said.

Simple scrutiny of the cancer and deformity lists made part of *The Bionetics Study* reveals that officials caught up in the chemical feast actually registered the following cancer-causers for use on food crops, regardless of the harmful, if not fatal, consequences: Aldrin, Aramite, Biphenyl, Captan, Captax, Chlorobenzilate,

Dieldrin, Gibberelic Acid, Heptochlor, Mirex, Monuron, PPDDD, PPDDT, Perthane, Piperonyl Butoxide, Piperonyl Sulfoxide, 2,4-D, 2,6-Dichloro-4, and Strobane. These names, generic and trade, are only aliases. There are hundreds of substances on the market that belong under each of those listed above, were proper extension of this roster to be accomplished.

I cite this inventory of information simply to make the point that toxic weed control has consequences that run well beyond the annihilation of weeds. Jack Doyle, the author of *Altered Harvest*, laid it out in spades when he spoke before a Gene Debate conference sponsored by the Danish environmental group NOAH, November 1, 1988. Jack Doyle's *Altered Harvest* identified the sickness of a research trend long before genetic manipulation became current coin. His work is both popular and documented, drawing on references by the thousands. Doyle delivered the paragraphs quoted below, and those used to backbone this chapter, as a spokesman for the Environmental Policy Institute, which has since merged with Friends of the Earth. His paper was entitled, *Herbicides and Biotechnology: Extending the Pesticide Era*, and he made the point that at a time when public policy should be getting rid of the herbicides, captains of industry were using considerable guile and cunning to extend their use. Doyle went on to cite a point in time when the modern herbicide era actually started, namely in 1941 in the botany laboratories of the University of Chicago.

> Scientists at the time were conducting research on plant hormones and synthetically produced chemicals that regulated various kinds of beneficial plant growth. These researchers were often frustrated in their work by the killing action of the growth regulators on the plants. But one scientist envisioned that these chemicals might work to kill weeds if purposely applied in toxic doses. And sure enough, the researchers soon discovered that certain of these compounds would indeed kill weeds.
>
> In Washington, this work soon came to the attention of the National Academy of Sciences' war research committee and the U.S. Army. The Army was then becoming interested in biological war-

fare research, and shortly recruited the leader of the University of Chicago botany laboratory to begin secret military research on herbicides at Fort Detrick in Maryland. Between 1944 and 1945, the Army tested the effects of more than one thousand different chemical compounds on living plants at Fort Detrick. The use of herbicides in warfare was seriously contemplated at that time, but never unleashed. [That sorry decision waited for the war in Vietnam.]

With the end of WWII, herbicides soon made their way to agricultural experiment stations, private companies, and farmers. In 1945, the American Chemical Paint Company (later named AmChem, which subsequently became part of Union Carbide) began selling the first systemic herbicide — 2,4-D under the brand name Weedone.

Two years later, 30 different preparations of herbicides containing 2,4-D were being sold in the United States. By 1949, about 23 million acres of agricultural land were treated with herbicides of all kinds. Ten years later, that figure rose to 59 million acres. Still, by 1962, only 14% of the $2 billion that farmers spent to control weeds was being spent to buy chemical herbicides.

Today, herbicide use in the United States and many other countries is exploding. As early as 1981, herbicides comprised more than 60% of all pesticides in U.S. agriculture. For some corporations, herbicides have become their single most lucrative product. In recent years, Monsanto has sold over $1 billion worth of herbicides worldwide in one year, nearly half of which derived from one popular herbicide named *Roundup*. When Eli Lilly's Treflan was riding high in the U.S. and other markets during the late 1970s, it alone comprised as much as 12% of the company's total earnings.

Laws, journalistic clout, and an atmosphere of intimidation in the colleges made seat-of-the-pants NPK fertilizers current coin. Blessed by a scientific priesthood, this image was swallowed hook, line and sinker by farmers. Oil company technology, after all, was an insurance policy for use of oil company rescue chemistry. Grants created suitable findings, and two unsound concepts swept farming — partial and imbalanced fertilization, and toxic rescue chemistry. Much of that rescue chemistry continues to be "rescue crops from weeds."

That anti-nature devices could produce bins and bushels became the supreme justification for fossil fuel technology in the early 1950s. That nature revolts against man's mistakes was less emphasized. Farmers were seldom told that plants without balanced hormone and enzyme systems summon the predators of the biotic pyramid so that misfits can be removed. But to save the crop from the penalty of agriculture's original sin, an almost unmentionable alchemy swept the scene — *the synthetic poisons.*

There have always been poisons in nature, frequently those associated with elements of heavy specific gravity, such as lead and mercury. Every child who reads *Alice in Wonderland* knows of the Mad Hatter's disease, that unhappy condition brought on when fumes from mercury used in the hatter's trade attacked the central nervous system, splitting amino acids, thereby creating proteins of a pathological character. Farmers have used compounds of arsenic, copper, lead, manganese, and zinc. They have used pyrethrum from dried chrysanthemums, nicotine sulfate from plants related to tobacco, rotenone from legumes in the East Indies. These natural poisons kill quickly and slowly, but they lack the deadly potential of man's inventions.

DDT was invented by a German chemist in 1874. Indeed, many of the miracle poisons of today can be found in some form in old German compendiums. At the end of WWI, many of the patents were handed to the world, and at the end of WWII, Paul Muller of Switzerland won the Nobel Prize for discovering insecticidal properties of DDT. At war's end, with many newsreels hailing the event, DDT was touted for stamping out insect-borne diseases and winning the farmer's war against crop destroyers. We now ask, just what is DDT? What are the chlorinated hydrocarbons? What are the phenoxy herbicides? What are organic and inorganic chemistry, for that matter?

It was Dmitri I. Mendeleyeff who first constructed a table of known elements in natural order, and supplied the periodicity of property and weight. His insight into the Creator's order was so great he supplied spaces where he believed an element should be to comply with the rhyme and reason of that supreme plan. That table still stands. The blank spots have been filled in. And the Periodic Chart of the Elements provided a simple and beautiful picture of order in the universe where we live. It did more. It opened chemistry and physics as never before, and made it possible for lesser minds to understand the structure of the atom. Moreover, it provided some facts agronomists could not ignore.

All the elements needed for life were listed as the first 53 of 92 natural elements on planet earth. Of these, all except one fell in order among the first 42, and all except two were listed among the first 34. There is also a natural order for abundance of elements, according to atomic weight and number. The heaviest elements are the rarest. Elements with even atomic numbers are more abundant than those with odd numbers in our universe. We don't know why, nor can we even guess.

The table itself is a veritable encyclopedia. There are series with missing electrons. As the eye moves from titanium to zinc, unfilled orbits change, an electron at a time. These transitions take place in natural order, moving across the table. There is also a vertical order to the table, weight increasing as each element is listed under the one above. There are groups that figure in biology and signal the entrance or exit of disease. Henry A. Schroeder, M.D., possibly the world's foremost authority on trace elements, told us that "a heavier metal can displace a lighter one in the same group in biological tissues and alter the reaction of the lighter one." He went on to say that tissues with an affinity for a certain element have an affinity for all other elements of the same group. Some elements are bone seekers. Some are thyroid seekers. All elements in two groups are liver and kidney seekers. These few data only hint at the vast complexity of the Creator's life plan. They also hint at how little of this vast knowledge has so far been uncovered, even though nature has been revealing herself for a long time.

A landmark event, in fact, took place in Berlin in 1828 when Friedrich Whöler discovered that ammonium cyanate could be transformed into urea by heat alone. The consternation of Justus von Liebig can be imagined. Here was a simple agent, heat, that could rearrange the atoms of a molecule into a different compound, yet still remain in possession of all the original atoms.

Hardly thirty years later, Friederick Kekule, in Ghent, conceptualized methane (CH_4) as a basis for organic compounds. Here was a hypothesis that explained the structural formulas for chain or aliphatic compounds common to fats and oils and petroleum. Benzene, however, remained unexplained. Benzene had been isolated from oil gas and from coal tar. Why didn't it fit the pattern? It belonged to a class known as hydrocarbons — compounds made up entirely of hydrogen and carbon, and characterized by a deficiency in hydrogen or carbon atom, to wit: C_6H_6. The story has been told that Kekule sat before his fireplace one evening and saw in the curling smoke a "vision" of gamboling carbon compounds, one figure of which grabbed its own tail — the hexagon. And so the riddle of benzene came clear. So did the riddle of hydrocarbons in general.

Junior high chemistry texts often use an illustration reproduced below. Students are asked to picture the basic element of the universe, carbon, aligned with hydrogen and/or chlorine.

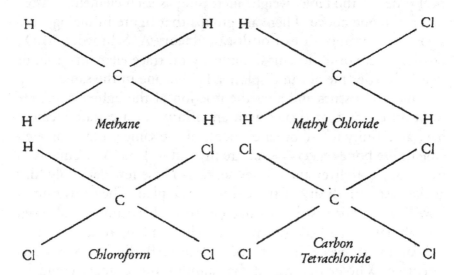

The basic element of the universe is carbon. Surround one atom of carbon with four atoms of hydrogen. This is the chemical structure for methane, the common gas of the swamps, the "original" hydrocarbon having atoms of only carbon and hydrogen. Now take away one of those hydrogen atoms, and substitute a chlorine atom, so that the one atom of carbon is surrounded by three hydrogen atoms and one chlorine atom. This is methyl chloride. Now take away three atoms of hydrogen and replace them with chlorine, and you have chloroform. Take away all the atoms of hydrogen, and replace them all with chlorine, around carbon, and you have carbon tetrachloride — the stuff in cleaning fluid and fire extinguishers. These simple formulas advanced chemistry by leaps and bounds. Yet they accounted for mere child's play compared to the benzene ring. When Kekule realized that a fourth valance could be absorbed intramolecularly, the door flew open. Aromatic hydrocarbons (so named because they smell) filled the compendiums, and caused man-made compounds to proliferate.

These simple illustrations give only the mildest hint of combinations possible and of the true complexity of the chemical world. There are rings and chains and branches, and figures grabbing their own arms and tails. A seemingly slight change in the Creator's formula can change the character of a substance. Many changes via heat, cold, pressure, mixes — whatever — have developed poisons of fantastic scope. It may be an oversimplification, but it is nevertheless a fact that the Creator's poisons wash away, and that man's poisons threaten to consume him. Nature's poisons do not easily pass through the placental wall. They obey Bertrand's Law. Some are essential. When man or animal intakes high concentrations that exceed the ability to repel or excrete the excess, these elements become toxic and lethal. They are governed by a principle known as homeostasis, and are said to be under homeostatic control. The man-made poisons are of a different stripe.

The role of the placental wall illustrates something about the natural order. Indeed, one of my first jobs at *Veterinary Medicine* magazine was to edit the work of George A. Young, D.V.M. In the mid-1950s, Young was working at the University of Nebraska. He found that newborn pigs are disease free, that they are protected by the mother's womb from the many diseases that hamper swine production. Once born, pigs become infected and usually they have not developed enough antibodies to survive in a swine producer's environment. Hence the high death rate of one- and two-week-old pigs. Young broke the disease barrier by taking piglets a couple of days before normal birth by hysterectomy. This classical work became the origin of specific pathogen free (SPF) hogs. The placental wall protected the young, and broke the disease cycle.

The placental wall cannot stop DDT and the chlorinated hydrocarbons. These synthetic poisons build up in fatty tissues and ultimately overwhelm the system. They break the amino acid chain and cause mutations. Many of the world's greatest scientists believe they have no safe level and no tolerance level. By offending the chromosomes, these substances tamper with the gene pool and the origin of life itself. All evidence says that the effects of these toxic genetic chemicals will be visited to the twentieth and thirtieth generation.

That is why Rachel Carson wrote, "We are rightly appalled by the genetic effects of radiation; how then can we be indifferent to the same effect in chemicals that we disseminate widely in our environment."

Rachel Carson meant the synthetic man-made poisons, and she also meant to compare these synthetics in mutogenic effect with atomic fallout. Later, Jerome Wiesner, a science adviser to President Kennedy, repeated the Rachel Carson statement when facing a United States Senate Commission assembled to examine *Silent Spring*. "Using agricultural pesticides," he said, "is more dangerous than atomic fallout."

Now the war on weeds becomes even more ominous. Do we really have to go after lambsquarters and Russian thistle with the equivalent of atomic energy? This is not hyperbole.

A few years ago, Americo Mosca of Torino, Italy, set out to illustrate how toxic genetic chemicals were in fact more dangerous than the atomic bomb. Add a word to your lexicon — *ionization*. This is the process used to add or subtract one or more electrons from an atom. The hydrogen atom is electrically neutral. It has a single electron traveling around a core. A violent impact can knock the electron out of the atom. This ionizes the atom and creates an ion pair. When atoms in human tissue are ionized, they are damaged. This damage can be minor, or so severe it kills a cell. Sick cells "have defective metabolic mechanisms that permit attack by bacterial and viral infections." Deranged cells "age more rapidly and may cause the appearance of these diseases of metabolism which are called cancer or thrombosis," noted Andre Voisin.

Chemicals used in agriculture have been ionized to subtract electrons from the hydrogen atoms of amino acids. They act in the same way as thermic, electric and radiant energy from an atomic bomb, said Mosca. "Therefore the damage caused by the ionization of atomic fallout and by chemical and physical agents are the same." The application of radioisotopes and fungicides based on Zineb in agriculture confirm this statement.

Knowing this much, Mosca computed the damage being done to human beings with the use of toxic genetic chemicals. Using power figures, he computed damage levels for farm chemicals in the United States and compared them to atomic bombs because he knew the degree of ionization of both nuclear fallout and farm chemicals.

To recite these details is not to suggest that official science agrees. As a matter of fact, official and government science say there is a safe level and a tolerance level for the synthetic chemicals, always on grounds that the concept of toxicity extant 200 years ago properly described man-made molecules.

Yet the fact is that toxic genetic chemicals do not qualify for homeostatic control, as do the natural compounds and sometimes lethal trace minerals. This is what Rachel Carson meant when she charged that all this is being done with the consent of scientists whose knowledge and concept of toxicity dates back to the Stone Age.

Publication of *Use of Pesticides* in 1963 didn't change the stand of the agri-chemists, nor did the statement by Jerome Wiesner that "using agricultural pesticides was more dangerous than atomic fallout."

It was not that some few random scientists didn't fail to stand up and be counted. "A false step from us may cause the complete destruction of soil fertility and anthropods will take advantage of the earth," a Syracuse University assembly concluded. "When the field becomes a factory," noted a panel of German and Netherlands scientists on the subject of pesticides of organic synthesis, "we are on the way to irremediable catastrophe."

This business of "getting" the weeds started writing its own biography, the gist of which was captured by Jack Doyle, when he spoke to that assembly in Copenhagen.

A significant increase in herbicide sales began in the mid-1970s with the increasing popularity of minimum and no-till agriculture, a system of crop farming in which chemicals are substituted for cultivation as the primary means of weed control. For example, some Chevron literature of a few years ago explains: "When you switch to no-tillage farming, you switch to an often total reliance on chemicals for control of unwanted vegetation." With low tillage methods there is reduced soil erosion, lower energy consumption, less runoff of fertilizer and pesticides, and increased moisture retention in the soil. Critics argue, however, that minimum-till crop residues increase pest and disease problems, resulting in greater pesticide use, increased costs for farmers, and additional groundwater pollution from pesticides.

Nevertheless, some predictions indicate that as much as 85% of all cultivated cropland will be in some form of so-called conservation tillage by the year 2000, and that means more herbicides. Not surprisingly, some chemical and pharmaceutical companies are gearing up their sales force and changing their sales pitch, casting themselves as conservationists. In April 1984, for example, Chevron announced that it would restructure its Ortho Agricultural Chemicals Division to focus more heavily on the trend toward minimum-till farming. Ortho's herbicide product manager is now called "product manager for conservation tillage."

In recent years, the seed and biotechnology industries have begun to research ways to protect seed and crops from the harsher side of herbicides: they have begun to adapt crops and seed to the likelihood of herbicide-treated soils.

One of the first products marketed to help crops tolerate high herbicide environments was "herbicide safened" seed. Ciba-Geigy, the Swiss pharmaceutical company, introduced one such product as early as 1979. Ciba-Geigy and its subsidiary, Funk Seeds International, acquired in 1974, called their product a herbicide antidote and named it Concep. Concep is a chemical coating applied to sorghum seeds to protect them from the damaging effects of herbicides such as Dual, Milocep and Bicep, all of which Ciba-Geigy sells.

Another problem with herbicides is that some of these chemicals kill crops, or linger too long in the soil, damaging crops that may follow in rotation. This phenomenon is known to farmers and herbicide makers as "residue carryover."

In Illinois, for example, about ten million acres of corn are treated each year with the herbicide atrazine. Corn can tolerate atrazine because it contains certain enzymes which detoxify the chemical inside the plant. Thus, corn is naturally resistant to atrazine's lethal effects. But this is not the case with soybeans, a crop often used in rotation with corn. And that can be a problem when atrazine is still present in the soil. A farmer using atrazine on corn, and then following that corn crop with a soybean crop, is likely to have atrazine-damaged soybeans and reduced yield because of atrazine soil residues. Other crops, such as alfalfa and small grains, are also sensitive to atrazine residues.

The same kind of problem exists with even the newer generation of low-dose herbicides, such as DuPont's wheat herbicide Glean. Only wheat, it seems, "knows" how to detoxify Glean or metabolize it into harmless (as far as we know) byproducts. Crops such as soybeans, sugarbeets, sunflowers, and corn that might follow wheat in rotation will be damaged by residues of Glean remaining in the soil. A few years ago, North Dakota farmer John Leppert remarked: "It would be at least four years in North Dakota before a field treated with Glean could be used for some broadleaf crops."

One solution to this problem has become clear with gene-splitting research: find the specific genes that enable a given crop to resist the ill effects of certain herbicides and move those genes into the sensitive crops. One plant biochemist, Charles Arntzen, leading a team of investigators at Michigan State University, spent three years pursuing protein chemistry techniques to unearth the mechanisms of atrazine resistance in weeds. Meanwhile, another group of investigators at the Harvard University laboratory of Lawrence Bogorad, was studying gene expression in plant chloroplasts. After collaboration, the two groups discovered that a single nucleotide change in one gene found in the chloroplast was the basis for the weed's resistance to atrazine. Presenting these results of the Miami Winter Symposium, Arntez suggested that such resistance could be genetically engineered into important crop plants, such as the soybean. A few years later, Arntzen would move to DuPont where he would head up the company's research effort to develop herbicide-resistant crop strains.

Scientists were asking only a few of the right questions as early corporate programs fell into full swing. Some decades ago, "some genetic engineers began to investigate the genetic and biochemical mechanisms in weeds that made them resistant to certain herbicides," Doyle told the Danish NOAH group. "By 1982, the first scientifc papers were presented which suggested that such resistance could be genetically engineered into important crop plants, such as the soybean. By this time, chemical and pharmaceutical companies had also begun their own programs of herbicide resistance research." In July 1982, *Chemical Week* wrote of a "slow but steady push" among herbicide makers toward the "genetic manipulation of corn, soybeans, and other crops to make them more resistant to herbicides. The theory is," explained the magazine, "that farmers would then be willing to use even more of the weeds killers, safe in the knowledge that their crop won't be damaged." At this point American Cyanamid struck a deal with Molecular Genetics, a biotechnology company, to develop new lines of hybrid corn resistant to a new class of experimental herbicides called imidazolinones. "The new lines of corn," reported *Chemical Week,* "are expected to increase the market for broad-spectrum herbicides, which otherwise have a limited potential when used with currant hybrids of corn."

In November 1982, Calgene, a California based biotechnology company, announced that it had cloned a gene for resistance to the world's most widely used herbicide, Monsanto's Roundup, chemically named glyphosate. Two years later, Calgene had contracts to develop herbicide-resistant crops with at least three major corporations: Kemira Oy, Finland's largest chemical company; Nestle, the world's largest food company; and Rhone-Poulenc, a major French agrichemical company.

By this time, DuPont had developed tobacco plants in the laboratory with resistance to its herbicide Glean — plants that were one hundred times more resistant to Glean than were normal plants. The company also cloned the gene for Glean resistance. Ciba-Geigy, meanwhile, was working with atrazine, and soon would hire a rising star in molecular biology — Mary Dell Chilton from Washington University — to head up Ciba-Geigy's biotechnology division in North Carolina. Ciba-Geigy was hoping to develop soybean varieties resistant to its old herbicide atrazine, and began work with a model system in tobacco, which it field tested in North Carolina in 1986.

According to the L. William Teweles consulting firm, the development of atrazine resistant soybeans would mean, for example, that atrazine use by farmers each year would double or triple over what it is now, increasing sales by about $120 million annually.

Some observers predict that the use of genetic engineering to develop herbicide-resistant crop plants will bring about a complete restructuring of the $2.4 billion-per-year U.S. herbicide market. For example, the L. William Teweles Company, a seed and biotechnology consulting firm, reports that some chemical companies are developing crops resistant to their herbicides "in the hope of selling the seed and chemical as a pair." Other companies are seeking herbicide resistance, according to Teweles, "as a way of gaining market share lost after a well known herbicide has declined in price and popularity . . . " In other words, the old herbicide will be sold in combination with a new seed resistant to it. Teweles' consultants also see herbicide resistant crops as creating "a complementary demand for both chemical and seed."

Since the early 1980s. a whole host of chemical, energy, pharmaceutical and biotechnology companies have begun research on herbicide resistance. As of the end of the 1980s, there were at least thirty-three companies involved.

In addition to this commercial activity, public funds from the Department of Energy, the National Science Foundation and the USDA have been used to support herbicide resistance research at a number of universities and agricultural experiment stations, including Auburn University, the University of California, Davis, the University of Chicago, Harvard, Louisiana State University, Michigan State University, Rutgers, and the University of Tennessee. In other instances, such as the work on atrazine resistance, university research has been supported or conducted in collaboration with private companies such as Ciba-Geigy and Shell Agricultural Chemicals. And while some of this research in the universities had been aimed at getting basic knowledge about plant molecular biology, much of it is now justified on the making of herbicide resistant crops and forest trees.

But is herbicide resistance research a good way to be "spending" biotechnology? Is it a good and safe investment for the rest of society? And should publicly-funded universities and research institutes be pursuing this line of research?

Industry officials and scientists say the making of herbicide resistant crops will only help herbicides to do their job more efficiently. Herbicide resistant crops, they say, will allow better targeted usage, as well as be safer for public health and the environment.

The bottom line is that American agriculture should be eliminating herbicide use rather than conjuring up new and exotic ways to extend and expand use through genetic engineering.

At this point we can only suggest the character of the box canyon agriculture is entering with its reliance on toxic genetic chemicals. These chemicals actually trigger weeds, order up new phylums and families and fertilize their progeny. Only a few have dared to ask the right questions. I think I have pointed the way in this little book. Admittedly, I have only scratched the surface.

Farm Chemicals Handbook lists some nine hundred toxic genetic chemicals. Each has its own biography. Possibly 50,000 different formulations of the possibilities routinely enter trade channels. They outshine each other in presenting a picture of purveyors and government run amok.

The baseball scores on herbicides would fill a manual big enough to enshrine the lives and averages of all the major league teams. Here I have merely abstracted and extracted from the record created by Jack Doyle and 67 other sources:

• In 1980, Canada suspended the use of nitrofen, produced by Rhom & Haas under the tradename TOK, after laboratory tests showed cancers and birth malformations in animals. In 1982, for example, *Science* magazine published an article on the teratogenic effects of nitrofen — mice born without heads. Shortly thereafter, Rohm & Haas pulled its TOK herbicide off the market because it said it didn't want to spend the money to do the required toxicity tests.

• Between 1982 and 1985, the EPA listed several popular herbicides for special review, indicating that testing on laboratory animals had shown these chemicals to be potential carcinogens.

• In June 1984, citing high dietary and applicator health risks, EPA placed the DuPont soybean herbicide linuron in a "restricted use" classification. DuPont data from 1980 showed the potential of linuron to cause benign, dose-related testicular tumors in rats and mice. After DuPont satisfied some EPA concerns for applicator safety, the agency lifted the restricted use of classification on linuron in September 1984, but kept the herbicide in special review because some tests showed dietary cancer risks.

• In late 1984, EPA announced a special review of Monsanto's herbicide alachlor, explaining that recent studies showed the chemical to cause at least four types of tumors when fed to laboratory animals. EPA banned the use of the chemical on potatoes as well as its application by aerial spraying. EPA also tightened the herbicide's labeling requirements, attempting to protect the

600,000 farmers and field workers who face a cancer risk of one in 10,000 from alachlor, according to the agency.

• Used widely on grains intended for human and livestock consumption, alachlor was, according to one EPA official at that time, likely to be present at some level in meat, milk, and poultry. The herbicide has also shown up in surface or groundwater in ten states, mostly in the east and midwest — in some places as high as 267 parts per billion — and human exposure through drinking water is likely.

• In April 1985, EPA moved on a third herbicide, cyanazine, produced by the Shell Chemical Company. Concerned that cyanazine might be contaminating groundwater and presenting a health risk to farmworkers, EPA announced a special review of the herbicide's safety. Cyanazine was found to cause birth defects in laboratory animals.

• Beyond their potential impact for human health, some herbicides also produce physiological changes in crop plants — such as reduced wax formation on leaves, and disruption of plant growth — that make the crops more susceptible to disease pathogens. The herbicide picloram increases the sugar-loving fungal pathogens, while 2,4-D reduces the sugar content of leaves, making them susceptible to other pathogens.

• The first genetically-engineered herbicide-resistant crop strains are expected to reach the market in within a year or two. A number of herbicide resistant or herbicide tolerant crop strains have already been field tested. Thirteen of the twenty-one field tests for genetically engineered crops approved by the USDA since late 1987 have been conducted by three chemical and pharmaceutical companies — Monsanto, Sandoz and DuPont — and over half of these were for herbicide-tolerant plants.

"Not everybody is thrilled about the prospect of herbicide-resistant crops," summarized Doyle. "If we create food crops with herbicide resistance," asks Sheldon Krimsky, a social scientist at Tufts University and former member of the NIH committee on recombinant DNA, "are we not going to reinforce the use of herbicides?

Are we not going to reinforce greater chemical use in food production at a time when people are increasingly questioning the agricultural use of chemicals?" Thomas Adamczyk, deputy chief of EPA's herbicide branch, noted that increased groundwater contamination is "inescapable," should biotechnology broaden the use of herbicides.

Let Jack Doyle continue. "By spreading more herbicides around in the environment, it is possible that more weeds will become resistant to herbicides because of the additional selection pressure on those weeds. In fact, one of the first noticeable problems to emerge with the widespread use of herbicides was the rise of genetically resistant weeds." The first report of weed resistance to 2,4-D came as early as 1959 in Hawaii. And for triazine herbicides, such as atrazine and simazine, scientists were surprised at the breadth of genetic resistance that emerged in weeds during the 1970s. "It has now become obvious," wrote Ciba-Giegy's H.M. LeBaron, "that the alleles for triazine resistance are more generally distributed (albeit at very low frequencies) than had been anticipated, both in terms of weeds as well as geographic distribution."

> Another problem, [wrote Jack Doyle] is the possibility that weed species sexually compatible with crop species will cross with the engineered crops, potentially resulting in the transfer of a herbicide resistant trait to one or more weed species. According to crop scientist Jack Harlan, most crops have one or more companions or cross-fertile weed species somewhere in the world, and many such cross-fertile weed species remain unknown and have not been identified for all crops. The sunflower has cross-fertilized weed species in the U.S. Sorghum has compatible weed species in the U.S. and Africa. And corn is cross-fertile with teosinte in Mexico. Biotechnologists, however, say that such an outcrossing can be controlled or avoided.

The first reports of triazine-resistant weeds came from Washington state in 1968, when massive doses of simazine in a conifer nursery no longer controlled the weed *Senecio vulgaris*. Atrazine resistance in specific weeds was reported in crop fields in Maryland in 1972, Ontario in 1973, Wisconsin in 1975, Massachusetts and Connecticut in 1976, California's San Joaquin Valley in 1977, Colorado in 1978, Virginia in 1979, and Michigan in 1980. Today, there are more than 30 weed species — once killed by atrazine or some other triazine — that have developed genetic resistance to one or more of these herbicides. Weed resistance or increased tolerance to other herbicides, has also been reported for specific weeds treated with 2,4-D, 2,4,5-T, diuron, dicamba, dalapon, paraquat, TCA, trifluralin, and others.

Some scientists say that their excursion into herbicide resistance will be short lived, and that the important thing is what is learned in the process about the chloroplast genome or the basic molecular biology of the plant. Yet capital is being invested, new herbicide factories will surely be built, and high-tech agriculture will not turn around overnight. The direction of this research is unmistakable.

In the seed and plant genetics industry, research priorities are already being reshuffled to accommodate herbicide-related traits in ways that may divert scientific attention away from more socially important kinds of research. There is some concern that plant scientists may be spending too much of their time to come up with genetically engineered varieties that will accommodate the use of chemicals, rather than developing disease or insect resistance in those crops. "Screening of cultivars for genetic resistance to new, highly potent herbicides," says Pioneer Hi-Bred corn breeder Don Duvick, "is becoming as important as screening the same cultivars for genetic resistance to prevalent disease and insect pests." Such priorities may well detract from, if not foreclose, other research that could lead us away from continued dependence on chemical pesticides.

So ends the quoted part of that report to NOAH in Copenhagen.

Having surveyed the weed connection with attention to nature's rules, we should be humbled indeed by our ignorance. William A. Albrecht — having examined weeds on the Gene Poirot farm in Lawrence County, Missouri — was forced to conclude that "Grass is of good feed quality only according to the fertility of the soil growing it." In other words, Albrecht said, ask the cow what she thinks.

Poirot discerned as much during WWII when his help went to war. He had to cut corners. Land was abandoned to grow what it would, weeds included. "The cattle chose the weeds where magnesium limestone and phosphate had been used as soil treatments and took them regularly in preference to the virgin prairie grass growing on the other side of the fence where no soil treatments had been use."

In *Are We Going to Grass?*, Albrecht drew conclusions that, in effect, tie the first chapter of this book to the last.

Here was testimony that weeds, including cockleburs, dock, briars, smartweed, ragweed, pigweed, Spanish needle and even nightshade, or what have you, growing on fertilized soil were preferred by the cattle rather than grass growing on the same type soil given no help to improve its fertility. Even the leguminous plants in the prairie were not chosen. The cattle disregarded native white clover and soybeans growing where remnants from cleaning the seed had been dumped only to grow up as a volunteer crop. Merely dumping legume seeds on the land does not mean choice feed even if the legume plants should be reputedly more proteinaceous, according to the claims of their pedigree. The fact that they can fix nitrogen from the atmosphere does not make them saviors in times of the feed troubles concerning protein shortages. Legumes in the virgin prairie were disregarded by the cattle. But non-legume plants, including what we commonly calls weeds, were chosen when these were growing on the abandoned crop land once given limestone and other fertilizers.

We use the plant species as the criterion. They use the nutritional quality, according as the soil fertility determines it, for their criterion as to whether the plant is a weed or not. Grasses in the virgin prairie on the Poirot farm were weeds in the cattle's judgment. They ruled them out of their consideration.

Albrecht observed that the cattle were suggesting a new definition for weeds. The cows would say "the weed is a plant that isn't of enough nutritional value, in their judgment, for them to eat it. In terms of this definition, they classified the prairie grasses as weeds. On the contrary, they classified the cockleburs, dock and other plants in the abandoned field as choice feed. Their classification is one radically different from ours. "Are we going to grass? Of course we are. But we shall go with success in capitalizing on it only under the careful attention to the fertility of the soil producing it. We shall go more successfully also by means of the selective approval of the cows that will help to make it a most economical asset for us in terms of the meat and milk we expect them to synthesize from it. With the cow assaying the soil for our decisions on the particular soil treatments needed to restore the fertility we may well be going to grass on a much greater scale. This will mean more protein food as well as more conservation of the basic resource — the soil — that creates it for us. Grass for the cover's sake must be the slogan of any grass program in soil conservation."

We can describe weeds and we can despise weeds, and we can praise their beauty in many cases. We can ask questions, and sometimes we can furnish answers. In a few instances we know which trace mineral, which condition, which factor is giving the farmer an unwanted guest. One day, not long after *Acres U.S.A.* was founded, William A. Albrecht gave me a short report he had written on broom sedge and tickle grass. Both weeds came to his attention because the cows said "such plant growth does not deliver enough feed value for her trouble of eating it," Albrecht's quote.

Poverty blue stem, or broom sedge, "is a mark of the kind of farming that fails to consider the fertility of the soil. . . ." he said. At that time tickle grass was also invading Sanborn Field at the University of Missouri. Chemical analysis of the weeds suggested itself.

As pounds per ton, broom sedge contained 2.14 of calcium, 2.18 of phosphorus and 88 of crude protein. For tickle grass the corresponding figures were 3.04, 1.9, and 69. In marked contrast for a mixture of clover and grass from fertile soil and at similar growth stage the corresponding values per ton were 26, 4, and 181 pounds . . . .

According to these simple soil differences, then, we can drive out broom sedge and tickle grass by lime, manure or other soil treatments offering better nourishment for better crops that will keep these pest crops out. That broom sedge and tickle grass should go out when you put soil fertility in is merely the converse of the fact that they come in when the fertility goes out.

Albrecht passed from the scene May 21, 1974. During the last several years of his life I was able to tape over one hundred hours of conversations with this first rate scientist, often mining his "visions" on a new approach to weeds.

Those visions duly found expression in several volumes styled *The Albrecht Papers*, which are kept in print by *Acres U.S.A.* Not as well known is a film Albrecht produced called *The Other Side of the Fence*. The key scene asked the question, *Why does the cow risk entanglement with barb wire to reach a tuft of grass on the other side?* And the answers to the other side's allure is both hinted at and proved out by the two paragraphs quoted above.

Over the years I and several of my associates have worked diligently at fleshing out the answers Albrecht provided. In the next chapter are many of the results of that effort, with possibly half the entries carrying definitive answers.

Judgement has to be the tag line. Reaching into the devil's pantry is simply bad judgment. Controlling weeds without poisons is quite the opposite.

Lambsquarters, Chenopodium album, *grows in high organic matter soil with good decay. It is a good indicator for phosphate being available on a daily meal basis. Shown here is a small plant (A); the floral spikes (B); flowers (C); utricle (D); and the seed (E).*

13
CAST OF CHARACTERS

Weeds have a nomenclature, much like a machine gun or an automobile. To keep it simple and still remain comprehensive, readers must be asked to master a few new vocabulary words. By now we are all familiar with common names for weeds. Spurge is such a name, one generally reserved for *Euphorbia serpens*, *Euphorbia heterophylla*, and *Euphorbia hexagons*. But there are other spurges: flowering spurge, or *Euphorbia corollata*; toothed spurge, *Euphorbia dentata*; leafy spurge, *Euphorbia escula*; mat spurge, *Euphorbia glyptosperma*; upright spurge, *Euphorbia hysopifolia*; spotted spurge, *Euphorbia maculata*; snow-on-the-mountain, *Euphorbia marginata*, etc. Usually, but not always, the scientific name will help separate and identify two weeds that have the same name.

In the thumbnail sketches that follow, I have selected the worst weeds, the selection being entirely subjective. Move over to another end of the country and the list will be different. Have someone else make up the list and it will be different still.

In any case, it will be necessary to say something about habitat, general appearance, flower color, leaves, fruits, smell and juice or poison. Habitat designations become wearisome enough: fields, waste places, lawns, dry areas, wetlands. General appearance will be described as grass, bushy, creeping, erect, mat and so on, none of the vocabulary being troublesome. Flowers, of course, have a color, and leaves are opposite, alternate, lobed, succulent, verticillate, basal, narrow, medium, and so on. None of this will prove troublesome for the average reader.

The description of fruit has its own vocabulary, and it has to be mastered up front. Here are the terms most likely to require definition.

Achene. A one-seeded, dry, indehiscent fruit.

Berry. A fruit that is fleshy with seeds in the flesh.

Bulbet. A small bulb, usually on the stem.

Calyx. The outer set of sterile floral leaves, or the sepals considered collectively.

Capsule. A dry fruit of more than one carpel which splits at maturity to release seeds.

Caryopsis. The grain or fruit of grasses.

Cone. A fruit with woody, overlapping scales.

Drupe. A fleshy or pulpy fruit in which the inner portion is strong.

Fleshy. Succulent, juicy.

Follicle. A podlike fruit opening along only one suture.

Indehiscent. Remaining persistently closed.

Legume. A podlike fruit composed of a solitary carpel, usually splitting open by both sutures.

Nutlet. A diminutive nut.

Pyxis. A capsule that comes open like a lid.

Utricle. A small, thin-walled, one-seeded fruit.

Other special terms used in this book are contained in the glossary.

As you read each entry in this cast of characters, remember that low biological activity is inherent in each weed problem. It is this lack of life in the soil that results in mineral imbalances. Each weed is keyed to a specific environment slotted for its proliferation. There are nutrient interactions and certain nutrients are needed to correct the weed problem. These may or may not be the nutrients indicated by the weed as deficient.

It has been noted that in a few hundred more years — considering the present rate of discovery — we will have all the answers on the role of trace minerals in crop production. Answers for the complexities that attend weed growth may take even longer.

The farmer needs to read his fields like an open book. Weeds help define exactly what is happening. The information offered here will help the commercial crop producer become independent of the allopathic system, but it also forces him to move out into the field. The skills that backbone these biographies cannot be learned through a windshield or from local radio stations blasting their herbicide messages into the tractor cab.

With these thoughts in tow, here are a few notes on specific weeds a farmer is likely to encounter.

BARNYARD GRASS, a.k.a., *watergrass, panic grass, cockspur grass, cocksfoot panicum.*

It is an annual, this Latin *Echinochloa crusgalli*, and it reproduces by seeds. A single plant can produce up to 40,000 seeds. In addition to the usual waste places, it also visits cultivated fields. Depending on moisture availability, this grass can grow to 4.5 feet in height, which it does along streams. Leaves alternate, are simple, broad and long without a ligule. The color is green to purplish. Spikelets are 1- or 2-flowered. The grain it produces is oval. There is a short awned version of barnyard grass, *Echinochloa crusgalli*, but the difference is almost academic. Barnyard grass is easily controlled with tillage early in its growth. Barnyard grass means inadequate

Barnyard grass.

calcium and phosphorus levels, the 2 nutrients that roll back more weeds than all the poisons put together. Potassium registers high when this grass takes over. There are other high readings that can be expected in magnesium, manganese, sulfate, boron, chlorine, selenium, zinc and copper. Repair of the disparity between calcium and the other elements will set the stage for another year. This grass also likes low organic matter soils and inadequate humus levels, all a consequence of sedimentation and eventual crusting. Simple mowing to prevent seed distribution is also effective. Barnyard grass can be grazed when young, but becomes unpalatable as it matures.

BEGGARTICKS, a.k.a. *Devils beggarticks.*

An annual herb which reproduces from seeds, beggarticks, *Bidens frondosa*, is found in rich, moist soils as well as cultivated areas, dry waste places, pastures, roadsides, gardens and damp open habitats. It has a shallow taproot with many branches. Smooth stems are somewhat 4-sided, branching near the top, and can grow to be up to 1 m tall. Leaves are opposite, 4-ranked, on petioles 1-6 cm long, lance shaped and serrated, and they are sometimes hairy on the bottom. The heads are saucer-shaped to hemispheric and the ray flowers orange-yellow. Beggarticks prefer moist soil and poorly drained

Devils beggarticks.

areas. As with many weeds, they signal calcium levels that are low along with low humus and bacteria. Beggarticks also indicate high levels of phosphate, magnesium, and aluminum.

BERMUDA GRASS, a.k.a., *wiregrass, devil grass, scutch grass, dogtooth grass, Bahama grass, vinegrass.*

Bermuda grass, *Cynodon dactylon* is a perennial that spreads by rhizomes and seeds as well as stolons. Although a lawn grass, it achieves weed status when it invades orchards, vineyards and neglected crop areas. Bermuda grass will not grow in shade. It looks a lot like crabgrass with shorter fingers. It has a ring of whitish hairs where the blade joins the sheath. Shallow

Bermuda grass.

plowing before the ground freezes is the remedy of choice. It has great value as an erosion prevention crop along highways. It can be propagated by chopping runners and inserting these in the soil and kept wet as well as by seeding.

HEDGE BINDWEED, a.k.a. *creeping bindweed, morning glory, climbing false buckwheat.*

This perennial, *Convolvulus sepium*, reproduces from both seeds and shallow creeping roots. It is a blood brother to field bindweed or morning glory, *Convolvulus arvensis*. The *sepium* brother is also known as climbing false buckwheat. It grows almost everywhere, even on eroded hillsides that are well drained. Bindweed is a typical reflector of an improper decay of

organic matter and excess accumulation of heavy soil metals. It may be that a bale of hay broke open in an area, and was left there. It may be that cattle were fed, and much organic matter was stomped into the ground. Morning glories function best in the presence of ample humus materials and an antagonistic decay system. Bindweeds tend to flourish more in an eroded low humus soil, which cannot support corrective decay systems for soil restoration. Low calcium, phosphorus, potassium and pH are benchmarks. Crusting and sticky soil are also consequences. Most creeping-vine-type weeds have extensive and fast growing rhizomes that develop to completely entrap the soil nutrient system in and around all the clusters of organic residues. The biological energies contained in these foul, rotting residues support numerous dominating hormone enzyme systems that are "just right" for the vine weed families, and "not just right" for other species of soil and plant life. Such conditions can occur within soils of high exchange capacity (clay) or low exchange capacity (sandy) — with low or high organic material content — always in soils that impose limitations on ferment and breakdown of organic residue in the desired direction. Such soils are unable to govern the humus system. They also lack the capacity to support the right kind of nutrition needed for better plant and animal food, chiefly because of the imbalanced hormone-enzyme system that is sustained by improper decay. Field bindweed, morning glory, creeping bindweed all dominate the plant kingdom because of a short circuit in the energy release of fouled decay systems. These limits are generated by an accumulation of dry-dead organic substances either under dry fall conditions, or in wet spring soil — with compaction, sedimentation, and improper tillage timing figuring in the equation. Cultural practices that relate to stress systems are greatly influenced by the pH character of the colloidal system involved and by the effect of drainage and air capacity of the decay medium. Correct these soil limitations through pH management and the bindweed-morning glory syndrome becomes completely dispersed. No herbicide chemical or fertilizer material can replace good soil management. Roots that go down 4 feet in the first year can't be chased by phenoxy herbicides. Hedge bindweed is easy to identify. High twining with smooth leaves that alternate, are simple, long-petioled, triangular ovate, the plant has white to pink to almost reddish flowers. The fruit is glabrous and covered with bracts and calyx. See illustration on page 28.

BLUEWEED, a.k.a., *blue sunflower.*

This is a perennial that reproduces by rhizomes and seeds. Its

Blueweed.

scientific name is *Helianthus ciliaris.* It grows in both cultivated fields and on prairie land, and rates attention as the most objectionable weed of the sunflower types. It has a bluish cast, grows about 3 feet high from a fibrous root. Toothed leaves are opposite. The flower is a typical sunflower with a small yellow disc and large yellow ray flowers. The bindweed remedy is indicated when this blue Texas denizen shows up outside its general bailiwick.

JAPANESE BROMEGRASS

Bromus japonicus grows just about everywhere except Florida and Maine, as far as I know. It is a winter annual that depends on

Japanese bromegrass.

seeds for reproduction. It really isn't too much trouble to agriculture, except cosmetic. *Bromus japonicus* germinates in the fall, producing a hairy turf that is palatable through the winter. After shoots appear in early spring, palatability vanishes like a Houdini rabbit. Stems seldom exceed 2 feet in height. A fibrous root system balances the plant underground. Leaves alternate and are very hairy. Many flowered spikelets characterize this weed. Japanese bromegrass is a wipeout when clean tillage is invoked in advance of corn or grain sorghum crops. Corn and sorghum root exudates seem to cancel out any *Bromus japonicus* right to life. The best bet for control in fields, lawns and waste places is to prevent seed formation by any clean and practical method. Nutrient adjustment is also indicated because both the calcium and phosphate levels will be too low, giving free rein to potassium, magnesium, copper, boron and selenium, all of which will register too high on any test.

BROOMWEED

Annual broomweed, *Amphiachyris dracunculoides*, reproduces by seeds. Broomweed is tough, woolly and freely branched. Flowers are yellow in composite heads. Note the fruit and seeds in the illustration. Livestock will not eat broomweed. The weed does best during drought. Moisture prompts important native grasses to crowd it out. Pasture management and fertility

Broomweed.

maintenance will do more to crowd out broomweed than any of the items in the devil's pantry. Aeration of a pasture with an Aerway implement helps keep it under control.

BUCKBRUSH, a.k.a., *coralberry*.

In home base Kansas, we called buckbrush by its common name, not *Symphoricarpos orbiculatus*, because frankly we didn't know about the sophisticated nomenclature. We knew it as a perennial that

The buckbrush weed.

obeyed the biblical injunction to increase and multiply via roots, runners and seeds, usually in pastures without climax status. Buckbrush seldom grew even 3 feet high. It had opposite leaves with a few teeth and white to pink flowers in terminal albeit interrupted spikes. Its pretty red berries stayed in place all winter. It had a light straw color and a finely longitudinal striate. We had a version of this weed-bush, *Symphoricarpos occidentalis* (snowberry) that could poison livestock, but animals would not eat it unless they were starving. Buckbrush becomes a problem when fields and hills are ignored year after year. It crowds out grass and therefore demands timely brushhogging. Mowing is best accomplished in May, when the plant is weakest and root reserves are low. Usually 2 years' attention with a mower annihilates buckbrush.

BUFFALO GOURD, a.k.a., *wild gourd, wild pumpkin, pumpkin vine, gourd vine, calabagilla, chili coyote.*

This perennial reproduces by roots and seeds, albeit seldom amid crops. *Cucurbita foetidissima*, sometimes called *Pepo foetidissima*, is a trailing plant that runs over 30 feet of vines from a large taproot. Leaves are ovate and cordate at the base. Flowers are orange, yellow or green, sometimes 4 inches across with pistils and stamens separate. The fruit is called a pepo and grows replete with green and yellow markings. It contains what might be styled mini-pumpkin seeds. In the old days sodium chlorate was considered the only practical method for eradication. Actu-

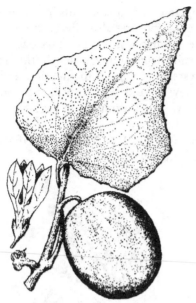

Buffalo gourd.

ally any chemical treatment is overkill because buffalo gourd is not a bad weed. Neglect of the land is the weed's ally just as hard chemistry is the amateur's crutch. A little vine spading might be in order. It invades cultivated fields only when they are neglected.

COMMON BURDOCK

Burdock, *Arctium minus*, is a biennial herb that reproduces by seed only. Its existence on a farm is generally a signal that the soil system is dominated by iron and is in need of calcium, and has a low pH. It is found all over the United States. Burdock has fantastically enormous roots, big leaves and burs that stick to animals as well as clothes of human beings. Common burdock, *Arctium minus*, is smaller than great burdock, *Arctium lappa*. Gypsum soils frequently exhibit burdock and it can be suggested that burdock is often a signal that soil has been incorrectly limed with magnesium carbonate or subdued with great applications of sulfate of ammonia and lime, giving the effect of calcium sulfate in the soil. Burdock is a good phosphate feeder. It has to have a good available source of phosphate. In the midwest there are a lot of soils low in calcium and high in magnesium, pH reading being on the low side. Many times farmers apply gypsum or ammonium sulfate on soils reading below pH 6.2. Unfortunately this has the effect of agitating the construction of the pH, driving it down to pH 5.8 or 5.7 in terms of a colloidal position. A colloidal position pH can be lower than the pH in terms of the entire environment, taking both colloidal and soluble form pH ingredients into consideration. Remember that magnesium will raise pH 1.4 times as high as the same amount of calcium. When gypsum, calcium sulfate, is put on soils at pH 6.2 or 6.1 — the resultant pH structure will still be too low to govern the proper release of trace minerals regulated by calcium. At such pH levels there are mineral releases on the surplus side. Often there is a surplus of aluminum. Moreover, there is a difference in gypsums, depending on whether and where they are mined, or whether they are by-products. As a rule byproduct gypsum is more easily broken down to influence the reconstruction of the pH equilibrium. It has a more fluffy particle surface (like a snowflake), which is quite different from the usual product which is textured much like a pearly smooth grain of sand. Many mined gypsums take a decade or more to break down. Heavy acid flushes both trace minerals and heavy metals out of the soil. When calcium levels are low, aluminum is flushed out very easily, as is iron. Burdock can tolerate more iron and aluminum than other weeds and crops, but it is still a good phosphate feeder. It has a capacity for tolerating this inventory of conditions without becoming toxic. By way of contrast, corn and grain crops cannot tolerate the releases of aluminum and iron made mandatory by very low pH systems. Burdock will proliferate in an environment of iron and aluminum that is killing off higher plants. In soils that are low in iron, or do not have a daily release of iron, burdock will not grow. Soils that have a proper decay system going — and this will not happen at low pH — will not give burdock permission for life. If a low pH soil is releasing a full complement of iron, burdock will function. Iron in relationship to manganese is also an important factor. High iron in the presence of low manganese regulates the kind of fungi that can

operate in that soil. This iron manganese posture also affects the bacterial processes that can occur, again determining which hormone systems are going to function and allow a weed seed to wake up and grow. See illustration on page 154.

BURWEED MARSH ELDER, a.k.a., *marsh elder.*

Burweed marsh elder.

With a poetic name, *Iva xanthifolia*, this burweed marsh elder is an annual that reproduces by seeds, albeit not often in tilled fields unless they are irrigated. It grows to 6 or 6.5 feet in height off a fibrous root. Leaves can be opposite or alternate, and are simple, ovate, toothed, long petioled and hairy. A few of the lower flowerheads pistillate, upper ones staminate, kicking out lots of pollen. The fruit is ovoid, ribbed longitudinally, gray brown to black. Because it is a hayfever plant, it demands control, even eradication. Mowing and cultivation are effective because burweed marsh elder does not do well if disturbed. The bottom line is that this is a weed of neglect.

CARPETWEED

A late-starting but quick-growing summer annual weed, Carpetweed (*Mollugo verticillata*) will quickly cover any fertile, bare soil; gardens, tilled crops, lawns, waste

Carpetweed.

places and sandy riverbanks. Carpetweed grows prostrate along the ground in all directions from the taproot, making large flat mats on the soil surface. The leaves are whorled at each joint of the stem. The flowers are small and white and the seeds are small, orange-red, somewhat kidney shaped and ridged on the back and sides. Carpetweed likes soils which are low in humus. Unlike many other weeds, calcium is not a problem

when this weed appears, but other elements are likely out of synch, most notably high levels of: phosphate, potassium, magnesium, iron, sulfate, copper, zinc and chloride.

CHEAT, a.k.a., *chess.*

Also known as *Bromus secalinus* in the old church tongue, cheat is a winter annual or annual geared to reproducing by seeds, which it produces in abundance. Winter wheat and rye are cheat stomping grounds. Originally it came from the Lower Volga and Eurasia, but nowadays cheat can be found al-

Cheat.

most everywhere. Cheat is a grass. It stands about 3 feet tall in solitary or tufted growth and has a fibrous root system. Leaves alternate. Spikelets are many flowered and narrow. Cheat's fruit is a caryopsis (grain), linear-obovate, deeply grooved, glossy, dark orange-brown. The old German remedy was to plant clean seed. When infestation rears its ugly head, don't be hard headed — use a rotation that will permit thorough cultivation in spring, namely corn, milo, soybeans. A plowpan or compaction figures in this weed's proliferation. Winter wheat or fall-sown crops should be fit into the rotation perhaps once in 3 or 4 years. Mowing ditches and the like can be effective if accomplished before seeds ripen. In loamy, energized soil, cheat seeds never work, whatever the source. Cheat is a shallow rooted plant that grows on the surface of the soil under dry conditions where there is compaction due to traffic or heavy pasturing. Light tillage in spring, when the soil is a little too wet, often figures. Many farmers like to fine-up a seedbed by going over the land with points removed. Often a heavy shower follows. Overworked, fine-textured soils tend to puddle and cement together. Moreover, without porosity or structure, the soil cannot handle the stresses of compaction. Once it dries, it tends to sediment on a shallow basis. There is little biological activity in such a soil. Cheat moves in when this degeneration occurs. The hazards of weather frequently figure in the establishment of cheat. This explains why a farmer will have the weed one year, not the next. After spring tillage, there is a very strategic time when rain on the soil is bad news. For instance, the first 12-23 hours after tillage are very critical. Often a farmer discs in the morning and finishes late at night. Then comes a 4:00 a.m. shower. The part of the field disced at 8:00 a.m. the morning before is probably OK. It may have melded together and positioned itself for rain. Not the afternoon acres. A rain within 12 hours will destroy the biological process in the stirred soil. That is why the time in which water falls can set up the conditions that permits cheat. In terms of fertility management, cheat calls for dramatic repair of low calcium and phosphate levels. Low levels of these major nutrients and a low pH conspire to activate boron, and this element seems to tilt the DNA computer toward cheat proliferation. Other Bromus plants that sometimes rate attention as weeds are Bromus racemosus, chess and upright chess; Bromus mollis; Bromus hordcaccus, soft chess; Bromus commutalus, hairy chess; and Bromus sterilis, barren bromegrass.

CHEAT GRASS, a.k.a., *downy brome, downy chess.*

All the above are names for *Bromus tectorum*, an annual that reproduces by seeds in untended or drought-stricken pastures. The purplish, awned spikelets, the ligules and floret are all hairy. The

Cheat grass.

fruit is a grain minutely striate, reddish-brown. Rotation to corn or milo and cultivation annihilates this weed. Proper grazing and repeated mowing suppress this weed. During drought, the awns on spikelets pack between the teeth and into nostrils of grazing animals. As with many weeds, cheat grass makes for good grazing early in the season, but is more like splinters later on.

CHICKWEED, a.k.a., *common chickweed, starwort, starweed, winterweed, satin flower.*

Chickweed is an annual or winter annual. In some cooler areas it survives through summer and behaves like a short-lived perennial. In the manuals they call it *Stellaria media*, but on the lawn it is a bearcat. It is weakly tufted. It reproduces by seeds and all sorts of creeping stems, rooting at the nodes. As a universal weed, chickweed grows from coast to coast, border to border, seemingly impervious to heat and snow. Once established, it can cover the soil like an army blanket, keeping out air and sunlight and water. Chickweed is the antithesis of crabgrass. Chickweed grows where there is a good amount of working organic matter on the surface of the soil — more so than at great depths. It is frequently a case of too much grass clippings not being consumed, a lot of peat or manure on a garden, with acids coming off organic matter flushing out minerals that become a little too hot for grasses or vegetables. This situation issues an invitation for chickweed to set up shop. Sometimes organic matter on a lawn decays for a week, dries up, gets wet again, and once more dries. With organic matter decaying in a detoured media, chickweed takes off if the pH is right, that is, not too low or too high. By way of contrast, crabgrass reflects soil that is tight, crusty and sedimentary. Acids from partially decayed organic material influence release of excess amounts of trace minerals that are needed, and it does this in a good colloidal way. It is possible to release the minerals but not have enough colloidal material in the soil to hold those minerals. They

Chickweed.

become water soluble and disperse, and the next stage of degeneration begins. Chickweed, crabgrass, quackgrass, nettles, plantain, buckhorn, dandelions and others grow the "green flags" of nature's system of limitations.

COCKLEBUR, a.k.a., *common cocklebur, clotbur.*

Cocklebur, *Xanthium pennsylvanicum,* is an annual that can grow in an environment with a high level of phosphorus available, and a reasonably good pH system. There is a great variation in shape, hairiness and spininess of mature burs. It is an annual that reproduces by seeds. This weed is bushy, rough and grows up to 4 feet in height. It has a fibrous root. Leaves

are alternate, simple, and toothed. Flowers cluster in upper leaf axils, a few of them pistillate. They are covered with curved, jawlike spines. Fruit is an achene, 2 of which are enclosed in a prickly involucre. Accordingly the names *Xanthium strumarium, Xanthium orientale* appear in the literature, as do *Xanthium canalense* and *Xanthium commune.* Phosphorus can only be available at good quality when the pH is somewhat in line. At the same time, this high level of phosphate tends to complex the zinc. And it is in this kind of environment that the cocklebur finds its hormone system activated, and nature telling it that it is its turn to grow. Taking one good look at this weed, a farmer can know enough not to fertilize with phosphate. Almost all cockleburs are similar to *Xanthium pennsylvanicum,* especially *Xanthium italicum, Xanthium commune,* with dense prickly hispid burs, and *Xanthium chinense* with glabrous burs. *Xanthium speciosum* has large fruits. *Xanthium spinosum* has spines in its leaf axils. All these species are related and often difficult to tell apart. Small grains tend to cancel out cocklebur, especially winter wheat. This weed, however, can become a problem in row crop acres. Cocklebur packs a 1-2 punch. One of its pair of seeds germinates the first season. Cocklebur has a poison in its cotyledons. See illustration on page 12.

CORN COCKLE, a.k.a., *white cockle.*

Corn cockle came to Kansas, then to the rest of the nation, with the arrival of Russian immigrants in the 1870s. Styled *Agrostemma githago*, it is a winter annual that reproduces by seeds, especially in winter wheat and rye. Unless its seeds are screened out of wheat, resultant pasta products taste awful, especially when home made. Kansas went after corn cockle with the majesty of the law in the 1930s. Corn cockle grows up to 3 feet in height, branching at the top. Its root system is fibrous. It has opposite leaves that are silky. Flowers are pink to lavender, with sepals longer than the petals and pointed. Its black seeds are triangular and rounded on the back. Corn cockle was a veritable bearcat in the old days because of seed wheat contamination. Properly screened wheat seed and good tillage practices easily eliminate the corn cockle problem. Corn cockle grows in soils that develop high salt concentrations, usually in high pH soils with the pH constructed to a marked degree on a magnesium, potassium and sodium basis. Phosphate levels tend to be low. Iron, sulfate, copper, zinc, chlorine and selenium releases tend to be high. Many high pH soils in the West require calcium, and corn cockle suggests a calcium flush is needed. See illustration on page 36.

CRABGRASS

This annual, *Digitaria sanguinalis* reproduces by stems rooting at the nodes and seeds. It usually dies with the first frost. It is tufted, mostly prostrate, and roots at the nodes. The fruit is a caryopsis. It literally blankets the United States, sparing no geographical area, yet is limited to environments that are right. Crabgrass simply says that the soil is low in calcium and that it cannot support decay starting with actinomycetes molds. It is usually possible to adjust the system in a year or two, putting a little calcium lime and sulfur or gypsum on the soil in order to restructure the pH. As this is accomplished, most of the infestation

Crabgrass.

dissipates, virtually rotting away. Usually applications can be computed on the basis of 1,500 pounds of high calcium lime per acre, 30-40 pounds of processed and active sulfur per acre. If ammonium sulfate is used, a little more calcium is required. On certain soils a mixture of calcium lime and gypsum is also good. As calcium exerts its adjusting capacity to correct the soil, a whole new array of rotting and decay organisms start eating at the roots of the crabgrass. Desirable humic acids are made available to release soil nutrients for lawn grasses. These can now begin to fill in eroded patches formerly occupied by crabgrass. *Digitaria ischaemum*, sometimes called smooth crabgrass, and *Digitaria filiformis* are somewhat similar, albeit with shorter and narrower fingers.

HOARY CRESS, a.k.a., *white top, perennial peppergrass.*

The plants with this name in any form are so closely related the species in effect dominates the genus — *Lepidium draba*. Whatever the moniker, tribe members are all perennials with extensive root systems, rhizomes and seeds. Stems are erect, branched and hairy, up to 30 inches in height. The illustration exhibits alternated leaves that are simple, oblong and toothed. Flowers are white in a globular shaped capsule. Again, the lessons learned in dealing with bindweed apply here. It takes the right organisms to attack the rhi-

Hoary cress above and below the soil.

zomes and annihilate them to the full depth of their soil penetration. In the old days farmers used a crude chemistry — sodium chlorate. The old Vermont farmer's insight on weeds in general applies here. Hoary cress can't stand prosperity. A proper calcium level with other cations in balance, plus biologicals that return life to the soil, are the best bet for non-toxic control. Reread the entry on field bindweed for insight into managing the draba species.

TEXAS CROTON

Croton texensis is a dangerous annual that reproduces by seeds. It causes most croton poisoning because animals eat it rather freely

Texas croton.

ballasts, in waste places. It grows up to 20 inches high from a taproot. Leaves are somewhat oval and fuzzy. The flower grows in a dense, fuzzy inflorescence, or remains generally inconspicuous. Seeds look a lot like castor oil plant seeds. Woolly croton is poisonous but it is also bitter, for which reason livestock avoid it unless starving. Mowing in pastures prevents seeding. The weed, however, should not be allowed to proliferate in waste places. We know very little

when compared to the other crotons. Texas croton grows up to 3 feet in height with hairy branches from a taproot. Its leaves are oblong and hairy. Flowers are very small and inconspicuous. The fruit is a warty globose capsule. Seeds are circular in outline and flat on the inner face. Texas croton is generally a product of neglect. Mowing debilitates the weed and prevents seed production. Commercial seeds contaminated with Texas croton must be avoided, especially in farmer to farmer deals.

WOOLLY CROTON, a.k.a., *hogwort.*

This annual herb, *Croton capitatus*, simply reproduces by seeds, often on prairie land, on railroad

Woolly croton.

about woolly croton, except that it can only survive when the calcium and phosphate levels are too low in terms of the Albrecht equation. How its DNA gets its marching orders is one of those mysteries for which we have no answer because we haven't been smart enough to ask the right questions. There is a brother woolly croton, *Croton glandulosus* tropic croton, which is not quite as aggressive in growth or poison production. It has leaves, and its seeds are a bit flatter, but there the distinction ends. As a practical matter, it is not often possible to fertilize waste places, hence the manager's penchant for using herbicide. The best advice is *don't!* A little mowing is safer for the worker and the environment.

DANDELION, a.k.a., *blowball, lion's tooth, puffball, milk witch, yellow Gowan, witch Gowan, doorhead clock, cankerwort, common dandelion.*

This weed, *Taraxacum officinale* needs no description. Of all the weeds, this one is most recognized by laymen who know no other weeds. It is a perennial. It is usually a symptom of overgrazing. Lawn aficionados go after the dandelion with a vengeance, as though it offended both the eye and the psyche of mankind. Yet on balance, the dandelion is a friendly weed. Its roots penetrate some 3 feet deep, transporting calcium and other minerals to the surface. Earthworms like the vicinity of the dandelion. Each time such a plant dies, remaining root channels become a conduit for worm travel and also a colloidal source of worm nutrition. The dandelion is a monoculture weed, an index of sedimentation, a biography of rain, root webbing, organic material forever in place

and unstirred. In every case calcium is colloidally weak or absent. The dandelion simply says organic matter residues are musty and are barricading the warehoused supplies of food. As the season goes along, dry weather usually weakens and subdues the dandelion. But if a quicker remedy is sought, the soil should be treated 6-7 inches deep with a supply of high calcium lime. Anyone really desperate will have to replant, but chances are the dandelion won't be back for a long time. It might be added parenthetically that astute lawn managers often regulate the availability of phosphorus to reduce the growth of grass and yet keep it strong in the absence of dandelions. The object is to restrict photosynthesis capacity of leaves by managing the conversion and release of phosphorus on a diet of "one meal" per day. Actually, we do not want a lot of soluble phosphorus on a lawn. It needs a good supply of zinc regulated by a calcium base, not too much nitrogen — just enough to etch the phosphate needed to grow a day at a time. The phosphorus should be lazy and slow, and at a balanced pH of 6.5. Never apply nitrogen or phosphorus fertilizer. Instead use gypsum and sulfur as needed to have a slow growing, healthy and vigorous lawn and watch neighbors wear out their lawn mowers. A pH range of 6.2-6.6 happens to preside over actinomycete mold balanced activity, mineral release — and as with all other weeds, there has to be a reference back to calcium and its colloidal function. The dandelion is not very important in crop production, and might be excluded from this roster except for its negative popularity. See illustration on page 162.

WOOLLY CUPGRASS

Woolly Cupgrass, *Eriochloa villosa*, is a tall annual with few to several racemes, the rachis and pedicels are very woolly. The blunt spikelets are about 5 mm long, more or less pubescent and grow singly or sometimes in pairs. Woolly Cupgrass signals low calcium, low humus and low porosity in soil; magnesium and soil moisture are high. Poor drainage and poor residue decay also contribute to conditions which nurture Woolly Cupgrass. Anaerobic bacteria prevails when this species is seen. Cupgrass has been cultivated and used for forage in some areas.

CURLY DOCK, a.k.a., *sour dock, curly leaf dock, narrowleaf dock, yellow dock, curly.*

The Latin brand name is *Rumex crispus*, according to Linnaeus. It is a perennial that reproduces by seeds in wild and tame places, coast to coast. My Dad's old coverless manual gives it top billing for Kansas. During the first year this plant forms a dense rosette of leaves on a stout taproot. Leaves are dark green, alternate, simple, crimped along the edges, petioled, with sheathing base. The illustration reveals small flowers in a terminal panicle of whorled ascending racemes, each flower having 3 tubercles. *Rumex crispus* and a sister (or brother) species, *Rumex altissimus* will invade cultivated fields, but are more damaging to pastures and legume acres, especially clover crops left in the field 2 or more years. The old timer's advice was to plow, both to tear out the fleshy roots and to aerate the soil and remove the plowpan, which is usually present. Corn and milo planted after thorough spring tillage send out auxins that close up shop for curly dock. Once that plant's DNA reads the script for the year, it settles back to await more correct conditions for it to increase and multiply. Curly dock bespeaks an incestuous relationship. In the far West, there are many docks other than curly dock, namely fiddle dock, golden dock, sheep's sorrel and willow dock. All are perennials except 1 annual, golden dock. Soils on the acid side with a wet season in tow or poor drainage and poor aeration tell this weed to wake up and claim the season. In terms of the baseball statistics on this weed, high and very high are signal words. The soils in which curly dock grows are very high in selenium, magnesium and phosphates, and high in chlorine, boron, zinc, copper, sulfate, iron and manganese. They are low in calcium. Heavy salt is also a factor. The high traces cry out for complexing action. Calcium is an important key to controlling this weed without poisons. See illustration on page 140.

TALL or PALE DOCK

This perennial, *Rumex altissimus,* is reproduced by seeds. It grows to 4.5 feet in height from a penetrating taproot. Leaves are simple and alternate. Flowers are small, albeit

Tall or pale dock.

in a conspicuous panicle sans petals. The fruit is coffee colored. It grows in high-moisture hardpan areas with a low pH or in hardpan areas with an improperly constructed pH. It damages pastures and non-rotated crop areas, such as clover acres. Seed crops contaminated by dock have been proscribed by a number of states. Frequent and intensive cultivation helps starve the root system, but the real remedy has to include cation exchange capacity management, hardpan repair, and rotation including row crops such as corn or milo. Tall or pale dock likes very low phosphate levels imbalanced by very high potassium, magnesium and manganese levels. Calcium will be low in tall dock territory. Iron, sulfate and copper also will be too high.

DODDER

This weed is an annual that reproces by seeds. It has several

Dodder on smartweed.

aliases, *Cuscuta cuspidata* and *Cuscuta glomerata*, but the one referred to here is *Cuscuta pentagona*. Dodder starts up as an independent plant, but soon enough establishes a parasitic relationship with the host crop, at which point almost all chlorophyll is lost. The dodder plant takes on a golden yellow color for its strings, which send small suckers into host plants. Dodder is unique in that its leaves are without chlorophyll. Dodder is a degenerative parasite that responds best to pH modification with calcium, magnesium, sodium and potassium in equilibrium, Albrecht style. Legislation against contamination in lespedeza seed may keep a few seeds away, but will do nothing to control the ample seed inventory already in the soil literally coast to coast.

DOGBANE, a.k.a., *Indian hemp*.

Apocynum cannabinum is another perennial that reproduces by roots, rhizomes and seeds. It stands as erect as a Coldstream guardsman, achieves a height of 3 feet and builds a bark that is tough and fibrous. Dogbane has a milky sap. Leaves grow opposite each other, are simple, lanceolate, short petioled, rounded or wedge-shaped at the base. It has small white flowers in terminal clusters. Dogbane has lots of seeds by August, the product of flower follicles. Extensive root systems are the key to both the plant and its eradication. Etching out the rhizomes with the ac-

The dogbane scene.

tive microorganisms of compost is first in dealing with the cause. A relative of milkweed, dogbane contains the same sticky, milky latex in roots, stems and leaves. Its seeds travel by way of wind. Allowed to spread, dogbane affects crop yields approximately the same as field bindweed. Varieties differ from one area to the next, not the consequences. Cultivation without biological intervention or root starvation will not handle old infestations. Since dogbane grows in soils with good cation exchange balances, it will fall victim to frequent mowing when infested land has been seeded to alfalfa. Soil aeration helps and — where possible — clean tillage does the same.

Injection of air into the soil will modify the dominance of anaerobic bacteria and repair faulty decay of residue, which in any case account for sticky and crusted soil and low humus. Soils in which dogbane grows have low calcium and phosphate levels, and very high overloads of potassium and magnesium. These conditions need repair. There is a blood brother to *Apocynum cannabinum* called *Apocynum sibiricum*, also called dogbane. Its stem leaves have a heart base and its seeds are a little longer. Non-toxic control is the same as for the other dogbane.

DROPSEED

Called *Sporobolus neglectus*, dropseed indeed drops its seeds and re-produces from seeds as an annual. It is a tufted grass, its seed a grain. It is basically a lawn weed that crowds out better grasses. It requires manual removal, and a good humate fix to cancel out the ample seed inventory left behind. *Sporobolus vaginiflorus*, styled wood and dropseed, is an annual very similar to *Sporobolus neglectus*, except that its leaves are hairy and seeds are larger in color. Review the lessons on climax grass production. In any real contest with climax pasture grass, dropseed fades out.

FLEABANE, a.k.a., *rough daisy fleabane*.

Erigeron ramosus, or fleabane, is an annual that reproduces by seed, usually in prairie settings. It achieves a height of 4 feet atop a fibrous root. Supple leaves alternate.

Dropseed.

Fleabane.

Disc flowers are dark, ray flowers are white. The fruit has a parachute of capillary bristles. Roots of this weed are shallow. Ordinary mowing and tillage offends the life of *Erigeron ramosus*. Fleabane also likes drought and apparently harvests its sustenance from the cosmos when the season is appropriate. Very low calcium and phosphate levels provide the enabling situation, with high zinc and boron the likely trigger mechanism. Potassium and magnesium juxtapose against calcium and phosphate by being very high. These conditions are present in many weed situations, and therefore we have to conclude that we're only guessing at the details, albeit not at the main premise.

CANADA FLEABANE, a.k.a., *mare's tail, horseweed.*

This relative of fleabane (a.k.a. rough daisy fleabane) is styled *Erigeron canadensis*. It is an annual that reproduces by seed, usually in grasslands, but also in waste places. The plant can be tiny and it can grow to 6 feet or more in height. Simple leaves alternate, are hairy, lanceolate and sessile. The tiny flowers have whitish discs and small white rays. Leaves and flowers contain a terpene that irritates the nostrils of horses. Fruit is an achene with a parachute of yellowish brown bristles. Canada fleabane takes over abandoned pastures with alacrity, but has a hard time of it

Canada fleabane.

when tillage, traffic and mowing are invoked.

FLOWER-OF-AN-HOUR, a.k.a., *Venice mallow, bladder ketmia, brown-eyed Susan, shoo-fly.*

Hibiscus trionum is the scientific name for the above more colorfully named weed which reproduces by seeds. The plant itself stands as erect as an Embassy guard, supported by a fibrous root system. Branches spread and are hairy. Leaves alternate and are simple. Cotyledons are round to heart shaped, light green and shiny. *Hibiscus trionum* grows up to 2 feet in height. Each leafstalk has a pair of awl-shaped stipules or appendages.

Flower-of-an-hour.

YELLOW FOXTAIL, a.k.a., *yellow bristlegrass, wild millet.*

This annual, *Setaria lutescens,* reproduces only by seeds in cultivated fields and other peripheral places. It stands erect, but remains compressed at the base, growing 3 feet or more in height, the plant's bulk tufted from a fibrous root. Simple leaves alternate and are glaucous. Spikelets are 1-flowered, each surrounded by 5 or more tawny, upwardly barbed bristles. The grain produced by yellow foxtail is broadly ovate. Its annual root system is quite shallow, making this weed an easy control object by ordinary cultivation. It is easily hoed or pulled up out of gardens. Animals love this weed when it is

Flowers are sulfur yellow to whitish with a purple center and dark veins. The fruit of *Hibiscus trionum* comes in capsules encased in a calyx or leaflike structure. This becomes papery and bladdery, as one of those colorful common names suggests. When maturity is achieved, the capsule opens, issuing kidney-shaped seeds. Clean cultivation as often and as late as the commercial crop permits is the best bet. In any case, toxic chemistry, with its short-falls, has little effect on seeds in soil storage, which remain viable for years. The best control approach can be developed by rereading chapter 2.

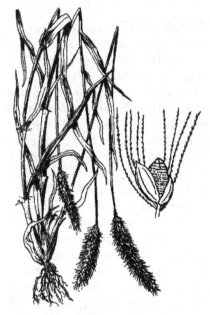

Yellow foxtail.

young and succulent. At this stage it can be grazed in stubble fields. Later on, yellow foxtail becomes dry and unpalatable. Withal, yellow foxtail is not a serious weed problem because of its utilization potential, although it is not something devoutly to be wished in alfalfa stands. Low calcium permits yellow foxtail to gain a toehold. Potassium and magnesium can be very high. A trace of selenium may figure in triggering this weed, which survives aluminum in the environment. Bacterial activity is anaerobic when yellow foxtail arrives. Withal, the foxtails rely on carbon dioxide for a seed triggering mechanism. See giant foxtail below.

GIANT FOXTAIL

Giant foxtail, *Setaria faberi*, is an annual and is therefore reproduced by seeds. It was introduced into the United States from China, possibly in millet seed. There was a time when giant foxtail was a serious problem only in Missouri, Illinois, parts of Tennessee, Kentucky, and Indiana. Since hard nitrogen has invaded the scene, giant foxtail has expanded its geographical domination. Mechanization and an improved capacity to destroy the basic character of the soil have speeded up the processes of deterioration, hence foxtail over most of the country. Anhydrous ammonia is almost an insurance policy for its proliferation. Foxtail grows in organic matter soil where there is a surplus of humic acid. Although pH adjustment has been front burner stuff so far, the topic has to surface in any discussion of the foxtail weed problem. Following faulty advice, farmers have been attempting pH adjustment with no more than ag lime for years. Most of the materials almost have always been a byproduct, a very coarse byproduct at that. These lime particles endure for many years, some of them for 25, 30, even 40 and 50 years. When farmers have paid little attention to the character of the lime, they have often ended up with dolomite, and this has in-

Giant foxtail.

creased the concentration of magnesium to a point where it tightened up the clay particles. As a result soils hold water longer. They do not warm up. And they are subject to more complexed conditions and thorough compaction. High capacity machinery is almost always a contributing factor. When a farmer works the soil a little on the wet side, heavy machinery tends to compact the soil underneath the surface. Even working with a light disc, tractor wheels will compact the soil 6 inches to several feet deep. It is this compaction that sets in motion the environment which induces the foxtail seed to germinate. The foxtail seed germinates in the absence of air and in the presence of an accumulation of carbon dioxide which cannot escape its airtight chamber. Magnesium is a contributing factor. It tends to keep the soil wet and it gets the clay particles to electrically bond themselves together tightly. The chemical-electrical bond on clay particles is very high when magnesium is in excess, and calcium is in deficiency. As a result of this, soil tends to hold itself together. Tractor traffic compacts it and presses out the air and as the soil begins to dry it cements together into a hard and germinous clod. This is the environment for the foxtail. This will partially explain why foxtail usually emerges a little later in the season, often after the final cultivation. The solution is obvious. Fertility management has to be used to regulate a compaction propensity out of the soil system. Lime in the right form is the key. But there is more. Weed seeds go into dormancy in the fall of the year. The length of day and night has a bearing on their life cycle. That is how nature controls all the living processes simultaneously — with kind of light, wavelengths of energy, angle or incidence to the sun, and how light factors are absorbed by hormones. Hormones must have enzyme partners, and enzyme systems fundamental in catalyzing these systems to work. Those same trace minerals govern bacteria and fungus and hormones. Hormones are the time clocks that regulate the sequence of life. They do this by absorbing seeds which can be digested in this way. There are other benefits. The soil will drain faster. There will be more air. It will be possible to plant on time. With a commercial crop off and running ahead of weed seed competition, the kingdom for the year is established. A final caution. If the soil is disced in the spring, allowed to set for a week, then disced again, new bunches of weed seeds are given a wake-up shock from light. It takes only a millionth of a second of light to trigger the process. Spring tillage often wakes up weed seeds. The more times it is done, the more difficult it is to manage weeds. One extra pass might make a fine seedbed, but this may not be the ultimate compatible objective of wholesome crop nutrition and production. Many times after planting there is a cold or wet weather break. The soil gets water-logged and stays cold for three weeks. This sets in motion a whole series of hazards. That last pass over the field may have fined the soil too much. Now it crusts over quickly. Foxtail, watergrass, nut-sedge — all grassy problem weeds now receive permission to take over. Introduction of air into the soil is a must. Here a picture is bet-ter than words. Caryopsis is usually greenish. Relatives are knotroot foxtail, *Setaria geniculata*; yellow foxtail, *Setaria glauca*; bristly fox-tail, *Setaria verticillata*; and green bristlegrass, *Setaria viridis*. Calci-um, soft rock phosphate, vitamin B-12, carbohydrates, and sulfates in some areas will reduce or elimi-nate this weed. Potassium chloride, hard chemical nitrogen and chemi-cal or manure salts often contrib-ute to giant foxtail growth.

GOATGRASS, a.k.a., *jointed goat-grass.*

Kansas laid claim to being the heartland for this weed, *Aegilops cy-lindrica*, but the fact is that goat-grass covers at least the Ohio Val-ley, Texas, Colorado, New Mexico and Utah, as well as parts of the East and West Coast, and if we look sharply it will likely be found elsewhere. Goatgrass arrived in the U.S. with Volga and Ukranian German immigrants, probably in

Goatgrass.

1876 or shortly thereafter. It is a winter annual that reproduces via seeds, and often becomes a nemesis in wheat fields. Simple leaves alter-nate with auricles at the base of the blade which can be smooth or hairy, according to variety. As the species name indicates, the two 4-flowered spikelets appear in a cy-lindrical spike, the uppermost spikelet being long-awned. Goat-grass grain ripens ahead of the wheat and shatters easily. Summer fallow procedures control goatgrass in wheat fields, and rotation of crops devastates *Aegilops cylindrica*. When wheat is grown continuous-ly, the control chore becomes more difficult. Goatgrass has the same lifestyle as winter wheat. It germi-nates in the fall and matures its seed immediately ahead of wheat. Continuous wheat therefore means plenty of seed. This seed in turn volunteers and grows with the next crop of wheat. Back crosses with wheat have been noted. Wheat grown with calcium and phosphate levels too low invites goatgrass. Such conditions, complicated by a hardpan barrier and low humus in the soil, give manganese and sulfate free rein, and allow high boron to coax the plant's DNA to come alive at a time when crop production demands a deep sleep.

GOOSEGRASS, a.k.a., *yardgrass, silver crabgrass, wiregrass.*

Eleusine indica, that's the Latinized name for the above weed grass. It is an annual that reproduces by seeds. It has hairy ligules, flowered spikelets and a grain fruit loosely enclosed in a reddish brown pericarp. Goosegrass is not a weed crop for cultivated fields. It is a nemesis in lawns, and also a suggestion of neglect. Proper lawn irrigation, cutting and fertilization is the mesmeric remedy for this weed.

GREEN AMARANTH, a.k.a., *palmer amaranth, careless weed, spleen amaranth, red amaranth, rough pigweed, smooth pigweed, pigweed.*

All the above named weeds are the same, which is an annual that reproduces from seed. Its Latinized name is *Amaranthus hybridus.* It is a toss-up whether the commonest name is green amaranth or careless weed. Hogs love it in its succulent

Goosegrass.

Green amaranth.

stage, but back off as the plant matures. They seem to know that the mature green amaranth can contain nitrate which becomes poisonous via enzyme action. Seed leaves exhibit a deep red underneath with many cross veins and a prominent midvein. Amaranthus hybridus can grow from 1-6 feet in height, erect as a garden trellis with a few ascending branches based on a shallow taproot. Egg-shaped leaves alternate, are elliptical, narrow and stem supported. The plant's greenish flowers are quite small and in leafless spikes, usually at the top of the plant. The chief spike is much longer than the lower part of the spike. It is this slender spike that distinguishes green amaranth from the many other pigweeds in the Amaranthus tribe. It grows under many conditions, but like other Amaranthus plants, it does not depend on phosphate and potassium fertilizers. As with other shallow rooted weeds, green amaranth is no big problem. Pulling and tillage make the most sense.

GROUND CHERRY, a.k.a., *bladder cherry, clammy ground cherry, lanternweed.*

It is a perennial that reproduces by both rhizomes and seeds, this *Physalis heterophylla.* It grows basically east of the continental divide in non-rotated crop areas. It has a low, clammy and hairy stem and a perennial root system. Simple leaves alternate and are ovate and

Ground cherry.

shallow lobed. Flowers are yellow in the axils of the leaves. The fruit is a yellow berry in a calyx. Seeds are light orange to straw colored, dull, granular, semicircular. The remedy is the same as for bindweed, which has been treated at greater length as the first entry in this section. Dad's pre-WWII manual says that 17 species were identified in Kansas before WWI, several of them prominent. They are prairie ground cherry, *Physalis lanceolata*; ground cherry, *Physalis longifolia*; low ground cherry, *Physalis pumila*; cutleaf ground cherry, *Physalis anagulata* and ground cherry, *Physalis rotundata, Physalis virginiana, Quincula lobata.* There are esoteric differences, but in the main stay in character, with *heterophylla.*

GUMWEED, a.k.a., *tarweed, Grindela.*

This is a short-lived perennial that accounts for progeny via offshoots, rhizomes and seeds. It grows some 3 feet high, has a brittle white or reddish stem. It has disc flowers with yellow rays. The bracts ooze a sticky substance. Fruit is an achene. Generally speaking, it would be correct to say *Grindelia squarrosa.* It cannot survive tillage. Spring and fall mowing controls this mildly poisonous weed. Animals avoid it because it tastes awful. There is a species called *Grindelia squarrosa nuda* that has very short rays.

Gumweed.

HEMP, a.k.a., *Indian hemp, marijuana, Mary Jane, and a raft of slang names that vary almost from county to county and time to time.*

Marijuana.

Cannabis sativa is almost as much a common name as it is scientific. The weed is an annual that reproduces by seeds in wild places. In this case, a picture is worth a thousand words. The male plant is quite different from the female. The leaves are lobed or toothed, hairy and petioled. Green flowers are in terminal clusters. Fruit is a typical achene. A resinous exudate is the source of marijuana or hashish. Two or 3 years of mowing close out heavy stands. Lawmakers have proscribed this plant and enforcement agents do their best to stamp it out. Once upon a time the plant's seeds were used in bird feed. Nowadays birds are on their own finding their Cannabis seeds.

HENBIT, a.k.a., *blind nettle, bee nettle, giraffe head, dead nettle.*

This member of the mint family, *Lamium amplexicaule* is a winter annual or short-lived perennial which reproduces by rooting stems, seeds and rhizomes. Leaves are simple and toothed, the upper sessile and clasping, the lower petioled. Flowers are blue to lavender in clusters, 1 type with 2-lipped corolla, the other hidden. The fruit grows as 4 single seed-up nutlets. As with any rhizome plant, the bindweed remedy has to be considered. The weed wouldn't be there except for the energy problem that supports it. Managing decay gases and rotting out rhizomes are the starting point.

HORSETAIL

Horsetail, *Equisetum arvense*, is a perennial. It reproduces by spores and rhizomes attached to small tu-

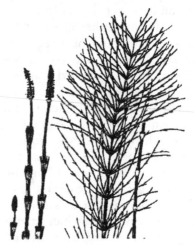

Field horsetail.

bers. Rhizomes are usually deep seated and long running. This one grows best in sandy or gravelly soils with a high ground water level, but it can also stand a dry summer. In general, it suggests improper drainage. Horsetail gained much attention with the publication of Louis Kervran's *Biological Transmutations* since this weed has a silica skeleton, as high as 80% of the ash. According to Kervran, silica transmutes into calcium making the organic silica in horsetail very valuable indeed. It will probably be

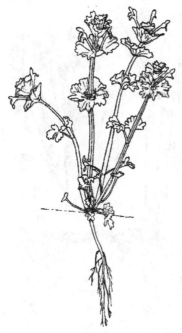

Henbit.

years before science formally identifies with what Kervran is saying. For now it is enough to reiterate his assertion that "Fresh green vegetables (young plants), radishes, etc., contain a large amount of silica. We know it is due to the ingestion of fresh grass that milk cows can excrete more calcium than they ingest, without decalcifying. The mother who breast feeds her baby may correct her diet by adding a small amount of horsetail to her food in order to avoid decalcification." Silica contained in horsetail has long been used as a tea remedy for various ailments, and biodynamic agriculture uses a 0.5-2.0% solution made by boiling such a tea for 10-15 minutes as a spray against mildew and fungi on grapes, vegetables, rose and fruit trees. Although not as strong as Bordeaux mixture, the biodynamic people report it swift and effective and kind to soil life. They point out, however, "that it should not be applied until the first course of fungus infection, too moist a stand of the infested plant is taken care of, too." Many books list horsetail as poisonous to livestock, including USDA's *Common Weeds of the United States*, causing equisetosis in horses, yet Ehrenfried Pfeiffer used it for kidney disturbances in cattle, horses and dogs. The "arvense" variety is quite different from other varieties. The "useless" varieties have a collar formed by black leaves. Field horsetail is green or perhaps slightly discolored.

Horsetail is seldom much of a weed problem. Early spring stems are without chlorophyll. Later these are green stems with whorls of scale-like leaves.

IRONWEED

I have never heard of another name for this perennial, officially styled *Veronia interior* in its Latinized version. It is a perennial propagated by rhizomes and seeds, often in pastures, just as often in native meadows and along fence rows. It is not found in cultivated fields very often. Ironweed grows to 4 feet in height and has a very fibrous root system. The fruit is a stubby achene surmounted by a

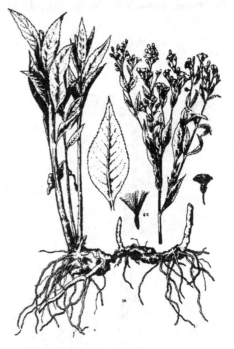

The ironweed complex.

parachute of capillary bristles within a row of small scales or stout bristles. This may be a mouthful to say, but the weed itself is no mouthful for livestock. All animals find it unpalatable. Ironweed is an early warning sign of degeneration. It easily vanishes under assault by the mowing machine, and fails to spread when pastures are aerated and treated with a nutrient flush answering a soil audit. The weakest stage for ironweed is early June, generally, when mowing should be pursued. This happens also to be the time frame when sumac and vervain — 2 other pasture invaders — should be mowed. Usually, it takes several years to kill off ironweed, unless a program of pasture regeneration is invoked. The classic weed remedy — repair of the calcium — stands out like a sore thumb when the soil in which ironweed grows is audited. Pasture regeneration requires total evaluation of this fact.

ITCHGRASS
Itchgrass, *Rottboellia exaltata*, is a coarse branching annual with broad flat blades and subcylindric racemes, dwindling toward the summit. Blades in robust specimens are as wide as 3 cm. The racemes are mostly 8-12 cm long and 3-4 mm thick, dwindling at the top. The sessile spikelet is 5-7 mm long. Itchgrass indicates soil low in calcium and humus and very high in magnesium. It also denotes low levels of manganese, iron

and zinc. Other factors that contribute to the growth of Itchgrass are anaerobic bacteria, poor residue decay and sticky soil with poor drainage. Aluminum is probably also present when you see this plant. The fragile hairs of the sheaths are irritating to the skin, hence the name Itchgrass.

JERUSALEM ARTICHOKE, a.k.a., *girasole*.
Jerusalem artichoke did not come from Jerusalem. It is designated as *Helianthus tuberosus*, and is a tuber bearing perennial of North America. It reproduces by rhizomes, tubers and seeds. It is often confused with the sunflower, *Helianthus annuus*. It grows up to 5.5 feet, usually in patches. The stem is smooth. Leaves are sometimes opposite, sometimes alternate, narrowly ovate, rough on top,

Jerusalem artichoke.

velvety underneath. Flowers are typical sunflowers, with small discs and large yellow rays. Hogs like to root out this tuber. As a weed it is unimportant. Commercial varieties have been grown for fuel alcohol and as livestock feed.

JIMSON WEED

Datura stramonium, or Jimson weed, is narcotic and poisonous. According to variety, stems of this plant are green, corolla white (variety *stramonium*) or stem purple, corolla lavender or pale violet (variety *tatula*). Jimson weed is the nemesis of every soybean grower in the nation. It may be that northern states, because of sun angle, are less likely to have Jimson weed. It will grow in a very actively decaying organic matter complex, the kind of system one might relate to buttonweed. Buttonweed grows where there is *methane* gas production. Jimson weed wakes up and grows where gas production is *ethane*. Decaying organic matter can sequester and accumulate and govern the availability of cobalt. Improper decay will allow these things more freedom. Again, when conditions are adverse to the lifestyle of actinomycete molds, decay takes the hydroxide direction. Typical is the case of soybeans following corn, lots of undecayed stalks being left over. It is frequently a case of working the soil a bit too late in the fall, or late tillage in the spring. Under warm conditions with excess organic matter, and in the ab-sence of bacterial activity taking decay in the proper direction, Jimson weed seeds are fired up and allowed to dominate. Of course if the calcium level were adequate, this alone would guarantee a different decay direction for trash. Thus the remedy is an improved calcium level in colloidal position, a regulated pH, and proper decay of organic matter. An injection of compost sees to it that decay proceeds in the right direction. This weed has a fibrous root, white to purplish flowers, and toothed leaves. See illustration on page 92.

JOHNSON GRASS

Johnson grass, *Sorghum halepense*, is an annual or perennial with both seed and rhizome reproduction. Its fibrous root system allows it to exercise a vicious reproduction cycle with few if any geographical limitations. Johnson grass prefers the rainbelt South nevertheless, especially where low organic matter, and worn-out soils prevail. This weed has 1-flowered spikelets in groups of 3 with large open panicles. The mature plant can be 2-8 feet tall, is always coarse and leafy with blades often 3 feet long. Inch-wide bright green leaf blades have whitish midveins. Johnson grass tends to grow in soils with a low calcium level regardless of pH. If the biological environment is favorable for crop production and has the proper decay organisms present, Johnson grass will not last. It can be given competition by planting small grain at the time an adjustment in pH is made. To control Johnson grass, it is necessary to set in motion biological processes that will attack the rhizome and make the root weaker. If a different stratum of bacteria is put in motion with timely application of well digested compost, it will etch out the rhizome system and ultimately clean out the weed. This may take a period of a year. Johnson grass grows where there is a reasonable level of available iron. The pH character of the soil governs iron release. Thus when small grain seeds are introduced to give Johnson grass competition, and pH adjustment is started at the same time, trace mineral release will invite a stratum of bacteria inimical to Johnson grass. Johnson grass is of the same family as quackgrass. Thistles have the same type of rootbase. Each is related to a different supply of trace minerals, the complex of trace minerals being what determines which weed family is to endure. Trace mineral release may shift an acre to quackgrass, and of course quackgrass and Johnson grass do not grow together. All these weeds are related to the iron to manganese ratio as released by other soil factors. If iron to manganese is kept in equilibrium, then the environment for almost all rhizome type weeds is removed. Basically, rhizomes have to be broken down by soil fungus diseases. When weeds such as John-

son grass grow, it simply means the soil does not have compatible fungus control for commercial crops. This means the crop is on the weaker side, and Johnson grass takes over. It sits at the table first and becomes a tremendous competitor to any grain crop or pasture grass. It also grows in sugar cane fields. Most sugar cane acres have imbalanced pH systems, excess iron, low manganese, or iron to manganese out of ratio to each other. The best way to control the situation is to introduce the type of byproducts that will energize bacteria — excellent composts or biologicals, for instance — thus subduing the soil life forms that are permitting that type of weed to dominate. When Johnson grass proliferates, potassium chloride, compaction, complexed zinc and pesticide interactions may be suspected. In such fields, calcium will be very low. Anaerobic bacteria will dominate, yielding poor residue decay and drainage. Sticky crusted soil with an aluminum problem will figure. Humus and porosity will be low. Potassium, magnesium, boron and sulfate will be high, with manganese, iron, copper, zinc, chlorine and selenium accounting for high readings or complexed relationships. A correcting remedy will likely include calcium, phosphates, copper, molybdenum, vitamins C and B-12, plus sugar and humic acid, all mixed to answer test readouts. See illustration on page 166.

JUNGLERICE

Like its relative Barnyard grass, *Echinochloa colonum*, or junglerice, is generally found in ditches and moist places. Its blades are rather lax, 3-6 mm wide and sometimes transversely zoned with purple. Spikelets are sessile and crowded. Like so many weeds, it indicates very low calcium and low humus in soil. If you are finding junglerice, magnesium, manganese, iron and boron levels are high in the soil. It especially likes hard, poorly drained soil with poor residue decay. Bringing calcium levels up and bringing the other nutrients in line will remedy the problem.

RUSSIAN KNAPWEED

A perennial that reproduces by roots, rhizomes and seeds, that's *Centaurea picris*, or *Centaurea repens*. Tradition says it came to the United States from Russia hidden in alfalfa seed. It still likes to travel that way, usually from Rocky Mountain and West Coast states. Before the age of hard chemistry, farmers controlled Russian knapweed exactly the way they handled field bindweed, with clean tillage and decay management. Faulty decay of organic matter is the culprit — in pastures because of over concentration of animals, in tilled fields because untreated soils impose limitations on the breakdown of organic matter. Inoculation of soil systems with predigested manures best manages this intruder

and its well-developed branching root system. Russian knapweed grows up to almost 3 feet in height. Stems branch at the base, are striate, woolly, hairy to glabrous. Leaves of new shoots alternate and are little toothed and whitish underneath. Flowers are numerous, tubular, rose to purple in color. Composite heads are flask shaped, usually over an inch long. Flowers identify Russian knapweed from June to August. Seeds start staking out new territory in August and September. This weed grows best in soils with low calcium, humus, bacterial activity; calcium will be low or complexed; potassi-

Russian knapweed, left to right, bracts, head, achene.

um, magnesium, manganese, chlorine will be high. Residual decay may be good, porosity high.

PROSTRATE KNOTWEED

As the name suggests, *Polygonum aviculare, Polygonum aviculare augustissimum,* and *Polygonum neglectum* comes to fruition in a prostrate position atop rambling thin taproots. It is an annual, sometimes a perennial that reproduces from seeds. Leaves are small and have a bluish cast. Small flowers mature in axilliary clusters. The fruit is 1-seeded, indehiscent, meaning persistently closed. *Polygonum buxiforme* is very similar, except that the stipules are more conspicuous. The mat character of prostrate knotweed makes mowing impossible. Reseeding may be indicated. Otherwise humate and sea-

Prostrate knotweed

weed extract treatment of the grass will cause prostrate knotweed to go dormant.

KOCHIA, a.k.a., *summer cypress, mock cypress, Mexican fireweed, red belvedere, burning bush.*

Kochia scoparia infests fields from Maine to the San Joaquin Valley. It is an annual that reproduces by seeds, especially in drought stricken and overgrazed pastures, but also in the usual waste places. Its long taproot can

Kochia.

support up to 6 feet of plant growth. Its green flowers ripen to a reddish tint in narrow spikes and terminal panicles. Its fruit is a reddish utricle, or thin-walled and one-seeded. There is a more feathery version called *Kochia tricophylla*. Kochia likes drought and hates clean cultivation. The whys and wherefores remain locked in its DNA. It produces a saponin, which is poisonous. Control suggests cut, pull, hoe and burn seed carrying plants in a safe place.

LADYSTHUMB

Ladysthumb, *Polygonum persicaria*, is an annual that reproduces by seeds. Stems are most likely smooth but sometimes hairy, simple to very branched, and up to 1 m tall. The leaves alternate and are lance-shaped, pointed at both ends, up to 15 cm long and 3 cm wide, with smooth edges and usually have a purple blotch in the middle. The sheath at the leaf base is fringed with short bristles. The flowering spikes are usually oblong to thick-cylindric and very dense. The flowers are pink, purplish or green and pink, and very rarely white. The mature sepals have prominently net-ted-veined bases. Ladysthumb can be found in cultivated ground and the usual waste places and roadsides, especially in moist soils with poor drainage. Jay McCaman suggests when ladysthumb appears very high selenium levels are likely. In addition, this weed indicates low calcium and high phosphate, manganese, and zinc.

LAMBSQUARTERS, a.k.a., *white goosefoot, pitseed goosefoot, mealweed, baconweed, wild spinach, white pigweed, fat hen, frostbite, chou grass, muckweed, dungweed.*

Lambsquarters, *Chenopodium album*, is not a serious weed, yet very common. Hogs and chickens love the plant in its succulent stage. It is an annual that reproduces from seed and generally indicates a rich, fertile soil. Potato acres in particular become infested with lambsquarters once the potato plant's specific requirements become unavailable. Otherwise the massive root structure of potatoes prevents lambsquarters growth. Pithy names tell something about how plants grow according to available light, temperature and geography. Lambsquarters sometimes grows 5 feet tall. It harbors a lot of nutrition for certain insects and

Ladysthumb.

stores a high quality of phosphate. It reflects the availability of good nutrition in the soil. Used in silage, it supplies needed nutrients. As a matter of fact, both pigweed and lambsquarters can become excellent silage. Both have a high protein content. Lambsquarters grows in a soil that has an appropriate decay system going, which of course has a direct bearing on release and catalyzing release of a good array of quality mineral nutrients. This weed does not depend on phosphate or potassium from fertilizers. Soil is intended to grow vegetative matter. Lambsquarters and redroot pigweed stand at the top of the ladder of the phylum of weeds that can grow under different soil conditions. They reflect almost ideal producing functions in an active biological soil system. There is no water insoak problem where lambsquarters and pigweed grow. Both of these weeds are easy to control. Neither have serious negative effects through auxin emission to growing crops. Indeed, there is a symbiotic relationship between redroot pigweed and lambsquarters and most plants. These weeds are the best possible laboratory analysis for phosphate being available on a daily meal basis. Where lambsquarters grows year after year, there is no need to buy phosphate fertilizers. There is no concern about buying potassium or about raising the levels of potassium, even though a soil audit might suggest that the till is not

quite full enough. Anatomically, lambsquarters is an annual that reproduces by seeds. It grows 5-6 feet in height from a taproot. Simple leaves alternate, are ovate in shape. This weed has green flowers in irregular spikes clustered in narrow panicles. Selenium, molybdenum, hydrogen peroxide, calcium, soft rock phosphate, vitamin C, sulfates and sugars — in some areas — put heavy stands of lambsquarters on the run. Potassium chloride, chemical nitrogen and magnesium may be contributing factors in this weed's more than normal proliferation. See illustration on page 192.

PRICKLY LETTUCE, a.k.a., *horse thistle, English thistle, milk thistle, common wild thistle, Chinese lettuce, compass plant, wild opium.*

Lactuca serriola (Lactuca serriola, Lactuca serriola integrata and *Lactuca virosa)* is quite a mouthful for a biennial, annual or winter annual that reproduces from seeds. It grows in all states in cultivated land, poorly maintained pastures, and in the usual waste places and gardens. It likes dry soils. It looks a bit like sowthistle, with which it is often confused. It has a milky juice serviced by a taproot system, creamy yellow ray flowers with heads in a paniculate cluster. Leaves alternate and have prickly margins. Whitish midribs with curved prickles are exhibited on the undersides. There is a twist to each leaf at the base. The fruit is

Prickly lettuce.

This perennial, *Lactuca pulchella*, reproduces via seeds and creeping roots. It stands atop a taproot system and produces a milky juice. Blue rag flowers that dry whitish in a racemose or paniculate cluster give this weed a distinct tint. The fruit with seeds is an oblong

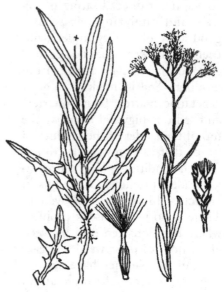

Wild blue lettuce.

ribbed. Livestock like this weed when it is young. Chickens relish prickly lettuce as a green. So do pigs. Unfortunately, it will taint milk. It won't survive repeated cutting if done before seeding. This weed grows in the presence of aluminum release, and therefore identifies with everything this condition implies — low aerobic activity, hardpan, crusted soil, low pH, etc. Calcium is always too low when prickly lettuce arrives. Magnesium is high, as is potassium. High manganese and iron releases also figure. The farmer faced with this inventory of conditions can respond accordingly.

achene with copious white capillary bristles. The bindweed remedy is indicated for this weed.

LITTLE BARLEY, a.k.a., *June-grass, albeit erroneously.*

Little barley, *Hordeum pusillum*, is a winter annual that reproduces by seeds in fields, waste places and abandoned land. It is erect or decumbent at the base, smooth and

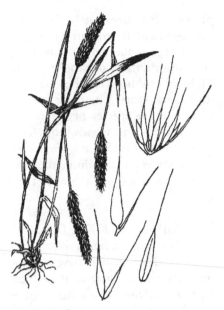

Little barley.

not over 1 foot in height. It has a fibrous root system. Spikelets are 3-flowered and closely aggregated. The grain it produces is long and narrowly obovate, hairy at the apex, and yellow. Little barley is a dry weather phenomenon. It seems to arrive in pastures in dry weather when other grasses are spent through overgrazing. Cattle will eat it early in the season, but by June the animals won't touch it. The control objective should be geared to prevention of seed formation and moisture preservation. Once seeds mature, spikelets shatter. Flame throwers have been somewhat successful in annihilating seeds, albeit not after shattering takes place. Low calcium must be dealt with, but both phosphates and potassium are high when little barley makes its stand. Magnesium is also very high. Zinc, boron and selenium appear to have a role in telling this weed to declare the kingdom for the year. As expected, low humus, porosity and bacterial activity influence the life and times of little barley.

LOCO, a.k.a., *stemless loco.*

Oxytropis lambertii, or loco, is a perennial reproduced by rhizomes and seeds. Supported by a taproot system with root tubercles, this loco stays very close to the soil. Leaves are long, white and hairy. The fruit pod has dark brown to black kidney-shaped seeds. *Oxytropis lambertii* is poisonous, but animals eat it only when pastures are lean. As with other forms of loco,

Stemless loco.

grubbing to a fair depth can keep a pasture free of weeds for up to 7 or more years. Pasture management and fertilization for higher phylum crops of forage are the best answer to this weed.

WOOLLY LOCO, a.k.a., *loco weed.*

As all good Western buffs know, loco weed, *Astragalus mollissimus,* sends a horse into crazy gyrations. It is a perennial that reproduces from both roots and seeds, and ruins pastures. It is a herbaceous bush that grows up to 16 inches in height from a penetrating root system. Leaves alternate and create a canopy of elliptical, fuzzy leaflets. Bluish to purple flowers are almost spikelike. The loco weed root goes deep, and does not respond to

Woolly loco.

physical measures easily. Fertility management to encourage desirable forage is the key to reduction and annihilation of woolly loco. Physical grubbing can be effective for several years. There are in fact several native species of *Astragalus* in grasslands and woods, not all of them locos. One, *Astragalus racemosus,* stores up selenium, the element identified with blind staggers.

CLIMBING MILKWEED, a.k.a., *sandvine, common milkweed.*

The milkweeds may have a common name, but there relationships end. *Gonolobus laevis* designates climbing milkweed, a perennial that reproduces from a succulent taproot system as well as from lateral roots and seeds. Gonolobus sometimes has 20-foot vines with twining stems. Leaves are opposite each other, simple, cordate, petioled. Flowers are white in peduncted auxiliary clusters. Seeds are winged and have a parachute of hairs folded in a pod. By August they are ready for distribution. Climbing milkweed often shares territory with field bindweed, and often outlives a successful bindweed control program. Climbing milkweed has many of the earmarks of common milkweed, but is much more destructive because of its root system. Still, seed pods are cancelled out when infested land is seeded to small grain crops. Small grain auxins simply cancel out *Gonolobus laevis.* Common

Climbing milkweed.

milkweed, a perennial called *Asclepias syriaca*, propagates from both seeds and spreading rhizomes. It turns up in soil with a near perfect cation exchange balance. It is seldom a problem in growing fields. Borders, fencerow waste areas, areas where there is not a lot of tillage — these are the sites where milkweed usually appears. It is here that the soil is constantly being challenged in its biological process, where it is not disturbed by compaction, tillage and traffic. This milkweed sometimes appears in ideal soil that is permitted to lay fallow for a period of time. It is easily managed by tillage, especially when its root reserves are low. This occurs at the time of seed maturity. *Asclepias syriaca* can be associated with a low humus level, a low aerobic bacteria count, and low moisture, and yet drainage may be good. Aluminum is generally a factor. Zinc, boron, chlorine, selenium and sulfate will register on the high side, along with manganese. Calcium and magnesium will dominate the exchange capacity sites available to cations. A calcium flush, carbohydrates and vitamin B-12 can chase this weed tribe right off the property. Poor electrolyte conditions help both types to grow. Use of potassium chloride helps fertilize this weed.

MISSOURI GOLDENROD

This perennial, *Solidago glaberrima*, grows well outside Missouri. It reproduces by offsets, rhizomes

Missouri goldenrod.

and seeds on plains, prairies, pastures. Flowers are in composite heads, and rays are yellow. The fruit and its seeds are tipped by a parachute of capillary bristles. This native goldenrod is not a bothersome weed. Missouri goldenrod starts its katabasis the moment the mower arrives. As with *Solidago canadensis* (Canada goldenrod), 2 or 3 mowings from midseason on closes out Missouri goldenrod's tenure.

WILD MORNING GLORY, a.k.a., *common morning glory, morning glory, tall morning glory.*

Formally named *Ipomoea purpurea,* this weed is an annual that reproduces by seeds in areas with poorly decaying organic matter. Its twining vine, with a fibrous root

Wild morning glory.

support, can climb a dozen feet or more. Doubtless its amply hairy stems and leaves are antennas — as Phil Callahan says — that balance cosmic energy to the special conditions poor decay manufactures. For practical purposes, it must be viewed along with field bindweed. Flowers have shades of pink, white, purple and blue, and ride along on a long axillary peduncle. The outer whorls of the flowers are oblong. Seeds are brownish to black. Since this weed is an annual, it is easily annihilated. Small grain crops set up the auxins that keep this prolific seed-producing weed from dominating the scene in field situations. The calcium level, of course, will be quite low when morning glory appears. The phosphate level also will be low. In turn the potassium level will be extremely high. A mixmaster combination of nutrient elements — high magnesium, iron, sulfate, copper, zinc, boron and selenium — governs the life and times of this wandering plant. All can be returned to perspective with a regulated lime application. A calcium flush will usually cause the wild morning glory to retreat and disappear from fields. Its preferred habitat is thickets and gardens carelessly tended in any case.

This information is fundamentally true for many of the other morning glory varieties such as: beach, blue, Japanese, bigroot, cypressvine, ivyleaf, smallflower and woolly.

COMMON MULLEIN, a.k.a., *velvet dock, great mullein, flannel leaf, big taper, candlewick, torches, Aaron's rod, Jacob's staff, hedge table, velvet plant, mullein, velvet mullein, torch plant.*

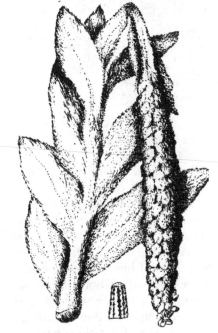

Common mullein.

This biennial, *Verbascum thapsus*, reproduces by seeds, chiefly in undisturbed places. The mature plant sends up its pyramid of foliage with a seeded antenna to a height of 5 feet at times, fuzz and hairs being a hallmark. Leaves alternate. Flowers are yellow to greenish white, about an inch wide, and crowded into a 3-foot-long spike. The plant's fruit is a many-seeded capsule. Seeds are co-

lumnar. Here, again, prevention of seed production is helpful. The best approach is to cancel out seeds in the soil with humic acid, fertilization and engineering a crop jump on weeds. Pasture eco-fertilization is always a good opening gun. Calcium, soft rock phosphate, sulfates, humates and potassium will help reduce or eliminate this weed. Use of potassium chloride and the resultant reduction in microbial activity are often factors that give the farmers this weed.

BLACK NIGHTSHADE

Found in waste places, roadsides, disturbed and cultivated fields, and beaches, *Solanum nigrum* is an annual without tubers, reproducing only by seeds. It is very difficult to distinguish from its cousin, *Solanum americanum* which is found

Black nightshade.

in rocky or dry open woods, thickets, shores, cultivated and waste areas. The unripe berries of some races are poisonous to sheep and other grazing animals. However, the ripe berries are often eaten raw or cooked for preserves or pies by humans. The stems are smooth or pubescent with simple leaves bluntly lobed at the base and oval in shape. The berries are green and turn black at maturity. The seeds are plentiful. These nightshades indicate soils low in calcium and very low in phosphate but very high in potassium and magnesium. Other elements found in high levels when Black nightshade appears are: manganese, sulfate, iron, boron, chloride, selenium and aluminum. Nightshade also indicates sticky, hard, moist soils with low porosity and humus along with anaerobic bacteria and poor residue decay.

CAROLINA NIGHTSHADE, a.k.a., *horse nettle, bull nettle.*

Solanum carolinense is a perennial reproduced by creeping roots, rhizomes and seeds. It often becomes established in overgrazed pastures, but is also a threat to cultivated fields as well as wasteland. It is a loosely branched weed with yellowish spines and short hairs. It grows 8-24 inches in height from its root system. Leaves alternate, are simple, petioled, broadly elliptic or ovate, wavy-toothed or lobed, and possessed of a few scattered prickles. Lavender flowers are tomato-like. Seeds are yellow to

Carolina nightshade.

light brown. *Solanum carolinense* yields to the control mechanism that annihilates almost all rhizome weeds, and therefore the field bindweed remedy rates consideration. Some of the symptoms that deliver field bindweed also exhibit themselves to analysis of *Solanum carolinense*, namely high potassium, low humus, poor decay system, a lack of aeration, hardpan, and so on. To deal with this weed it is necessary to introduce air into the soil and to set in motion biological systems antagonistic to rhizome development. Often this weed gains a toehold in imbalanced soil systems via seed contamination in alfalfa, clover and lespedeza. Such contamination is of little consequence if proper cation balances are maintained and if soil carbon to nitrogen is in equilibrium. For the record it is enough to say that this weed grows best when calcium, magnesium and potassium are out of equilibrium, with calcium too low, potassium and magnesium too high. The phosphate level is always too low when this weed proliferates. As an aside, selenium must be noted as a factor when Carolina nightshade appears. Bacteria, cancelled out by low moisture, are on vacation when this weed proliferates. Humus reaches a vanishing point, even though porosity may be high and the soil sandy.

PRICKLY NIGHTSHADE, a.k.a., *buffalo bur.*

Solanum rostratum is the official name for prickly nightshade, an annual that reproduces by seeds. It grows almost anywhere if left undisturbed. It grows up bushy and

Prickly nightshade.

prickly, seldom over 20 inches in height atop a fibrous root system. Leaves alternate. The calyx is prickly. A bur encloses the fruit of the plant, which is a circular berry that is dull, pitted and brown-black. The shallow root system gives control a handle, and it can be swung with gusto as tillage before seeds are set. No one loves prickly nightshade because it hurts on contact and creates problems in alfalfa, clover and Sudan grass seed packages. When the bur attaches itself to wool, price and grade are seriously affected. In the Dust Bowl 30s, it grew around the buffalo wallows still evident on Dad's north steppe. Disturb this weed at all and it doesn't make it very far. Oh, for a weedeater when the wallows were still evident!

SILVERLEAF NIGHTSHADE, a.k.a., *nightshade, bull nettle, prairie berry, sand briar, silver horsenettle, trompillo, white horsenettle.*

It is pretty in flower, this *Solanum elaeagnifolium* of the nightshade family. It is a perennial that stakes its claim on territory via creeping root, rhizome and seed propagation. It once called the high plains its habitat, but now has moved across the country, even as far as the San Joaquin Valley — Kern County included — and the Coachella and Imperial Valleys in California. Leaves alternate on this weed, are long, simple, elliptic, petioled and armed

Silverleaf nightshade.

with prickles and silver, star-shaped hairs. The pretty flower is violet. The fruit is many seeded, yellow or orange. The seed itself is flattened and nearly circular. It germinates at 59° F. Seed production is prodigious, something like 4,000 seeds per square yard when infestation is heavy. The control of choice is the same as for Carolina nightshade, *Solanum carolinense.* In terms of baseball stats, you can expect extremely low calcium and phosphate levels when silverleaf nightshade makes the playing field. In turn potassium, magnesium and manganese will be too high, with iron, sulfate and copper also on the high side. These are merely dead chemistry stats speaking. Actually the plant is telling the farmer that

the anaerobes have taken over, and therefore some attention should be given to the earlier discussion on field bindweed.

YELLOW NUTSEDGE

Found all over the United States in cultivated fields, gardens, grainfields, rich or sandy soils, Yellow nutsedge, *Cyperus esculentus,* is a serious perennial weed. It reproduces by seeds and weak thread-like stolons that end by hard tubers. Stems of this weed are tall, simple and triangular in shape; the pale green leaves are 3-ranked, about as long as the stem, with closed sheaths mostly at base. Yellow nutsedge produces spikelets 0.5-3 cm long and 1.5-3 mm wide that are yellow to golden-brown, strongly flattened, mostly 4-ranked along the wing-angled rachis, blunt, the tip acute to round. Ap-

Yellow nutsedge.

pearance of nutsedge indicates soils seriously out of sorts with very low levels of calcium and phosphate and very high levels of potassium and magnesium. Iron, sulfate, boron, selenium, salt and aluminum levels are likely to be high. Soils are also likely to have low humus and porosity, high moisture, anaerobic bacteria, and poor drainage and residual decay.

FALL PANICUM

This tough grass that jams up machinery and cuts cornfield production is styled *Panicum dichotomiflorum*. It is an annual that branches from the base and nodes. It likes moist ground, and can

Fall panicum.

therefore be found along streams and waste areas where compacted, wet anaerobic soil conditions prevail. If a field provides the tight compacted soil that puts foxtail on the march in early summer, it will likely support fall panicum later on in the year if herbicides manage to erase the foxtail weed. Fall panicum indicates ongoing soil degeneration. It represents a lower phylum of life than foxtail. As a matter of fact, if foxtail are allowed to grow, there will be no fall panicum. But if foxtail are attacked by herbicides, this takes away the auxins from the foxtail that usually cancel out fall panicum. Foxtail can dominate the fall panicum through auxin root residues. This makes fall panicum a herbicide-caused weed — a consequence of a living system building resistance to herbicides. Fall panicum is worse than foxtail. Since it depends on higher temperatures, it usually arrives after corn is cultivated in mid June or July. It dominates the environment in which it grows. Since it is a gnarled, knotted and disjointed plant, it has the angles to go anywhere and choke anything. It pulls down corn plants, messes up snappers and cutting bars, and often claims life and limbs when farmers try to cuss it out of harvest machinery. We curse fall panicum, often forgetting that this is nature's way of preventing sick nutrient material from getting into the life stream. Corn that grows up with fall panicum is bound to be sickly or at least subclinically deficient. Usually it will die early and fail to mature its grain. Based on a fibrous root, fall panicum has a grain and sheaths of leaves rather loose.

Browntop panicum, *Panicum fasciculatum*, is an annual in the same family as Fall Panicum. It thrives in areas of low calcium, low humus, low porosity and anaerobic bacteria activity. Hard or sticky soils which contain aluminum, along with poor drainage and poor residue decay add to the problem. Appearance of Browntop Panicum also indicates that the following elements are high: potassium oxide, magnesium, and manganese.

TEXAS PANICUM, a.k.a., *Texas millet*.

Texas Panicum, *Panicum texanum*, can be found in waste places, low lands, along streams but also, like Fall Panicum, in fields. This panicum indicates very low levels of calcium and potassium. Unlike the other panicums in this book, Texas Panicum prefers low selenium to high as well as good drainage as opposed to poor and is more likely to be found in less moist soils than its cousins. Low bacteria levels adds to the conditions for sustaining Texas Panicum.

PENNYCRESS, a.k.a., *Frenchweed, stinkweed, field pennycress*.

This annual or winter annual reproduces by seeds. It was styled *Thlaspi arvense* by Linnaeus. It grows up to 20 inches in height and has alternate toothed leaves. A bruise reveals a garlic-like odor. Flowers are white. The fruit is a winged capsule containing dark reddish-brown seeds with granular ridges on each side. This plant is a seed machine, and its progeny in storage stays viable for years. *Thlaspi arvense* taints milk, butter and cheese and accounts for grass eggs, a consequence of essential oil of mustard contained therein. Withal, it bows to tillage easily in the fall, less so in spring. Mowing before a shower of seeds is ready makes the most sense. High levels of selenium, sulfate, magnesium, potassium against very low levels of calcium and phosphate seem to set up the launching pad for pennycress. There is also a chlorine factor when this weed appears. The aerobic bacteria count tends to be very low under pennycress conditions. Repair of the calcium-phosphate

Pennycress.

level is the key in terms of biology, but as a practical matter a little clean tillage and aeration is devoutly to be wished.

PEPPERGRASS

The chief style in peppergrass is identified as *Lepidium densiflorum*. It stands 10 inches high and has toothed or deeply lobed leaves. Flowers for *densiflorum* are usually without petals. The fruit is a flat capsule that is almost circular and contains granular dull orange seeds. Cattle like peppergrass, which taints milk, cheese and but-

ter, this happens especially in dry years. The chief difference between *densiflorum* and *virginianum* is that the first came to the U.S. with the Volga Germans, the last is native and has petals.

PROSTRATE PIGWEED, a.k.a., *pigweed*.

Amaranthus blitoides is an annual that reproduces by seeds. It has a prostrate stem 1-1.5 feet long, and is based on a long taproot. Seed leaves or cotyledons are narrow,

Prostrate pigweed.

Peppergrass.

pointed and up to 8 times as long as wide. Leaves have a magenta tinge on the underside. Flowers have no petals and are inconspicuous in axillary clusters. Pigweed is a member of the amaranth family. It is not very obnoxious — indeed, it furnishes a good hog and poultry feed when in its succulent stage. Soils that produce this weed are generally well balanced. Humus may be low and drought stress to crops triggers its hormone systems for growth. This pigweed gravitates more to sandy soil than its other relatives in the amaranthus tribe. Withal, potassium and manganese may be a shade high, with iron release still higher. Ditto for zinc. In the main, low moisture seems to be more a problem than soil balance.

WHITE PIGWEED, a.k.a., *tumbleweed.*

Amaranthus graecizans is very much a brother or sister to *Amaranthus blitoides*, both being annuals that reproduce by seeds. Much like Russian thistle (no kin), white pigweed is called tumbleweed because as a mature weed it breaks away from its roots and tumbles in the wind, spreading seeds with reckless abandon. White pigweed sometimes grows 2 feet high from

White pigweed or tumbleweed.

an ample taproot. Its leaves are small, alternate, simple and broad near the tip. Flowers cluster in leaf axils. The white pigweed tumbler can't stand tillage. It, much like Russian thistle, is a dry weather phenomenon. It spreads an indecent amount of seeds, relying on climatic conditions to touch off its hormone and enzyme system for life and growth. Unlike *Amaranthus blitoides, Amaranthus graecizans* suggests a few fertility problems: low calcium and phosphate, high potash and copper, aerobic bacteria off duty because of hardpan, low moisture, low humus, low porosity.

REDROOT PIGWEED, a.k.a., *green pigweed, Chinaman's greens, careless weed, green amaranth, redroot, rough pigweed.*

Redroot pigweed is a member of the Amaranth genus, specifically *Amaranthus retroflexus*. It is an annual that reproduces from seeds and can prove quite troublesome in cultivated crops, orchards, vineyards, etc. As with *Amaranthus hybridus, Amaranthus retroflexus* can cause nitrate poisoning of livestock when mature. *Amaranthus retroflexus* stands 4-6 feet high, and branches freely. The taproot of redroot pigweed is quite red. Flowers are small and green and grouped in spikes. Seeds are black, glossy and lens-shaped or oval. Leaf tips are notched with the midvein reaching the notch with a temporary bristle. *Amaranthus retroflexus* is easy to control. Joe Cocannouer, in *Weeds, Guardians of the Soil*, did not see redroot pigweed as a big nemesis, even though it signals a calcium-potassium ratio out of whack, potassium too high, calcium too low, with a resultant shortfall in humus. The phosphate complex also needs attention when the weed proliferates. Calcium, phosphorus, copper, molybdenum, carbohydrates, humates and vitamin C in some areas will reduce or chase away this weed when it dominates a field. Chemicals and salts in undigested manures, magnesium and potassium chloride often contribute to redroot proliferation. See illustration on page *viii*.

Blackseed plantain.

BLACKSEED PLANTAIN, a.k.a., *rugel, purple-stemmed plantain.*

This plantain is *Plantago rugelii*. Specifically, an annual and sometimes perennial that reproduces by seeds, shoots and roots. It is full tufted with leaves in a basal rosette. Leaves are wavey toothed. Green flowers are in a dense, terminal spike. A pyxis or capsule holds 4-10 seeds. Cultivation can destroy the root system, and therefore rotation is indicated.

BRACTED PLANTAIN

The above weed is known as *Plantago aristata*. It is an annual that reproduces by seed and rears its head in run-down pastures. It grows up to 10 inches, secure atop a fibrous root system. Stems and

Bracted plantain.

Cast of Characters 245

leaves are hairy. Flowers are whitish in a dense spike. The fruit is a 2-celled, 2-seeded affair known as a pyxis. The capsule is brown, boot-shaped and grooved. Bracted plantain seldom shows up in cultivated fields. In pastures it bows to fertility management and to nothing else. Climax native grasses usually crowd it out.

POISON OAK

Its genus and species are *Rhus quercifolia; Toxicodendron quercifolium*, which is quite a handle. Poison oak is a perennial that reproduces from seeds and spreads via subterranean stolons, which are a nightmare to eradicate. Leaves are 3-parted on velvety petioles far out on the stem. Leaflets are elliptic, rhombic and hairy above, velvety below, changing to glabrous, obtuse or rounded above. These are deep-teethed or lobed similar to oak leaves. Flowers are greenish white. Fruit is a drupe, meaning a fleshy affair in which the inner part is hard as a rock. The goat, and sometimes sheep, come into their own controlling poison oak. Cut and grub attacks on leaves soon starve roots. Poison sprays rely on this principle when dealing with poison oak. The folk remedy for people who are susceptible and exposed to poison oak is to wash quickly with laundry soap in hot water, or in solvents such as benzene, kerosene or turpentine. A hot potassium permanganate solution also will oxidize poison in blisters that form. Hydrogen peroxide recommends itself. A physician should treat poison oak, but unfortunately many cannot recognize the syndrome. Otherwise the best Boy Scout advice is, "leaflets 3, let them be."

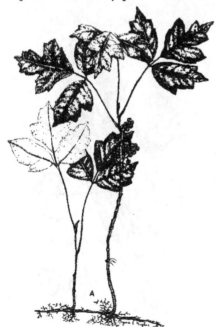

Poison oak.

POORJOE

Found in abandoned fields, along roadsides and in waste places, Poorjoe or *Diodia teres*, sends out slender shallow roots from a large taproot. Circular, slightly hairy stems branch as this annual gains height. Leaves are opposite, long and lance-shaped; stipules are fused and form several long bristles. Poorjoe's flowers are perfect,

always in pastures, on abandoned land and in undisturbed areas. It grows as a bush about 3 feet high and has red, prickly stems. There are usually 9-toothed and hairy leaflets. Flowers are pink. A rose hip encloses the fruit or nutlets. Heavily infested fields can be han-

Poorjoe.

meaning they produce both pollen and ovary, whitish-pink to lavender and funnel-shaped with 4 short lobes. They have a 4-toothed calyx fused to the ovary and 4 stamens attached to the corolla. The seedpods and seeds are hairy and the seeds are oval, light-brown to grayish-brown. Poorjoe especially likes sandy soils that are low in moisture and humus. The appearance of this weed announces very low levels of calcium and phosphate and very high levels of potassium and magnesium. Its arrival also indicates high levels of selenium and sulfate.

PRAIRIE ROSE

Rosa suffulta is more easily recited than separated from other wild roses that often infest a field. *Rosa suffulta* is a perennial that reproduces by roots and seeds, almost

Prairie rose.

dled with a routine of following and cultivation with duckfoot or other suitable implements. Above soil growth has to be bladed.

PRICKLY SIDA, a.k.a., *teaweed.*

An annual herb, prickly sida, *Sida spinosa*, is found in waste places, cultivated fields, open ground, gardens and pastures. It puts out a slender, branching and long taproot and reproduces by seeds. The stems are tall, softly

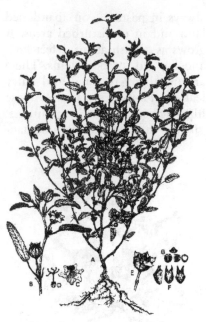

Prickly sida.

PRICKLY PEAR

During Dust Bowl days, we singed the needles off prickly pear and fed the fleshy parts to livestock. Prickly pear — there are several species of Opuntia, 1 of *echinocereus*, 4 of *neomammilara* in Kansas, others elsewhere — can't stand prosperity. They grow when land is overgrazed and drought has fastened itself on the countryside. Take Opuntia species and its barbed bristles. Flowers are a sulfur yellow, up to 3 inches across, with stamens open for a day. Seeds are circular, straw colored, the coiled embryo elevating the surface in an arc. Prickly pear can't stand even ordinary cultivation. When I was a youngster, farmers fought this cactus plant with fire, but fire — it turned out — merely set up better

hairy, and many branched with alternating oval/lance shaped serrated leaves. Flowers are solitary or clustered in the axils of the leaves with a thin, star-shaped calyx and pale, yellow petals; they produce an oval-shaped seed pod with two sharp spines at the top. The seeds are 1-2 mm long, egg shaped, dull and dark reddish-brown. Prickly sida thrives in highly porous soils with good drainage and low levels of moisture, humus and bacterial activity. The soils that sustain this weed are likely to be low in calcium, iron, and sulfate; very low in phosphate; very high in potassium; and high in copper.

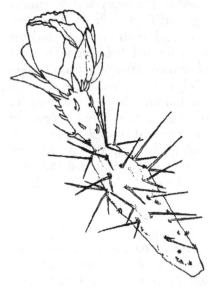

A typical prickly pear.

seed reproduction, adding insult to injury already caused by stem propagation of this perennial. There used to be more prickly pear before the big jackrabbit kills of the 1950s and later havoc wrought on jackrabbit progeny by toxic farm chemistry. Jacks ate mature cactus fruit and spread seeds that easily survived digestion.

PUNCTURE VINE, a.k.a., *goathead, bullhead, caltrop, puncture weed, burnut, ground burnut.*

All these names go with *Tribulus terrestris,* an annual that reproduces from seeds. It invades cultivated fields, but so-called waste areas are a more common habitat. Basically, puncture vine — by whatever name — is a prostrate plant. Several stems of various lengths grow from a taproot, which services this hairy creature. Cotyledons are thick, very wide and brittle. Bright green leaves are elliptical, gray on the undersides. Yellow flowers are small, hardly a quarter of an inch across. Seeds — evident from July until frost — form in a cluster of carpels, 5-angled, bony, each with 2 divergent stout horns, separating at maturity. Each bur has 2-4 seeds. There is 1 seed in each compartment. When this weed ages and dries, its burs become a menace to all who venture near. Its horns penetrate rubber tires, either directly or indirectly. Puncture vine burs often reduce the quality of wool in western states. This shallow-rooted weed is easy to control when young. A youngster can pull it up. A grub hoe or tiller reduces it to zilch quickly and efficiently. A low calcium and a very low phosphate level is the benchmark for this weed's existence and control. In turn potassium, magnesium and manganese levels will read high when this weed grows. So will selenium, chlorine and sulfate, even though drainage and residue decay may be good to excellent. *Tribulus terrestris,* unfortunately, poses more questions than it answers. See page 40 for illustration.

PURPLE-FLOWERED OYSTER, a.k.a., *salsify, goatsbeard.*

This particular goatsbeard, *Tragopogon porrifolius* is quite similar to *Tragopogon pratensis* except

Purple-flowered oyster.

that its ray flowers are blue to purple and not as long as the longest involucral bracts — also, the peduncle is dilated and hollow below the head. It is a biennial that reproduces by seed. Mowing and tillage are indicated, with mowing as soon as flowers appear the most effective.

PURSLANE, a.k.a., *pursley, pussley, common purslane, pursley duckweed, wild portulaca.*

Purslane, *Portulaca oleracca*, is an annual that reproduces by seed. It is sometimes used for greens. Pigs and chickens love it as a succulent. Purslane grows down close in a mat about a foot in diameter from a shallow fibrous root system. Smooth leaves cluster, are simple and broadest near the apex. Small, yellow flowers are in the axils.

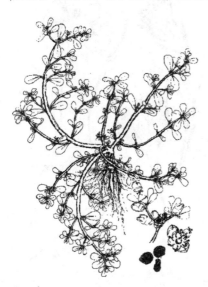

Purslane.

Fruit is a capsule. Control is simple during the early stages, but even physical removal serves up a phenomenon — the plant continuing to live and mature seeds after being uprooted. Seeds cannot endure and set new plants if cation balance is achieved and pH is properly structured with calcium, magnesium and potassium in an Albrecht equilibrium. Even more important is regular introduction of air into the soil. Cation balances are sometimes difficult to achieve because purslane soils have high potassium and magnesium levels. High iron and copper releases also figure when this weed declares the kingdom for the season. Calcium and phosphate levels are always low in purslane territory. Aerobes go off duty under low porosity and low moisture conditions, hence acid soil release of iron and copper. Review of Chapter 2 will suggest a plan of attack on purslane. Horse purslane is much the same weed, with round leaves and diced prominent veins.

FLORIDA PURSLANE, a.k.a. *Florida pusley, Mexican clover.*

Richardia scabra is an annual that reproduces by seeds and is particularly fond of sandy soils with good drainage and low humus. The stems are round, hairy and branching. The leaves are opposite with flat blades in an oblong shape. The flowers white and funnel-shaped. As with other purslanes (see above) this plant indi-

Florida Purslane.

cates a calcium deficiency in the soil.

QUACKGRASS, a.k.a., *couchgrass.*
Quackgrass, *Agropyron repens,* is a perennial that reproduces by seeds and extensively creeping underground rhizomes. In fact, seeds are relatively unimportant for reproduction much of the time. Examination of ears often reveals seeds to be nonexistent or sterile. Although considered a noxious weed in the United States, rhizomes from this plant have herbal qualities and are used as extracts in treating urinary disorders. Rhizome propagation makes clean tillage hazardous. Each little broken piece of root or stem promptly becomes another thriving plant when moisture conditions so decree. Dealing with this weed means

structuring a proper decay system in the soil, one that invites actinomycetes and several other species of molds, acidiomycetes included. In order to endure, these beneficial molds must have a well-aerated soil and adequate calcium. No one seems to have trouble identifying quackgrass. Spikelets are pendulous, glumes smooth, lemmata with stiff brown hairs at the base. Copper, manganese, soft rock phosphate, vitamin B-12, calcium, molasses, soil aeration and use of sulfates in some areas will reduce or eliminate this weed, the recipe to be determined by scanner. Potassium chloride, sterile soil conditions and compaction help this weed proliferate. See illustration on page 8.

RAGWEED
Linnaeus named it *Ambrosia elatior,* possibly as a joke because of its offensive odor. It is an annual

Ragweed.

that reproduces by seeds, sometimes in cultivated fields, sometimes in run-down pastures. This weed is bushy and hairy atop a fibrous root. Leaves alternate in general and are deeply bipinnated, variable and also hairy. Flowers are very small in terminal clusters. Some few heads at the base have pistillate flowers. The upper flowers are staminate. The fruit is an achene in a woody enclosure, with tubercles straw-colored to brown. Drought and poor moisture reserves in the soil cause a shortfall in the potassium processing system. This signals ragweed to have at it for the season. Cultivation and mowing will annihilate ragweed. It has to be an object of control because of the misery it delivers to human beings. Cattle should be kept from ragweed because it taints milk. Ragweed out of control can be managed with manganese, copper, vitamins C and B-12, calcium, phosphate and sugar in a solution, recipe to be worked out on-scene according to test readings. Potassium chloride, compaction, complexed zinc, low bio-activity, and chemical toxicity usually figure when this weed gets out of hand.

BUR RAGWEED, a.k.a., *lagoon-weed.*

The Latinized name is *Franseria tomentosa* for this perennial that reproduces via rhizomes and seeds. The term *lagoon* suggests its general habitat. It grows erect to 2 feet

Bur ragweed.

in height as a purplish-white weed. Leaves alternate and are broadly ovate, pinnately 3- to 5-parted, long petioled and dusty white. Lower flowers pistillate, upper ones staminate. Seeds have hooked spines that enable them to travel without a ticket on the coats of passing animals and human beings. By September, generally speaking, seeds are ready to travel. In addition to being a moisture thief, bur ragweed is a hayfever plant. It responds to control systems that prove effective for field bindweed. Bur ragweed grows in hardpan soils with little bacterial activity and low humus. Such soils have an aluminum problem. Calcium and magnesium levels are low or complexed, and potassium is high. There are relatives in the *Franseria aeanthocarpa* and *Franseria tenuifolia* tribes, plains dwellers and residents of pasture land. Low calcium, low or unavailable phosphorus, low potassium and general disequilibrium brought on by drought support bur ragweed's right to life.

COMMON RAGWEED, *Ambrosia artemisiifolia*

COMMON RAGWEED, *Ambrosia artemisiifolia* is a shallow-rooted annual herb widespread throughout the United States. It is found in old pastures, wasteland, roadsides, vacant lots, stubble fields,

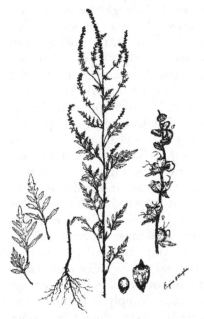

Common ragweed.

cultivated lands and seashore locations. Like its cousins in the ambrosia family, its abundant pollen causes sneezing and suffering. *Ambrosia elatior* is a variety of common ragweed, *Ambrosia artemisi-*

ifolia, which is an especially varied and pernicious species.

GIANT RAGWEED, a.k.a., *buffalo weed*

GIANT RAGWEED, a.k.a., *buffalo weed.*

This "ambrosia" weed was styled *Ambrosia trifida* by Linnaeus. It is simply another ragweed that reproduces by seeds whenever the moisture conditions, or lack thereof, are right. Again, potassium is complexed by drought or dry crusted soil conditions when giant ragweed appears. Scanner readouts say that calcium and phosphates are high enough, with magnesium, manganese, iron, sulfate, copper, zinc, boron, chlorine, aluminum and selenium also registering high. But complexed potassium seems to be more of a key to an energized seed.

Giant ragweed.

Lack of air in the soil, and capillary return of water, more than most other considerations give this weed permission for life. This weed branches superbly, yet stands erect. It grows between 1 and 10 feet in height. Simple opposite leaves have 3 palmate lobes and are rough and hairy. Lower flowers pistillate, upper ones staminate. The product of giant ragweed is pollen in great abundance. Fruit is enclosed in an involucre, is whitish or mottled. There is a central protuberance with smaller ones surrounding it for floating. Cultivation and mowing are indicated. It has been and remains the premier hayfever irritant in the United States.

WESTERN RAGWEED, a.k.a., *perennial ragweed.*

This particular "ambrosia" is styled *Ambrosia coronopifolia*. It is a perennial reproduced by rhizomes and seeds on pastures and prairies. It grows up to 20 inches high, and is always hairy and bushy. Leaves are less lobed than *Ambrosia elatior*. Lower flower heads pistillate, upper heads staminate. Fruit is much like *Ambrosia elatior*, but usually with fewer protuberances. This weed is a hayfever dandy. It takes *stick-to-itiveness* to keep it under control or to eradicate it. Mowing to prevent seed spread is a must. The bindweed approach to cancellation of rhizome spread — with well-digested compost — merits review and implementation. Needless to say, dry soil

fires up this weed's hormone system and states the potassium shortfall that gives it permission to life. Farm crops do best when they can get their potassium in a simple colloidally energized form. But when conditions of soil dryness prevail, when the soil's refinery process isn't hitting on all cylinders, potassium comes off in a hard-to-take colloidally complexed form. This form is just right for ragweed. It might be noted that smartweed has an opposite index card. In the early spring, and sometimes shortly after harvest, cool, cloudy weather sets in. Fields become waterlogged. More complexed forms of potassium take over. Colloidally energized potassium is not available for good crop growth. Under wet conditions, smartweed gets its signal to germinate and grow, and under dry conditions ragweed declares its domain. It is the Creator's rule that potassium must be activated, released and catalyzed by bacterial processes. Under dry conditions this is not possible. So when the potassium supply is minimal, enzyme processes trigger hormones that tell the ragweed seed to move along. One can conclude from all this the significance of having a good capillary water system. When a living soil gets too wet or too dry, too cold or too warm, it means problems, and specific weed families tell all about the symptoms. We have only to make the proper diagnosis to determine an enduring corrective treatment. See illustration on page 58.

REDVINE, a.k.a., *buckwheatvine*.

This perennial, woody, tendril-bearing vine known as *Brunnichia cirrhosa* in the Latinate, is found largely along riverbanks and in coastal areas. The stems are high climbing and many-stemmed and

Redvine.

up to 2 cm thick. The leaves alternate and are deciduous and have a long lance shape. Flowers produce an indehiscent winged fruit. the arrival of this climber, as with so many weeds, indicates unbalanced soil. Calcium, phosphate and humus levels are low while potassium, magnesium, and aluminum are high when redvine is present.

RED RICE

Oryza sativa, is an annual (sometime perennial) found in areas which are low in calcium and potassium. Soil in which this plant is found are likely to be low in humus with poor soil porosity or sticky, hard soil having poor drainage and poor residual decay. High magnesium and high anaerobic activity also help sustain this plant. Stems are erect 1-2 m tall; blades are elongated with a dense, drooping panicle 15-40 cm long. Spikelets are 7-10 mm long, 3-4 mm wide; the outer and inner bracts

Red rice.

are rough with scattered, appressed hairs. This plant is cultivated in all warm countries at low altitudes where there is enough moisture. It is one of the world's most important food plants.

ANNUAL RYEGRASS, a.k.a., *Italian ryegrass, Australian ryegrass.*

Annual ryegrass, *Lolium multiflorum*, along with its cousin, perennial ryegrass, is one of the most important of the European forage grasses. Both species are used in the United States to a limited extent for meadow, pasture, and lawn. They are of importance in the South for winter forage. In the Eastern States the ryegrasses are

Annual ryegrass.

often sown in mixtures for parks or public grounds, where a vigorous growth is required. The young plants can be distinguished from bluegrass by the glossy, dark-green foliage. Annual ryegrass grows to 1 m tall and is pale or yellowish at its base. It has prominent auricles at summit of sheaths with spikelets that are 10- to 20-flowered, 1.5- 2.5 cm long; the outer bracts are 7-8 mm long. This plant is closely related to *Lolium perenne*, but generally thought to be agriculturally distinct. It grows well in hard soil low in calcium and iron, and high in magnesium. It also tolerates aluminum in the soil.

PERENNIAL RYEGRASS, a.k.a., *English ryegrass.*

A short-lived perennial ryegrass, *Lolium perenne*, is quite similar to annual ryegrass (see above). It was the first meadow grass to be cultivated in Europe as a distinct and species. Before its cultivation the meadows and pastures were native. Like annual ryegrass it is used to a limited extent in the United States. Its stems are erect or decumbent at the reddish base, 30-60 cm tall. It is a glossy grass with blades 2-4 mm wide. The spike is often slightly sickle shaped around 15-25 cm long; spikelets have between 6 and 10 flowers. The outer bracts are 5-7 mm and are not bristly. It grows in meadows and waste places, especially if they are high in magnesium and low in boron.

SANDBUR, a.k.a., *field sandbur.*

Cenchrus incertus is an annual that reproduces via seeds protected in the plant's spiny burs. As the name implies, this weed likes sandy soil low in calcium, phosphate, humus and carbon. Its appearance in cultivated fields generally means sloppy farming. Sandbur is easy to recognize. It has flattened stems that branch to perhaps 20 inches in height. Often it forms large mats up and out from a fibrous root system. Leaves alternate and stay close to the soil. Sandbur becomes an easy victim to tillage, which in any case should be accomplished before seeds mature. Mowing is not effective. Oddly enough, sandbur is palatable and grazing animals prefer the weed to less nutritious grasses during the

The sandbur weed.

early stages before burs are formed. High aluminum seems to have a directing role when this weed appears. Calcium is always very low, as is the case with many weed species. Magnesium and manganese register high or very high, as do sulfates, boron and chlorine. But high zinc, copper, selenium, iron, potassium and manganese seem to figure in the governing role.

SHATTERCANE, a.k.a., *wildcane.*

Shattercane, *Sorghum bicolor*, is an annual grass that is common in sticky soils with poor drainage. Its appearance signals very low calcium and phosphate levels and very high levels of potassium and magnesium along with high levels of manganese, iron, sulfate, copper, zinc and boron. Usually humus and soil porosity are low, bacterial activity is anaerobic, and residue decay is poor.

SHEPHERD'S PURSE, a.k.a., *lady's purse, pepper plant, St. James weed, shepherd's pouch, mother's heart.*

Officially *Capsella bursa-pastoris*, this annual or winter annual reproduces by seed in many habitats. It annihilates poor pastures during drought. It has small white flowers in a raceme which elongates. The fruit is a thin flat capsule. Its grasses are relished by poultry in spring. Sometimes shepherd's purse gives egg yolks an olive color. Sheep are a good mowing machine for shep-

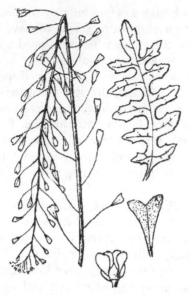

Shepherd's purse.

herd's purse. In any case, mowing and attention to fertility management will control this weed.

BROADLEAF SIGNALGRASS

Broadleaf Signalgrass, *Brachiaria platyphylla*, is an annual found in low, sandy, open ground. Rooting occurs at lower nodes; blades are thick, 4-12 cm long, 6-12 mm wide; the panicle is shortexserted or included at the base. Signalgrass thrives when calcium is very low and magnesium is very high; phosphate, potassium oxide, manganese, iron, sulfate and zinc levels are also high when this weed appears. Porous soil and low humus round out the conditions that support this plant.

SMALLFLOWER GALINSOGA

This annual reproduces by seeds and is found in weedy gardens, dooryards, lowland fields and waste places, especially in damp areas with rich soil. Also known as *Galinsoga parviflora*, it is a cosmopolitan weed found all over the United States. The stems are spreading with many branches; leaves are opposite, oval to lance-oval serrated and pointed at the tip. The flower heads are small and numerous, scattered at the ends of the branches; the ray flowers are very small and white, surrounding the small yellow disk flowers. Hard, moist soils with low humus and porosity attract this plant as does anaerobic bacteria, poor residue decay and poor soil drainage. Calcium is low and potassium and

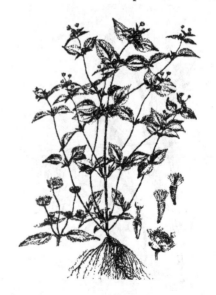

Smallflower galinsoga.

manganese are high when it appears.

PENNSYLVANIA SMART-WEED, a.k.a., *Jim McHale's weed.*

The Latin for this one is *Polygonum pensylvanicum.* At *Acres U.S.A.* we call it Jim McHale's weed after the former Secretary of Agriculture for the Commonwealth of Pennsylvania. It is an annual that produces by seeds, usually in wet or swampy places. It shoots up a stem about 3 feet from a well-developed root system. Leaves alternate. Flowers are pink, sometimes white, in a dense short spike. The fruit is reddish-brown to black, glossy, very granular, almost orbicular. Mowing and cutting are indicated. If this smartweed infests a stubble field, discing before seed production takes place

in late summer. Jim McHale's weed is a low calcium territory weed. It also calls attention to a very low phosphate and magnesium level. Potassium, on the other hand, tends to be high. High releases of manganese, sulfate, zinc, boron, chlorine and selenium are also factors. Review the principles in Chapter 2 as a diagnostic aid in determining nutrient shortfalls or imbalances. See Western ragweed.

SWAMP SMARTWEED

Its name says it all, even though Latinized designations shave the

Smartweed root and plant parts.

Pennsylvania smartweed.

fine points in terms of genus and species: *Polygonum coccineum pratincolum*. Moisture is the key, and this condition can be found in fertile bottom fields as well as ditches and along meandering streams. Swamp smartweed grows 12-16 inches high, and is supported by a fibrous root system. It is a perennial that reproduces by rhizomes, seldom by seeds, and is of small consequence in dry or drained fields. Its leaves alternate. Its pink flowers have no petals, but exhibit their splendor as terminal spikes. Again, the controls proved effective for bindweeds are operative in controlling this denizen of the swamps, except that swamp smarweed is by no means confined to poorly drained soil. It relies on poorly decayed organic matter and complexed potassium for its permission to life, and therefore suggests calcium, aeration and compost injection into its rhizome systems. High chlorine, iron and selenium figure in the swamp smartweed equation. Sulfate is often very high. Calcium and phosphate levels are usually too low, and potassium and magnesium levels are too high, all classical weed invitation patterns. Good creek- and river-bottom land can become badly infested when inattention permits swamp smartweed to increase and multiply.

SNOW-ON-THE-MOUNTAIN

This weed has an official nomenclature that bespeaks many

Snow-on-the-mountain.

authors — *Euphorbia marginata Lepadena marginata,* and *Dichrophyllum marginatum*. It is an annual that reproduces by seeds. It has a taproot system, produces a milky juice, and exhibits oblong leaves that are both hairy and crowded. Flowers are bordered by bracts and white marginal leaves. The fruit is a capsule and seeds are light gray to brown. Snow-on-the-mountain is less a weed than an ornamental in the east. In a farm context the weed is somewhat dangerous since it can poison hungry livestock. The plant does not survive easily on plowed land. It is easily controlled in pastures by mowing before seeds drop.

RED SORREL, a.k.a., *sheep's sorrel, dock.*

This perennial reproduces by shallow creeping rhizomes and seeds. Sorrel, *Rumex acetosella*, is a fertility level weed. It grows 4-10 inches, keeping its leaves close to the soil. Leaves are lanceolate and exhibit a pair of basal lobes. Flowers have a yellow staminate, and a somewhat red pistillate. This weed cannot survive intensive cultivation. Even though it is reproduced by creeping roots and seeds, its roots starve easily compared to bindweed. One of the problems with red sorrel and buckhorn is that they can't be killed with either a hammer or hoe when growth conditions are right. Tear off a stem, then shower it with a little water, and it will stand up like a member of the guard. Like a cancer, it is almost always impossible to get it all, and the part that survives grows in wild proliferation. The answer is to get the decay process going again with managed levels of calcium, and a balance of the other basic cations — magnesium, sodium and potassium — and the phosphate level up. As pastures become acid because of faltering fertility, sorrels and docks find an environment in which their seeds can take off. The distance from seed to rhizome is very short, measured on any scale. Sorrel is rich in oxalates, or salts that are not readily digested. Because of this sorrel has a reputation for being poisonous to

Red sorrel.

horses. Redwood forests always have a companion weed called oxalate. The term oxalate also designates a mild organic acid that keeps etching mineral nutrients out of native rock and lignated carbon residues to sustain redwood nutrition. Only lignated leaves and bark contribute the organic matter. The function of the oxalate root, and its auxins, is to produce oxalic acid needed in that decay process. High carbon lignins in a redwood forest need to be recycled. Oxalic acid is required to keep the mineral supplies coming, the ferns and fungi working. Some of those redwood trees are 3,500 years old, having been born well before the time of Christ. So it can be seen that the whole system works, year after year, without the aid of synthetic nitrogen, bagged fertilizer or toxic rescue chemistry. Red sorrel grows in acid soils, and it contains oxalic acid. The weed suggests soils that have not been cultivated, aerated or maintained properly, soils with a subdued biological process, certainly not with enough biotic activity to stimulate a good rotation of life. Often as not, wood and high-fiber organic matter figures in this weed pattern. Under acid conditions with low calcium, there is little actinomycetes activity. Buckhorn is a prolific weed, albeit in aerated soils that would otherwise support sorrel. It all relates back to wood, wood decay (usually wood shavings in the soil), old bedding, or accumulations of heavy amounts of horse manure, which is high in fiber. When the soil is aerated, buckhorn takes off, and sorrel remains subdued.

RED SPRANGLETOP

Leptochloa filiformis is an annual grass that grows on open or shady ground and is a common weed in gardens and fields. The name Leptochloa is from the Greek and literally means slender grass. It is found where soils are low in humus and calcium; high in copper, potassium, and phosphate; and very high in magnesium. Soils with poor residue decay and sticky soils are also likely places where Leptochloa will be found. The foliage and panicle are reddish or purple in color, hence the name -red sprangletop. Culms are erect or branching and bent below, 40-70 cm tall, or often dwarf; sheaths are somewhat hairy. The blades are flat and thin, as much as 1 cm wide; panicle is somewhat sticky with many approximate slender racemes 5-15 cm long, on an axis mostly about half the entire length of the stem. Spikelets are 3- to 4-flowered, 1-2 mm long. The glumes are tapering, longer than the first floret, often as long as the spikelet; lemmas are without bristles with fine hair along the veins growing to approximately 1.5 mm long.

Red sprangletop.

PROSTRATE SPURGE

Euphorbia supina (sometimes known as *Euphorbia maculata*) is found in dry, gravelly or sandy fields, sterile waste places and roadsides. This native annual reproduces by seeds. The stems are slender and prostrate or ascending, branching from near the base and forming mats that are soft and smooth, often reddish in color, with a milky juice. Leaves are op-

Prostrate spurge.

posite and elliptic-oblong in shape, serrated, covered sparsely with long, fine hairs, often mottled with a purple color. Prostrate spurge grows in sticky soils with low humus, low porosity, anaerobic bacteria, with low levels of calcium and phosphate and high levels of potassium, magnesium and salt.

SPOTTED SPURGE, a.k.a., *milk spurge.*

Spotted spurge is an annual that reproduces by seeds. Its handle is *Euphorbia maculata*, a.k.a. *Chamaesyce maculata*. The plant is a hairy-mat-former. Note the taproot. Leaves are both hairy and toothed. Both staminate and pistillate flowers grow in axillary clusters. Seeds grow in a hairy capsule and are pitted and brown to reddish. *Euphorbia maculata* won't grow when there is a climax crop of grass, and it won't survive tillage. If it is allowed to mature it produces a poisonous milky juice, but since it is a matted plant animals rarely eat it. Although it succumbs to tillage, mere foot traffic abuse won't dent it. It grows best from Colorado to the East coast,

Spotted spurge.

and the West coast from Washington to mid-California.

SQUIRRELTAIL

Known as *Sitanion hystrix*, squirreltail is a perennial that reproduces from both seeds and rhizomes. This tufted grass grows to 20 inches in height. Flowers are spiked, long awned and jointed. Cattle will graze this grass while it is

Squirreltail.

young. But when the fruit arrives, the grass joints break up like splinters, tormenting animals between teeth, in the nose, etc. The awn develops rasplike edges. Close grazing first, then mowing is the best remedy.

STINKGRASS, a.k.a., *skunkgrass, lovegrass, matrimony grass.*

This is a common fall weed, an annual that reproduces by seeds and is often found on cultivated land. Styled *Eragrostis cilianensis,*

Stinkgrass.

stinkgrass is a low-tufted grass with flowering stems. Its numerous leaves are generally near the soil. The plant exhibits between 25 and 70 flowers in a dense panicle. Stinkgrass grain is long and oval, slightly flattened, orange-red to reddish brown. It has a shallow root system and thus yields to cultivation and weeding. Stinkgrass has to have its annual fix of seeds or it self-destructs. Stinkgrass is mildly poisonous, but really not a problem except on neglected farms. Attention to the calcium level and tillage are the most effective remedies.

SMOOTH SUMAC

Rhus glabra is sometimes considered a weed. It reproduces from seeds and rootstocks. It is in fact a shrub that steals grassland, often

Smooth sumac.

winterkills. The leaves are well illustrated here. Flowers are greenish-white or yellow. Drupes are covered with red hairs. Smooth sumac should not be a problem. It can be dragged to extinction with a rail or mowed down easily when tender and young.

SUNFLOWER, a.k.a., *common sunflower, annual sunflower, wild sunflower.*

Styled *Helianthus annuus*, the sunflower is sometimes treated as a separate species, *Helianthus lenticularis*. In my youth, we called it the Landon button flower, after genial Alf Landon who ran for president in 1936. It is an annual that reproduces by seeds and produces seeds for birds. It has a rough stem, a quite fibrous root, and stays small or grows to 8.5 feet, according to conditions. Leaves alternate, are simple, ovate, lower cordate and long petioled. Flowers form a dark brown disc center, and ray out with bright yellow corollas. Abundant and nutritious seed production is seated in the disc center. Although well known and easily recognized, the sunflower is not an important weed. Its tap root is assisted by only a few lateral roots, and this makes control in all but waste places a simple tillage procedure. This weed will not grow easily in cultivated fields, although at times it can be troublesome to small grain producers. In terms of basics, the sunflower requires the same low calcium and phosphate levels required by many weeds. When this condition is matched by high potassium and magnesium levels, the flash point for this colorful weed is reached. Several other nutrients tend to measure high when the sunflower has its dry weather — iron, sulfate, copper, zinc, manganese. Sometimes it seems a shame to annihilate the sunflower. It is, after all, a very pretty flower. See illustration on page xvi.

PLAINS SUNFLOWER, a.k.a., *sand sunflower.*

Plains sunflower.

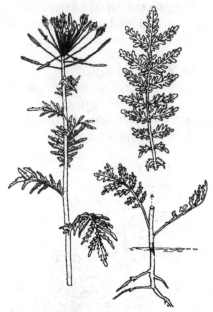

Tansy mustard.

This high plains plant, *Helianthus petiolaris*, is a great deal like the so-called common sunflower, except that the tips of the chaff are gray-brown and conspicious. It does not usually grow as tall as *Helianthus annuus*. Control is exactly the same as for *Helianthus annuus*.

TANSY MUSTARD

Tansy mustard has several handles, *Descurainia intermedia* being the chief one. It is an annual that reproduces by seeds. There are many varieties, notably *Descurainia pinnata* and *Descurainia sophia* (flixweed). Tansy mustard grows up to 28 inches in height from a fibrous root. Leaves alternate. Flowers are yellow in terminal racemes. Clean tillage is effective and cheap-

er than chemical remedies. It is not a serious weed problem. Nevertheless, it speaks of calcium and phosphate levels that are way too low; potassium, magnesium and manganese levels way too high; iron, sulfate, copper, zinc, boron, chlorine and selenium way too active. Calcium and phosphate levels brought up to equilibrium would best solve the problem, but this is not always practical when the weed problem is minor.

TANSY ASTER

It has a longer name, *Machaeranthera tanacelifolia*. It is an annual that reproduces by seeds. It usually stands 2.5 feet high, has small flowers in composite heads. Discs

Tansy aster.

Bull thistle.

are dark, ray flowers blue to purple. The fruit is gray and has a parachute of capillary bristles. Its importance is near absolute zero. Mowing keeps this native in tow.

BULL THISTLE

This weed, *Cirsium lanceolatum,* is a biennial that reproduces by seeds. It grows up to 4 feet high off a fleshy root. Leaves are rough on top, hairy below and spiny. Flowers are light pink. It has the usual parachute bristles. Although the bull thistle will not persist under tillage, it can substitute its presence for grass. Manganese is the nutrient in short supply when the thistle wins out over pasture grass. A wet spring and moist soil also helps wake up this plant's seeds with a message to declare the kingdom for the year. As with other thistles, the bull thistle is easily annihilated when flowers are in their glory and root reserves are low.

CANADA THISTLE, a.k.a., *Canadian thistle.*

This perennial herb is known as *Cirsium arvense.* It reproduces by both roots and seeds and is a problem in cultivated crops, often standing 4 feet high. It branches freely, has a fibrous and ranging root system. Simple leaves alternate and are spiny-toothed, hairy when young and dark green. Ample flowers are white to rose colored. Fruit with seeds in light to dark brown, tipped with a parachute of bristles. The control is the same as for bindweed. Canada thistle is sometimes mistaken for ordinary pasture thistles. The thistle crowd responds to manganese. All thistles exhaust their root reserves exactly at the time they are the prettiest. Mowing at that time is lethal.

Canada thistle likes low calcium levels in its soils, and extremely low manganese. Poor residue decay and anaerobic bacte¬ria domination are classic when this weed appears.

Canadian thistle, *Cirsium arvense,* likes an environment in which iron is depressing manganese availability. It might be noted that an environment that will support burdock is exactly opposite of the environment that will support thistle. Thistles have prickly leaves. Biennials of the species send down great taproots and concentrate potassium. They grow almost everywhere. Canadian thistle has long, creeping root-stocks. The field sowthistle, *Sonchus arvensis,* has very deep creeping roots that put this weed in a class by itself. Common sowthistle, *Sonchus oleraceous,* is edible and is cultivated in some parts of Europe. Blessed thistle, *Cnicus benedictus,* as the name implies, is used as a bitter extract for Benedictine Liqueur.

Thistle likes high iron, low calcium, and a poor organic matter structure in the soil. If the calcium is inadequate to govern release of trace minerals, and the colloidal pH is improperly positioned, metals are released in excess amounts. High amounts of nitrogen applied to soils low in calcium leave the soil without a governor, and the inevitable result is an excess flushing out of minerals. This sets in motion a lot of hormonal processes that affect the character of weeds that can grow and regulates their ability to germinate and achieve their genetic potential. If a weed is missing certain nutritional requirements, this affects its genetic mutation. Organic material decaying improperly with the wrong fungus systems in tow and a lack of actinomycetes molds all figure in setting the stage for the thistle. In the West, where pH is often built with high levels of sodium and potassium, but with low levels of calcium and magnesium, the pH may read near neutral, but still provide the environment for thistles.

Thistles have a tremendous root system. These rhizomes build themselves in a mat, much like a strawberry plant, and dominate the environment. They have a fantastic auxin production which subdues anything else, including grain crops. They grow rapidly with big leaves and shade out any other crop established at the same time. Here again, construction of pH figures first. Generally speaking, it is necessary to change the construction of pH by increasing calcium and magnesium, and complexing sodium and potassium, all to put a governor in charge again. This adjustment will regulate the iron to manganese relationship, and the release of other heavy metals. It is not necessary to measure cadmium, lead and chlorine. It is enough to control the practices that tend to flush them out.

In the presence of high iron and low manganese, a whole strata of fungi that like mineral imbalance increase and multiply, and these are favorable to thistle root development. Thistle roots are also rhizomes that function well below the plow level. This means it is not physically possible to tear them out or penetrate them with herbicides. They can be subdued only by in¬creasing the supply of manganese and regulating the manganese to iron profile. This much accomplished, a whole different strata of bacterial mold systems is invited, and these are antagonistic to the thistle rhizome. They rot it out, usually in a period of 3-6 months.

Deionized sulfur is one of the things that will permit regulation of the manganese to iron ratio. Ordinary sulfur or sulfur contained in salt fertilizers is quite soluble and can be obliterated quickly. Ammonium sulfate will provide sulfur that has only a fleeting acid action. It is quickly absorbed and neutralized. The moment it is made soluble it becomes quite active and agitates the imbalance even further. If there is an excess of iron, it will increase the excess many times over. Sulfate salt or ammonia can flush out a lot of iron, and it is this flushing out that creates toxicity to many plants and sets in motion hormone processes that invite the weeds that thrive in the type of environment in which they find themselves.

Poison sprays just kill the tops and never get to the roots. As a consequence, auxins remain to do their handy work. Clean tillage is sometimes effective if the thistle can be cut at a certain stage of its metabolic life system. Folklore observers have noted that the position of the moon and its magnetic effect have a bearing on how plants react to being cut. Although this inventory of observations has never achieved high science status, many successful farmers have kept their own records and picked up patterns they believe to be successful. See illustration on page 108.

Pasture thistle.

PASTURE THISTLE, a.k.a., *field thistle, tall thistle.*

This thistle, *Cirsium altissimum*, reproduces from seeds, sometimes in neglected fields. It grows to 6 feet in height atop a fleshy taproot. Leaves are slightly toothed with weak prickles. Flowers are rose colored and terminal on the branches. Fruit with seeds is tipped with a parachute of plumose capillary bristles. The weed is easily expungable by the mowing machine, especially when this is done before seeds drop. This is not a serious problem weed, although the sharp spines are objectionable. Root reserves are lowest when the flowers are prettiest. Cutting at that time is lethal to the plant.

RUSSIAN THISTLE, a.k.a., *wind witch, common saltwort, Russian tumbleweed, tumbleweed, witch weed, saltwort, Russian cactus, prickly glaswort.*

Even in the Latin identification system, Russian thistle has its aliases. There are some 60 species worldwide, 20 of them in the U.S. The most common scientific designation is *Salsola kali*, which USDA lists also as *Salsola pestifer*. There is also *Salsola australis*, a member of the goosefoot family. Another Latin designation is *Salsola iberica*, and there are at least 17 more such names in the United States alone. Whatever the name, Russian thistle, variety *tenuifolia*, is the one that the West, particularly Kansas and Colorado, made famous. It's an annual seed machine and it provides weed lore with answers because its ubiquitous presence asked the right questions. As with Canadian thistle, the manganese to iron ratio is key.

Recognition is seldom a problem. Basically, this annual reproduces by seeds, usually in overgrazed pastures and drought stricken terrain. The plant has a spiny stem with reddish markings. It can grow up to 4.5 feet in height. Leaves alternate and for a time are succulent. Greenish flowers are not conspicuous.

I have stayed on to express the above notes because the plant is so well known and such a good teacher of the right questions. Managing the iron levels and cultivation, as with Canadian thistle, is the best strategy against this stubborn specimen. Russian thistle demands combat because it hosts the sugarbeet leafhopper, which in turn harbors the virus that confers curly top disease on beets and certain vegetable crops such as tomatoes, green beans, squash, cantaloupes, spinach, red beets, and many other receptive truck crops grown in the same soils. Rainbelt farmers do not need to worry about this weed. See illustration on page *vi*.

TRUMPET CREEPER, a.k.a., *Virginia creeper.*

An aggressive, widely distributed native weed, *Campsis radicans*, is a perennial vine that reproduces both by seed and vigorous running roots. The stems are woody and leaves are pinnately compound with oval to lance-shaped leaves that have toothed edges. The flowers are bell-shaped, orange to scarlet, rarely yellow and

Trumpet creeper.

produce a winged seed. This creeper will grow in fields, yards, roadsides, waste places, woods, on trees, posts and old buildings. It is also cultivated as an ornamental. Soils very low in calcium appeal to Trumpet creeper, but other elements such as magnesium, manganese, sulfate, copper, zinc, boron and selenium are high when this plant appears. Low humus, low residue decay and anaerobic bacteria all contrive to support the creeper's growth.

VELVETLEAF a.k.a., *Indian mallow, butterprint.*
This annual is a troublesome weed in all but the coldest areas. It reproduces by seeds, usually in culti-vated fields, and just about every-where else except climax prairie sod. *Abutilon theophrasti*, as the name implies, has the velvet touch with soft hairs all over the leaves. Crushed, these leaves have an unpleasant odor. From a penetrating taproot system, plants stand erect. Simple leaves alternate, are petioled and cordate at the base. They achieve 4- to 12-inch widths. Flowers are orange-yellow and seated on short leafstalk peduncles. The fruit of velvetleaf splits open at maturity. This weed can't make it in small grain fields for reasons still to be identified. It proves troublesome in row crops. The remedy is cultivation, cutting or pulling. Old timers recommended burning seedpods, even if immature. Poisons are not particularly helpful because seeds retain their vitality for over 50 years. Only the well-inoculated compost pile will kill them. The appearance of velvetleaf is an early warning system with specifics attached. It says decay has gone in the wrong direction, with methane rather than carbon dioxide, the byproduct. Phosphates in the soil are all complexed, and aerobic microorganisms have gone off duty. Velvetleaf soils also have a carbon problem. Fertilization with muriate of potash and hard nitrogen is almost always an insurance policy for having this weed. Herbicides also support velvetleaf proliferation. Calcium and phosphate levels are low or complexed when velvetleaf appears. Potassium and

magnesium are high, as is the case with selenium. With anaerobes in command, manganese, iron, sulfate, copper, boron and chlorine are cut loose and achieve a high profile. Low humus, low porosity and poor decay translate into high moisture, crusted and sticky soils and aluminum release. High salt does the rest. It will take a mixture of correcting materials that includes calcium, phosphorus, molybdenum, silicon, vitamin B-12, molasses, humates and sulfates in some areas to correct the soil, the recipe to be determined in each case, possibly by scanner. See illustration on page 78.

HOARY VERVAIN, a.k.a., *verbena*.
This perennial reproduces by rhizomes and seeds. Academia knows it as *Verbena stricta*, and farmers know it as a denizen of worn pasture land and farm waste places. It has stout stems and seldom grows over 4 feet in height. These stems are simple or branched above, velvet hairy. Leaves are prominently toothed, simple, sessile, broadly ovate, with whitish hairs and pinnately veined. Flowers are blue to purple in a spike. Early June is the time to mow hoary vervain because this is the weakest stage of the root system, and just at the edge of the bloom stage. Simple eradication via mowing works in 2-3 years, but the weed is a harbinger of oncoming degeneration, and suggests better pasture fertility management, especially attention to the calcium fix.

Hoary vervain.

As one might expect, both the calcium and phosphate levels will be low when hoary vervain rears its head. Potassium and magnesium will be very high. Some of the trace elements will be high, namely zinc, boron, chlorine, selenium, generally a consequence of a low pH. Hardpan conditions can be expected. Calcium will be too low for crop comfort in hoary vervain territory.

In any case, bacteria will be too inactive for proper regulation of the trace nutrients that must be kept in check with a dignified poverty, much like a Roman bureaucrat.

Prostrate vervain.

PROSTRATE VERVAIN, a.k.a., *large bracted verbena*.

An annual, sometimes perennial, that reproduces by both seeds and runner roots, that's *Verbena bracteata* and *Verbena bracteosa*. This lawn weed is rough and hairy with free branches and a meandering taproot. Leaves are wedge shaped. Purple flowers ride along on a spike with long bracts. Seeds come in 4 single-seeded nutlets that are oblong. The bindweed remedy works best because control has to deal with roots as well as seeds. Humate treatment of infested lawns unravels prostrate vervain. Scattered plants should be removed, but this will have minimal effect unless fertility management is invoked.

VOLUNTEER BARLEY

Volunteer Barley, *Hordeum vulgare*, is an annual cultivated for grain and sometimes appears spontaneously in fields and waste places, but it is usually not persistent. The stems are erect, 60-120 cm tall; blades are flat and between 4-15 mm wide with well-developed auricles. The spike is nearly

Volunteer barley.

erect or erect growing between 2 and 10 cm long, excluding the awns. This barley produces 3 spikelets which lack a petiole or stalk. The bracts are narrow and without veins, growing out to a stout awn. There are two groups of cultivated barleys. In the 2-rowed forms the lateral spikelets are fairly well-developed but sterile. In the second group all the spikelets produce large seeds; these are called 6-rowed, or, if the lateral florets overlap, 4-rowed barleys. In some varieties the seed is naked.

VOLUNTEER RYE

Volunteer Rye or *Secale cereale*, is a commonly cultivated annual re-sembling wheat, but usually taller with a more slender spike that is on the average longer than wheat. Rye grows erect, with flat blades and dense spikes. It usually volunteers in fields and waste places. The spikelets are normally solitary and 2-flowered. The rachilla are disjointed above the glumes and produced beyond the upper floret as a minute stipe. The glumes are narrow, rigid, tapering and pointed; lemmas are broader and sharply keeled. There is a 5-nerved ciliate on the keel and exposed margins that tapers into a long awn.

VOLUNTEER WHEAT

Volunteer wheat, *Triticum aestivum*, is a commonly cultivated an-

Volunteer rye.

Volunteer wheat.

nual crop plant. It volunteers in fields and waste places, especially in the vicinity of grain elevators. It can be low or tall with flat blades and thick spikes. The wheat culms are erect, freely branching at base, 60-100 cm tall. The blades are 1-2 cm wide, spikes mostly 5-12 cm long; internodes of rachis are 3-6 mm long. The spikelets are broad and smooth or with fine hair. Depending on the plant, the spikelets are also long-awned or awnless. Wheat glumes are usually strongly keeled toward one side, the keel extending into a point, the other side usually angled at the apex. The origin of wheat is unknown, partly because there is not a native species like any of the cultivated forms.

White prickly poppy.

WHITE PRICKLY POPPY

An annual that reproduces by seeds, that's *Argemone intermedia*. It is considered a pasture and orchard weed with blue-green leaves. Flowers are short-peduncled. Fruit is an oblong capsule which contains globular, black seeds. The plant is poisonous, but cattle won't eat it because of its prickly nature. It can grow in cultivated fields that are neglected. Pulling or mowing before seed formation is most effective.

WILD BUCKWHEAT, a.k.a., *knot bindweed, black bindweed, bear bind, ivy bindweed, climbing bindweed, cornbind.*

Polygonum convolvulus is an annual that reproduces seed. From a fibrous root it first grows erect,

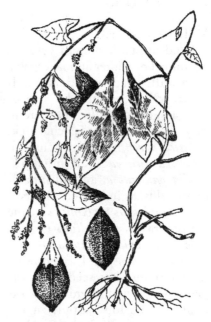

Wild buckwheat.

then twines around any support or creeps. Simple leaves alternate. Flowers are whitish in axillary clusters. The one-seeded fruit is dull black and granular. This shallow rooted plant is easily eradicated by cultivation. Rotation for the purpose of introducing new root auxins — to corn or milo — is indicated since wild buckwheat thrives in small grain crops. Especially when the calcium and phosphate levels are too low in the presence of high iron and magnesium release. Potassium is no problem. Hardpan and poor residue decay with resultant crusted and sticky soil — exacerbated by anaerobic bacteria domination — all dovetail to give wild buckwheat a shot at wrecking small grain stands.

WILD MUSTARD

Wild mustard, *Brassica kaber*, is an annual or winter annual capable of prolific seed reproduction. It grows well in grainfields, particularly amid oat stands. There are in fact several mustards: charlock, *Brassica arvensis*; Indian mustard, *Brassica juncea*; ball mustard, *Neslia paniculata*; and all inhabit grain fields, as indeed do wild radishes, *Raphanus raphanistrum*; the peppergrasses (*Lepidium virginicum* and *Lepidium apetalum* and *Lepidium campestre*). It is, however, in oat fields that seeds of these plants wake up and grow, first exhausting the food supply in the seed, next invading the nutrient bank account of the commercial

crop. A lot depends on how trash behind the harvest is handled, since this will have a bearing on which mold and fungus will be invited to that table. Also, a lot relates to the supply of juices, vitamins, minerals, sugars present in the organic material returned to the soil. Prompt tillage of harvested residues will capture all these goodies and stimulate quick fall fermentation and a cleaner rootbed the following spring. Wild mustard is usually related to a field planted to small grain. Most grain crops follow crops that leave a lot of stubble from the year before, and frequently the field is not worked in the fall. It is usually a case of mulching in the stubble during a spring when soils are cold. That's a common habit in putting out small grains. An accumulation of trash that winters over on top of the soil is conducive to slime mold production. These slimes make the soil sour and waterlogged. Even if that soil is given a shot of air, slime mold works its mischief for a week or 10 days. Warmer temperatures might come along and invite a new mold to take over. Nitrogen use figures in all this. Nitrogen goes to calcium first, then to phosphorus, taking the nutritional supply away, and this situation has a bearing on which of the fusarium molds will function. If the undesirable fusarium molds take over, they put into motion hormone processes that fire up mustard, wild radish, and weeds of that ilk. This is the reason that stover must be turned in as soon after harvest as possible in the fall. Slime mold is not likely to take hold in trash on the surface if the decay system is functioning under proper aerated conditions. It is almost impossible to find wild mustard in the better soil areas of a field unless spring tillage jumps the "start." More commonly the weed grows in an area stressed due to poor drainage and poor structure. It is usually a consequence of working the ground early under poor drainage conditions. Everything has been done pretty wrong when mustard covers an entire field. It might be pointed out that small grains have a different auxin effect than coarse grains. As soon as they germinate they put out their auxins, and these are sometimes complementary to stimulation of fusarium molds. Stem rust, root mold and the like are always associated with the same areas as wild mustard because both are manufactured by a sequence of weather factors. The advice on wild mustard comes down to this. If good compost is not available, it is best to use some nitrogen to get the decay process moving. This should be applied with a fall mulch of crop residues. Nitrogen is not necessary if compost is available because good compost can hand over something like 100 pounds of nitrogen per ton — all of it in colloidal form, not leachable, never wasted. Leaves are coarsely toothed; flowers have yel-

low petals. See illustration on page 124.

WILD OATS

Wild oats, *Avena fatua*, are hardy annuals, and a most troublesome weed crop reproduced by seeds. Seeds usually ripen before the wheat and drop to the ground before harvest. Since they are not taken off the field, they perpetuate themselves. Wild oats are a prob-

Wild oats.

lem over most of the West, especially California. This weed relates to soil areas that are overly wet and poorly drained. Cold seedbed temperatures usually figure, and there are usually sedimentation problems due to poor surface porosity or surface tension of soil particles. These particles tend to filter down causing sedimentary barriers in the lower levels of soil surfaces. Likely as not they've been agitated by working the soil on the wet side, working the ground early while trying to get the wheat planted early. It is almost always a cost of rushing field work before many areas in the field are ready for machine tillage. Draws, swells, low pockets, poorly drained areas, sometimes a slope with a seep coming from above — all need air to warm the soil. It is usually a case of a farmer working a ridge, discing mealy soil — then the disc hits that wet spot. Almost every field has susceptible areas that are wild oats soil conditions. Here again pH figures in preventing the target area from getting proper drainage. Soils planted on the wet side seal over easily following a shower. The problem can be corrected by adjusting the calcium load in seal areas. Anyone who goes to the trouble of getting a soil audit will usually discover a deficiency in calcium, low magnesium, high sodium and high potassium. There are plenty of farms with 1,000 to 2,000 pounds of sodium per acre. These acres exhibit a high

pH — sometimes pH 8 or more — but this reading represents a false character pH. Sodium is an active element with a high position on the periodic chart. It can be made soluble with good, ionized, active sulfur and another cation injected to take the place of sodium — calcium, magnesium, potassium, or humic acid for instance. The sodium or excess cation will be flushed off the colloid and mobilized to a water soluble form. It will end up as dry powder on top of the soil, or it will leach into the subsoil and reduce the concentration and saturation of the colloidal remains. Plants live off the colloidal position, and elements that are water soluble won't interfere. Plants depend on energy exchangeable nutrient forms. Water does not wash nutrients into the plant. The water soluble fertilizer requirement of state agencies is — as Bill Albrecht said — "a damn fool idea." Another way of dealing with oats is to use good, ready-to-go-to-work compost materials, or special soil wetting agents such as Amway, WEX or Basic H. These things will reduce surface tension and permit the soil to get rid of excess water. It might be redundant to note that if a farmer would wait until the soil warmed up in the super-wet areas being discussed here, he would not irritate the system, and there would be no wild oats. The seeds would simply stay dormant. Thus the general remedy: treat those areas in the fall of the year with surfactants, pH modifiers and compost, and correct the structure of the soil so that it drains better. In the spring, simply delay tillage of those areas until they are dry and ready. If the field is to be plowed or deep tilled, it would be well to disc and scratch those areas before plowing to take off the surface tension. Sealed areas will always suck water to the top. As soon as surface tension of the sealed over area is reduced, water tends to sink and go down faster. On chemical farms, potassium chlorine use and complexed zinc plus NO_3 may be suspected. A good bio-remedy is a calcium flush together with phosphates, NH_4, copper, SO_4, molybdenum, vitamins C and B-12, the recipe to answer scanner diagnosis.

WILD ONION, GARLIC

Allium canadense, as pointed out on page 6, is a perennial that reproduces by bulbs, bulblets and seeds with equal alacrity. Stems are simple, smooth and about 1 foot in height and the plant has what botanists call an alliaceous bulb odor. Flowers are pinkish with 6 perianth segments, 6 stamens and 1 superior pistil. Fruit of *Allium canadense* is a marvel of design. Its 3-valved capsule has 3-6 glossy, ovoid, black seeds with a small wing-like ridge around the seed, a sort of Saturn effect. Although seeds are a backup reproduction mechanism, they seldom account for progeny. That task is performed

Wild onion.

by bulblets. *Allium canadense* gives that garlic taste to milk, a problem that can be remedied by removing cows from infested pastures at least 6 hours before milking. The calcium treatment is almost always a help, since wild onion and garlic pastures speak of dead soil, a faltering microorganism population, and a pH badly in need of modification. Usually, decay is going in the wrong direction, and this means the cation equilibrium needs adjustment with attention to Albrecht's formula (see page 61). There are other native onions, notably *Allium mutabile* (leek) and *Allium nuttalli* (called simply wild onion or wild garlic). Leek is a simple, narrow bulb with broad keeled flat leaves, a pithy stem bearing a dense terminal of pink flowers and black seeds. Allium is a perennial reproduced by bulbs and bulblets, seldom by seeds. *Allium vineale* has 2 styles of bulbs — a soft bulb which sets new life in motion the first fall, and a hard bulb for overwintering. Leaves are slender, hollow, grooved and usually numerous. Flowers are green or purple. It doesn't matter. They seldom reproduce. *Allium canadense* means very low calcium, high magnesium, poor drainage, low humus, aerobes off duty, anaerobes dominating. An aluminum problem also is indicated. *Allium vineale* means the same low calcium, very high potassium and magnesium with high iron, zinc, boron, chlorine and selenium a fabricator of the soil profile. High chlorine and low bacteria activity round out the picture. Control for all the onions is somewhat the same — cation balance, not poisons, being the key.

Wild potato vine.

out the root system, and this means well-digested compost. Seeds are dark brown to black and hairy. But it is the root system that is awesome, especially on fertile bottom land and in cultivated fields. Calcium adjustment to the maximum per base exchange capacity helps.

WILD POTATO VINE, a.k.a., *man-of-the-earth*.

This weed is more difficult to control than the farmer's chief nemesis, bindweed. It is called *Ipomoea pandurata* in the Latinate, which more or less telegraphs the fact that this summer-blooming morning glory has an enormous taproot which can weigh between 80 and 100 pounds fresh. Digging is futile, cultivation useless. Only a new inventory of microorganisms can rot

WILD PROSO MILLET a.k.a., *broomcorn millet, hog millet.*

Wild millet, *Panicum miliaceum*, is commonly cultivated in Europe and Asia and sometimes cultivated in the United States as forage, occasionally the seed is used as feed for hogs. It grows in waste places, often where it has escaped from cultivation. Wild millet is a stout-stemmed plant that can be erect or decumbent at base growing 20-100 cm tall; blades can be smooth

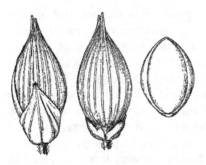

Wild proso millet, spikelets and floret.

to slightly hairy and up to 30 cm long and 2 cm wide. It has numerous ascending branches which are very rough and bear oval spikelets toward the ends. The fruit is straw-colored to reddish brown. According to Jay McCaman, wild proso millet indicates very low calcium and phosphate levels and very high levels of potassium, magnesium, copper, zinc and selenium. There are also likely to be high levels of manganese, iron, boron, aluminum and chloride when millet appears. Low bacterial activity, poor residue decay, and sandy soil all contribute to growth of millet.

WIRESTEM MUHLY

Wirestem muhly, *Muhlenbergia frondosa* is a perennial that spreads by its creeping, scaly rhizomes. It can be found growing in thickets, low ground, and waste places. The stems are stout and smooth and the plant often takes root at the lower nodes and freely branching from all of the nodes. The branches are ascending and spreading and the plants become top-heavy and

Wirestem muhly.

bushy at 40-100 cm long. The grass blades are flat and rough, usually not more than 10-15 cm long and 3-7 mm wide. Wirestem muhly has numerous inflorescence, terminal and axillary, the largest growing to 10 cm long. These inflorescence are narrow and loose, the branches ascending and densely flowered from the base. You are most likely to find wirestem muhly growing in sticky soils with high levels of aluminum, low humus and very low calcium.

WITCHGRASS

Witchgrass, *Panicum capillare*, grows in open ground and waste places and is often found in cultivated ground. Its stems are erect or somewhat spreading at base, 20-80 cm tall; sheaths are hairy and blades are 10-25 cm long, 5-15

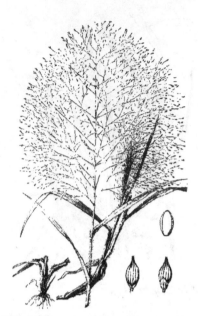

Witchgrass.

It produces a taproot and numerous stems from a crown which grow tall, branched near the top, and can be smooth, angular or ridged. The leaves are long, pinnately divided with bottom leaves consisting of a large terminal lobe, forming a dense rosette, the stem leaves becoming progressively shorter. Flowers form in spike-like racemes at the end of each branch,

Yellow rocket.

mm wide and hairy on all surfaces. The plant is densely flowered, often half the entire length of the plant and at maturing the whole inflorescence will often break away and roll before the wind. Jay McCaman tells us that witchgrass will be found in sticky soils with low humus and high porosity. Very low calcium levels are indicated along with very high levels of magnesium. Aluminum, chloride, and selenium levels most likely are high also when witchgrass appears.

YELLOW ROCKET, a.k.a., *wintercress.*

Yellow Rocket, *Barbarea vulgaris,* is a short-lived perennial, reproducing by seeds and sometimes by new shoots from the old crowns.

they are 4-petaled and bright lemon-yellow. Yellow rocket is native and can be found in new meadows, along roadsides, in fields. Soils where this weed is found are low in calcium and very low in phosphate. High levels of potassium, magnesium, manganese, iron, sulfate, copper, zinc, boron, chloride, and selenium guarantee conditions in which yellow rocket flourishes.

YELLOW SALSIFY, a.k.a., *yellow goatsbeard, oysterplant.*

It is a biennial that reproduces by seeds. Styled *Tragopogon pretensis*, yellow salsify grows to about 3 feet in height atop a taproot. It has a milky juice. Flowers are in composite head with rays longer than involucral bracts. Fruit appears as a rough-ridged achene with a parachute of brown capillary bristles. Mowing at regular intervals is the best solution, starting when flowers first appear.

Yellow salsify.

WEEDS BY COMMON NAME

Aaron's rod . . . . see common mullein
Agave . . . . *Agave lecheguilla*
Amomum . . . . see iris
Annual knawel . . . . *Scleranthus annuus*
Annual meadow-grass . . . . *Poa annua*
Annual ryegrass . . . . *Lolium multiflorum*
Annual sunflower . . . . see sunflower
Argentina bahia grass . . . . Arisaema genus, several species
Arrow-leaved wild lettuce . . . . Lactura genus, several species
Arrowhead . . . . *Sagittaria latifolia*
Autumn crocus . . . . Colchicum genus, several species
Autumnal hawkbit . . . . *Leontodon autumnalis*
Baby's breath flower . . . . *Gypsophila paniculata*
Bachelor's button . . . . *Centaurea cyanus*
Baconweed . . . . see lambsquarters
Bahama grass . . . . see Bermuda grass
Ball mustard . . . . *Neslia paniculata*
Balloonvine . . . . *Cardiospermum haliccacabum*
Barnaby's thistle . . . . *Centaurea solstitialis*
Barnyard grass . . . . *Echinochloa crusgalli*
Bay laurel . . . . *Umbellularia californica*
Beaked hawksbeard . . . . *Crepis taraxacifolia*
Bear bind . . . . see wild buckwheat
Bedstraw . . . . *Galium aparine*
Bee nettle . . . . see henbit
Beggarticks . . . . *Bidens frondosa*
Bent awn . . . . *Erianthus contortus*
Bent grass . . . . Agrostis genus, several species
Bermuda grass . . . . *Cymodon dactylon*
Big taper . . . . see common mullein
Bindweed . . . . *Convolvulus arvensis*
Bindweed . . . . *Convolvulus repens*
Bindweed . . . . see field bindweed
Bird's foot trefoil . . . . *Lotus corniculatus*
Bitterweed . . . . *Helenium tenuifolium*
Black bent . . . . *Alopecurus agrestis*

Black bindweed . . . . *Polygonum convolvulus*
Black cohosh . . . . *Cimicifuga racemosa*
Black haw. . . . . *Viburnum prunifolium*
Black nightshade . . . . *Solanum nigrum*
Blackseed plantain . . . . *Plantago rugelii*
Bladder campion . . . . *Silene inflata*
Bladder cherry . . . . see ground cherry
Bladder ketmia. . . . . see flower-of-an-hour
Blind nettle . . . . see henbit
Bloodroot. . . . . *Sanguinaria canadensis*
Blowball. . . . . see dandelion
Blue bur. . . . . *Lappula echinata*
Blue gum . . . . see eucalyptus
Blue sunflower . . . . see blueweed
Blueweed . . . . *Helianthus ciliaris*
Boneset . . . . *Eupatorium perfoliatum*
Bouncing bet . . . . *Saponaria officinalis*
Bracken . . . . *Pteridium acquilinum*
Bracken fern. . . . . *Pteris aquilina*
Bracted plantain. . . . . *Plantago aristata*
Bristly foxtail . . . . *Setaria verticillata*
Bristly starbur. . . . . *Acanthospermum hispidum*
Broad dock. . . . . *Rumex obtusisfolius*
Broadleaf dock . . . . *Rumex obtusifolius*
Broadleaf signal grass . . . . *Brachiaria platyphylla*
Broom brush . . . . see scotch brush
Broom sedge. . . . . *Andropogon virginicus*
Broomweed . . . . *Amphiachyris dracuniculoides*
Brown-eyed Susan . . . . see flower-of-an-hour
Browntop panicum . . . . *Panicum fasciculatum*
Buckbrush . . . . *Symphoricarpos orbiculatus*
Buckhorn plantain . . . . see ribbed plantain
Buckwheat . . . . *Polygonum convolvulus*
Buffalo bur. . . . . see prickly nightshade
Buffalo gourd. . . . . *Cucurbita foetidissima*
Buffalo gourd. . . . . *Pepo foetidissima*
Buffalo grass. *Buchloo dactyloides*
Buffaloweed . . . . see giant ragweed
Bulbous buttercup . . . . *Ranunculus bulbosus*
Bull nettle . . . . see Carolina nightshade
Bull thistle . . . . *Cirsium lanceolatum*
Bull thistle . . . . *Cirsium vulgare*

Bullhead. . . . . see puncture vine
Bur cucumber . . . . *Sicyos angulatus*
Bur marsh elder . . . . *Iva xanthifolia*
Bur ragweed . . . . *Franseria tomentosa*
Burdock. . . . . *Arctium lappa*
Burning bush . . . . see kochia
Burnut. . . . . see puncture vine
Butter-and-eggs . . . . .see toadflax
Buttercup. . . . . *Ranunculus acris*
Butterprint. . . . . .see velvetleaf
Buttonweed . . . . *Diodia teres*
Calabagilla . . . . see buffalo gourd
Caltrop. . . . . see puncture vine
Camomile . . . . *Matricaria chamomilla*
Canada fleabane. . . . . *Erigeron canadensis*
Canada goldenrod . . . . *Solidago canadensis*
Canada thistle . . . . *Cirsium arvense*
Candlewick . . . . see common mullein
Cankerwort . . . . see dandelion
Caper spurge .Euphorbia genus, several species
Careless weed . . . . see green amaranthum
Carolina nightshade. . . . . *Solanum carolinense*
Carpetweed . . . . *Mollugo verticillata*
Cascara segrada . . . .*Rhamnus purshiana*
Cat's ear . . . . *Hypochaeris radicata*
Catnip herb . . . .*Nepeta cataria*
Cattails. . . . . *Typha latifolia*
Celandine. . . . . .Chelidonium genus, several species
Chaparral. . . . .*Larrea tridentata*
Chaparral. . . . . *Larrea mexicana*
Charlock . . . . *Brassica arvensis*
Cheat. . . . . *Bromus secalinus*
Cheat grass. . . . . *Bromus tectorum*
Cheeses . . . . see roundleaf mallow
Cherokee rose. . . . . *Rosa bracteata*
Chervil. . . . . *Chaerophyllum procumbens*
Chess . . . . .see cheat
Chickweed . . . . *Stellaria media*
Chicory . . . .*Cichorium intybus*
Chili coyote . . . . see buffalo gourd
Chinese lettuce. . . . . see prickly lettuce
Chives . . . . see wild onion

Chou grass . . . . see lambsquarters
Chrysanthemum . . . .*Chrysanthemum morifolium*
Cinquefoil . . . . .Potentilla genus, several species
Clammy. . . . . ground cherry see ground cherry
Cleavers . . . . *Galium aparine*
Climbing bindweed . . . . .see wild buckwheat
Climbing false buckwheat . . . . see hedge bindweed
Climbing milkweed . . . . *Gonolobus laevis*
Clotbur . . . . see cocklebur
Cocklebur . . . . Xanthium genus, several species
Cocksfoot panicum . . . . .see barnyard grass
Cockspur grass. . . . . .see barnyard grass
Coltsfoot . . . . *Tussilago farfara*
Common burdock . . . . *Arctium minus*
Common chickweed . . . . .see chickweed
Common cocklebur. . . . . see cocklebur
Common dandelion. . . . . see dandelion
Common horehound. . . . .*Marrubium vulgare*
Common milkweed . . . . see climbing milkweed
Common morning glory .see wild morning glory
Common mullein. . . . . *Verbascum thapsus*
Common peppergrass. . . . .*Lepidium virginicum*
Common purslane . . . . see purslane
Common ragweed . . . . *Ambrosia artemisiifolia*
Common sunflower. . . . . see sunflower
Common wild thistle . . . . see prickly lettuce
Compass plant . . . . see prickly lettuce
Coneflower. . . . . *Echinacea angustifolia*
Confederate violet . . . . Viola genus, several species
Coralberry . . . . .see buckbrush
Corn buttercup . . . .*Ranunculus arvensis*
Corn camomile . . . . *Anthemis arvensis*
Corn campanula. . . . . *Legousia hybrida*
Corn cockle . . . . *Lychnis githago*
Corn cockle . . . .*Agrostemma githago*
Corn gromwell. . . . . *Lithospermum arvense*
Corn growwell . . . .*Veronica persica*
Corn marigold . . . . *Chrysanthemum segetum*
Corn mint . . . .*Mentha arvensis*
Corn sowthistle . . . . *Sonchus arvensis*
Cornbud . . . . .see wild buckwheat
Couchgrass. . . . . .see quackgrass

Creeping bindweed .... see hedge bindweed
Creeping buttercup .... *Ranunculus repens*
Creeping jenny.......................... *Convolvulus arvensis*
Creeping thistle .... *Chenopodium arvense*
Creeping thistle .... *Cirsium arvense*
Crested wheatgrass .... *Agropyron cristatum*
Crotalarea.......................... *Crotalaria spectabilis*
Cuckoo flower .... see meadow pink
Cudweed .... *Filago germanica*
Curled dock.......................... *Rumex crispus*
Curly .... see curly dock
Curly dock.......................... *Rumex crispus*
Curly leaf dock.......................... see curly dock
Cut-leaf geranium .... *Geranium dissectum*
Cypress spurge .... *Galarrhoeus cyparissias*
Daisy .... *Bellis perennis*
Daisy .... *Chrysanthemum leucanthemum pinnatifidum*
Dallis grass.......................... *Paspalum dilatatum*
Dandelion .... *Taraxacum officinale*
Dandelion .... *Taraxacum vulgare*
Darnel .... *Lolium temulentum*
Dayflower.......................... *Commelina* genus, several species
Dead nettle .... see henbit
Death camas.......................... *Zigadenus* genus, several species
Devil grass .... see Bermuda grass
Devil's club.......................... *Oplopanax horridum*
Devil's paint brush .... *Hieracium aurantiacum*
Dock .... see red sorrel
Dodder.......................... *Cuscuta pentagona*
Dodder.......................... *Cuscuta* genus, several species
Dog daisy.......................... *Chrysanthemum leucanthemum*
Dog fennel.......................... see mayweed
Dogbane .... *Apocynum cannabinum*
Dogtooth grass.......................... see Bermuda grass
Door-head clock.......................... see dandelion
Dove's foot.......................... *Geranium molle*
Downy brome .... see cheat grass
Downy chess .... see cheat grass
Dropseed .... *Sporobolus neglectus*
Dungweed .... see lambsquarters
Dwarf black sumac.......................... see poison sumac
Dwarf spurge .... *Euphorbia exigua*

Echinacea . . . . *Echinacea angustifolia*
Elder flower . . . . Sambucus genus, several species
English thistle . . . . see prickly lettuce
Eucalyptus . . . . *Eucalyptus globulus*
Eyebright . . . . *Euphrasia officinalis*
Facelis . . . . *Panicum dichotomiflerum*
Fall panicum . . . . *Panicum dichotomiflorum*
False brome . . . . *Brachypodium sylbaticum*
False hellebore . . . . *Veratum veride*
Fat hen . . . . see lambsquarters
Feverweed . . . . see Joe-Pye weed
Field alkanet . . . . *Lycopsis arvensis*
Field bindweed . . . . *Convolvulus arvensis*
Field forget-me-not . . . . *Myosotis arvensis*
Field madder . . . . *Sheradia arvensis*
Field mustard . . . . *Brassica sinapis*
Field pansy . . . . *Viola tricolor*
Field peppergrass . . . . *Lepidium campestre*
Field sandbur . . . . see sandbur
Field scabious . . . . *Scabious arvensis*
Field speedwell . . . . *Veronica agrestis*
Field speedwell . . . . *Veronica officinalis*
Field thistle . . . . see pasture thistle
Flannel leaf . . . . see common mullein
Fleabane . . . . *Erigeron ramosus*
Flixweed . . . . see tansy mustard
Florida beggarweed . . . . *Desmodium tortiasum*
Florida purslane . . . . *Richardia scabra*
Flower-of-an-hour . . . . *Hibiscus trionum*
Flowered peppergrass . . . . *Lepidium apetalum*
Flowering spurge . . . . *Euphorbia corollata*
Flowering spurge . . . . *Euphorbia escula*
Forget-me-not . . . . *Myosotis arvensis*
Fox sedge . . . . *Carex vulpinoidea*
Foxglove . . . . Digitalis genus, several species
Foxtail . . . . see giant foxtail
Foxtail barley . . . . *Hordeum jubatum*
Frenchweed . . . . see pennycress
Frostbite . . . . see lambsquarters
Fumitory . . . . *Fumaria officinalis*
Galinsoga . . . . *Galinsoga ciliata*
Garden nightshade . . . . see black nightshade

Garlic . . . . *Allium vineale*
Geranium . . . . *Geranium molle*
Geranium . . . . *Geranium pratense*
Geranium . . . . *Geranium pusillum*
Giant foxtai . . . . *Setaria faberi*
Giant ragweed . . . . *Ambrosia trifida*
Ginseng . . . . *Panax quinquefolium*
Giraffe head . . . . see henbit
Girasole . . . . see Jerusalem artichoke
Goatgrass . . . . *Aegilops cylindrica*
Goathead . . . . see puncture vine
Goatsbeard . . . . .see purple-flowered oyster
Goldenrod . . . . *Solidago canadensis*
Goldenrod . . . . Solidago genus, several species
Goldenseal . . . . *Hydrastis canadensis*
Goosegrass . . . . *Eleusine indica*
Goosegrass . . . . *Galium aparine*
Goosegrass plantain . . . . *Eleusine indica*
Gourd vine . . . . see buffalo gourd
Great mullein . . . . see common mullein
Greater knapweed . . . . *Centaurea scabiosa*
Greater plantain . . . . Plantago genus, several species
Green amaranth . . . . *Amaranthus hybridus*
Green bristlegrass . . . . Setaria viridis
Green flowered peppergrass . . . . *Lepidium apetalum*
Grindella . . . . see gumweed
Ground burnut . . . . see puncture vine
Ground cherry . . . . *Physalis hetrophylla*
Groundsel . . . . *Senecio vulgaris*
Gumweed . . . . *Grindella squarrosa*
Hardhead . . . . *Centaruea nigra*
Hare's ear mustard . . . . *Conringia orientalis*
Hawkweed .Hieracium genus, several species
Heavy sedge . . . . *Carex gravida*
Hedge bindweed . . . . *Convolvulus sepium*
Hedge mustard . . . .*Sisymbrium officinale*
Hedge table . . . . see common mullein
Helen's tear plant . . . . *Inula helenium*
Hellebore . . . . *Veratrum viride*
Hemlock . . . . *Conium maculatum*
Hemp . . . . *Cannabis sativa*
Henbit . . . . *Lamium amplexicaule*

Hoary cress . . . .*Lepidium draba*
Hoary plantain . . . . *Plantago media*
Hoary vervain . . . .*Verbena stricta*
Hogweed . . . .*Heracleum sphondylium*
Hop clover . . . .*Medicago lupulina*
Horse elder . . . . *Inula helenium*
Horse nettle . . . . see Carolina nightshade
Horse thistle . . . . see prickly lettuce
Horsebush . . . . see horseweed
Horsebrush . . . . Tetradymia genus, several species
Horseshoe vetch . . . . *Hippocrepis comosa*
Horsetail . . . . *Equisetum arvense*
Horseweed . . . . see Canada fleabane
Huckleberry foliage . . . .*Vaccinium ovatum*
Huffcaps . . . . *Aira caepitosa*
Indian hemp .see dogbane, see also hemp
Indian mallow . . . . .see velvetleaf
Indian mustard . . . . *Brassica juncea*
Iris . . . .*Viola odorata*
Ironweed . . . . Veronica genus, several species
Itchgrass . . . . *Rottboellia exaltata*
Ivy bindweed . . . . .see wild buckwheat
Ivy-leaf speedwell . . . . *Veronica hederaefolia*
Jacob's staff . . . . see common mullein
Japanese bromegrass . . . .*Bromus japonicus*
Japanese hedge parsley . . . .*Aethusa cynapium*
Jerusalem artichoke . . . . *Helianthus tuberosus*
Jesuit tea . . . . see wormwood
Jim McHale's weed . . . . see Pennsylvania smartweed
Jimson weed . . . .*Datura stramonium*
Joe-Pye weed . . . . *Eupatorium purpureum*
Johnson grass . . . .*Sorghum halepense*
Jointed goatgrass . . . . see goatgrass
Junglerice . . . .*Echinochloa colonum*
Kochia . . . . *Kochia scoparia*
Knapweed . . . .*Centaurea nigra*
Knot bindweed . . . . .see wild buckwheat
Knotgrass . . . .*Paspalum distichum*
Knotgrass . . . . *Polygonum aviculare*
Knotroot foxtail . . . . *Setaria geniculata*
Köku . . . . see iris
Kudzu . . . . *Pueraria lobata*

Lagoonweed. . . . . see bur ragweed
Lady's mantle . . . . *Alchemilla arvensis*
Lady's purse . . . . see shepherd's purse
Lady's smock . . . . *Cardamine pratensis*
Ladysthumb. . . . . see spotted knotweed
Lamb's lettuce. . . . . *Valerianella olitoria*
Lambsquarters . . . . *Chenopodium album*
Lambsquarters . . . . *Brassica sinapis*
Lantana . . . .*Lactuca scariola*
Lanternweed. . . . . .see ground cherry
Large bracted plantain . . . . .see greater plantain
Large bracted verbena. . . . . see prostrate vervain
Large field speedwell. . . . . *Veronica tournefortii*
Larkspur. . . . . Delphinium genus, several species
Leafy spurge. . . . .*Euphorbia esula*
Lechugiulla. Agave genus, several species
Leek. . . . . see wild onion
Lion's tooth . . . . see dandelions
Little barley . . . .*Hordeum pusillum*
Lobelia herb. . . . .*Lobelia inflata*
Loco. . . . . *Oxytropis lambertii*
Loco weed . . . . see wolly loco
Lousewort . . . . .Pedicularis genus, several species
Lovegrass . . . . see stinkgrass
Mallow. . . . . *Malva neglecta*
Man-of-the-earth . . . . see wild potato vine
Mandrake. . . . . *Podophyllum peltatum*
Mare's tail. . . . . see Canada fleabane
Marigold, corn . . . . *Chrysanthemum segetum*
Marijuana. . . . . see hemp
Marsh cudweed . . . . *Gnaphalium uliginosum*
Marsh elder . . . . .see burweed marsh elder
Marsh mallow . . . . see mallow
Mary Jane. . . . . see hemp
Mat spurge. *Euphorbia glyptosperma*
Matrimony grass . . . . see stinkgrass
Mayapple. . . . .*Podophllum peltatum*
Maypop. . . . . *Passiflora incarnata*
Mayweed . . . .*Anthemis cotula*
Meadow fescue. . . . . *Festuca elatior*
Meadow pink. . . . . *Lychnis floscuculi*
Meadowsweet. . . . . Spiraea genus, several species

Mealweed..................................... see lambsquarters
Mexican firewood.................................see kochia
Mexican tea .... see wormwood
Mild water pepper ....*Polygonum hydropiperoides*
Milk spurge ....see spotted spurge
Milk thistle.............................. see prickly lettuce
Milk witch .... see dandelion
Milkweed.................... Ascelepias genus, several species
Milkwort .... *Polygala vulgaris*
Missouri goldenrod ....*Solidago glaberrima*
Mock cypress ....see kochia
Mormon tea................................. *Ephedra nevadensis*
Morning glory .... *Convolvulus arvensis*
Morning glory ....*Ipomoea hederacea*
Morning glory .... see hedge bindweed
Morning glory ....see wild morning glory
Mother's heart .... see shepherd's purse
Mouse-ear-chickweed.................... *Cerastium vulgatum*
Mouse-ear-hawkweed...................... *Hieracium pilosella*
Muckweed .... see lambsquarters
Mullein ....*Verbascum thapsiforme*
Mullein .... see common mullein
Musk thistle............................ *Carduus nutans*
Mustard .... Brassica genus, several species
Mustard .... *Sinapis arvensis*
Narrow leaf dock ....see curly dock
Narrow-leaf sneezeweed ....see bitterweed
Nettle...................... Urtica genus, several species
Nightshade............................ see silverleaf nightshade
Nipplewort........................... *Lapsana communis*
Nutsedge .... see purple nut sedge
Nutsedge .... see yellow nut sedge
Nutshade .... *Cyperus esculentus*
Onions..................................*Allium canadense*
Orache............................ *Atriplex patula*
Orchard grass............................ *Dactylis glomerata*
Oregon grape............................*Berberis aquifolium*
Orrisroot .... see iris
Oxeye daisy .... see daisy
Oysterplant ....see yellow salsify
Pale poppy............................ *Papaver argemone*
Palmer amaranth ....see green amaranth

Papaver. . . . . see poppy
Panic grass . . . . see barnyard grass
Parsley fern. . . . . *Petroselinum sativum*
Partridge pea . . . . *Cassis fasciculata*
Passion flower herb. . . . . *Passiflora caerulea*
Pasture thistle. . . . . *Cirsium altissimum*
Pencil tree. . . . . Euphorbia genus, several species
Pennsylvania smartweed . . . . *Polygonum pensylvanicum*
Pennycress . . . . *Thlaspi arvense*
Pennywort . . . . Hydrocotyle genus, several species
Pepper plant. . . . . see shepherd's purse
Peppergrass. . . . . Lepidium genus, several species
Perennial bristlegrass. *Setaria geniculate*
Perennial lettuce. . . . . see wild blue lettuce
Perennial peppergrass . . . . see hoary cress
Perennial ragweed. see Western ragweed
Perennial ryegrass . . . . *Lolium perenne*
Persecaria . . . . Polygonum genus, many species
Petty spurge . . . . *Euphorbia peplus*
Pignut . . . . *Conopodium denudatum*
Pigweed . . . . Amaranthus genus, several species
Pigweed . . . . see redroot pigweed
Pineapple weed. *Matricaria suaveolens*
Pitseed goosefoot . . . . see lambsquarters
Plains sunflower . . . . *Helianthus petiolaris*
Plantain . . . . Plantago genus, several species
Poinsettia . . . . Euphorbia genus, several species
Poison ivy. . . . . *Rhus radicans*
Poison oak . . . . *Rhus quercifolia*
Poison oak . . . . Rhus toxicodendron quercifolium
Poison sumac . . . . *Rhus copallina*
Pokeweed . . . . Phytolacca genus, several species
Pondweed. . . . . Potamogeton genus, several species
Poorjoe. . . . . *Diodia teres*
Poppy. . . . . *Papaver argemone*
Poppy. . . . . *Argemone intermedia*
Poverty weed . . . . see broom sedge
Prairie berry . . . . see silverleaf night
Prairie rose . . . . *Rosa suffulta*
Prairie sunflower. *Helianthus petiolaris*
Prickly glasswort . . . . see Russian thistle
Prickly lettuce. . . . . Lactuca genus, several species

Prickly nightshade . . . . *Solanum rostratum*
Prickly pear . . . . *Opuntia humifusa*
Prickly pear .Echinocereus genus, several species
Prickly pear . . . . Neomammilaragenus, several species
Prickly pear . . . . Opuntia genus, several species
Prickly sida. . . . .*Sida spinosa*
Prince's pine herb . . . . *Chimaphila umbellate*
Prostrate knotweed. . . . . Polygonum genus, several species
Prostrate pigweed . . . .*Amaranthus blitoides*
Prostrate spurge . . . . *Euphorbia supina*
Prostrate vervain. . . . . .Verbena genus, several species
Puffball. . . . . see dandelion
Pumpkin vine. . . . . see buffalo gourd
Puncture vine . . . . *Tribulus terrestris*
Puncture weed . . . . see puncture vine
Purging flax . . . . *Linum catharticum*
Purple cockle . . . . see corn cockle
Purple coneflower. . . . . Echinacea genus, several species
Purple nut sedge. . . . . *Cyperus rotundus*
Purple-flowered oyster . . . . .Tragopogon genus, several species
Purple-stemmed plantain . . . . .see blackseed plantain
Purslane . . . . *Portulaca olenacca*
Purslane speedwell . . . . *Veronica peregrina*
Pursley . . . . see purslane
Pursley duckweed. . . . . see purslane
Pussley . . . . see purslane
Pussywillow . . . .*Salix nigra*
Quackgrass. . . . . *Agropyron repens*
Quaker grass. . . . . *Briza maxima*
Ragged robin . . . . *Lychnis floscuculi*
Ragweed. . . . . Ambrosia genus, several species
Ramsons. . . . .*Allium ursinum*
Red amaranth. . . . . .see green amaranth
Red bartsia . . . . *Bartsia odontites*
Red belvedere. . . . . see kochia
Red campion . . . . *Lychnis dioica*
Red deadnettle . . . . *Lamium purpureum*
Red poppy . . . .*Papaver rhoeas*
Red rice . . . . *Oryza sativa*
Red sorrel. . . . . *Rumex acetosella*
Redroot pigweed . . . .*Amaranthus retroflexus*
Redvine . . . .*Brunnichia cirrhosa*

Rest harrow . . . . *Onomis repens*
Ribbed plantain . . . . *Plantago lanceolata*
Red sprangletop . . . . *Leptochloa filiformis*
Ribwort plantain . . . . *Plantago lanceolata*
Rice cutgrass. . . . . *Leersia oryzoides*
Rose bay. . . . . *Chyrsanthemum morifolium*
Rough daisy . . . . see fleabane
Rough pigweed. . . . . see green amaranth
Round-leaved toadflax . . . . *Linaria spuria*
Rugel . . . . see blackseed plantain
Russian cactus . . . . see Russian thistle
Russian knapweed . . . . *Centauren repens*
Russian thistle . . . . *Salsola kali*
Ryegrass . . . . Elymus genus, several species
Sage . . . . *Artemisia vulgaris*
Sage grass . . . . *Artemisia fugida*
Salsify. . . . . see purple flowered oyster
Salt grass . . . . *Distichlis stricta*
Saltwort . . . . see Russian thistle
Sand briar. . . . . see silverleaf nightshade
Sand sunflower. . . . . see plains sunflower
Sandbur . . . . *Cenchrus pauciflorus*
Sandvine . . . . see climbing milkweed
Sandwort . . . . *Arenaria serpyllifolia*
Sassafras rootbark. . . . . *Sassafras albidum*
Satin flower . . . . see chickweed
Saw palmetto . . . . *Serenoa serrulata*
Saw palmetto berries . . . . *Serenoa repens*
Scabious. . . . . *Scaiosa arvensis*
Scarlet pimpernel . . . . *Anagallis arvensis*
Scentless mayweed . . . . *Matricaria inodora*
Scotch broom. . . . . *Cytisus scoparius*
Scutch grass . . . . see bermuda grass
Sedge . . . . see broom sedge
Sedge . . . . see fox sedge
Sedge . . . . see heavy sedge
Selfheal. . . . . *Prunella vulgaris*
Shattercane. . . . . *Sorghum bicolor*
Shave grass . . . . see horsetail
Sheep's sorrel . . . . see red sorrel
Shepherd's needle . . . . *Scandix pecten*
Shepherd's pouch . . . . see shepherd's purse

Shepherd's purse. . . . . *Capsella bursapastoris*
Shoo-fly . . . . see flower-of-an-hour
Sickle grass . . . . *Parapholis incurva*
Sickle pod . . . . *Ajuga replans*
Sickle pod . . . . *Cassia obtusifolia*
Silver crabgrass. . . . . see goosegrass
Silver horsenettle . . . . see silverleaf nightshade
Silverleaf nightshade. . . . . *Solanum claeagnifolium*
Silverweed . . . . *Potentilla anserina*
Skunkgrass. . . . . see stinkgrass
Slender fescue. . . . . *Festuca octoflora*
Slender foxtail . . . . *Alopecurus agrestis*
Slender nettle . . . . see stinging nettle
Small crane's bill. . . . . *Geranium pusillum*
Small nettle . . . . *Urtica urens*
Smallflower Galinsoga . . . . *Galinsoga parviflora*
Smartweed . . . . *Polygonum pennsylvanicum*
Smooth sumac . . . . *Rhus glabra*
Snow-on-the-mountain . . . . *Euphorbia marginata*
Snow-on-the-mountain . . . . *Lepadena marginata*
Soft brome . . . . *Bromus mollis*
Soft crane's bill . . . . *Geranium molle*
Sorrel . . . . see sheep's sorrel
Sow thistle . . . . Sonchus genus, several species
Spanish needle . . . . *Bidens bipinnata*
Spleen amaranth. . . . . see green amaranth
Spotted knotweed. . . . . *Polygonum persicaria*
Spotted spurge . . . . *Euphorbia maculata*
Spotted spurge . . . . *Chamaesyce maculata*
Spring amaranth. . . . . *Amaranthus spinosus*
Spurge . . . . Euphorbia genus, several species
Spurry . . . . *Spergula arvensis*
Squirreltail . . . . *Sitanion hystrix*
St. Augustine . . . . *Paspartum distichum*
St. James weed . . . . see shepherd's purse
St. Johnswort . . . . *Hypericum perforatum*
Starweed. . . . . see chickweed
Starwort . . . . see chickweed
Stemless loco . . . . .see loco
Stinging nettle . . . . *Urtica procera*
Stinkgrass. . . . . *Eragrostis cilianensisi*
Stinking mayweed . . . . *Anthemis cotula*

Stinking Willie. . . . . *Senecio jacobaea*
Sulfur cinquefoil. . . . .*Potentilla recta*
Summer cypress . . . . see kochia
Sun spurge . . . . *Euphorbia helioscopia*
Sundews. . . . . *Drosea rotundifolia*
Sunflower. . . . .*Helianthus annuus*
Swamp smartweed . . . . *Polygonum coccineum pratincolum*
Swampy horsetail . . . . see horsetail
Sweet birch. . . . .*Betula lenta*
Swinecress . . . . *Senebiera coronopus*
Tall buttercup. . . . . *Ranunculus acris*
Tall thistle . . . . see pasture thistle
Tansy . . . . *Chrysanthemum segetum*
Tansy . . . .*Tanacetum vulgare*
Tansy aster . . . . *Machaeranthera tanacelifolia*
Tansy mustard . . . . *Descurainia intermedia*
Tansy ragwort. . . . . *Senecio jacobaea*
Tarweed. . . . . see gumweed
Teaweed. . . . . *Chenopodium ambrosioides*
Texas croton. . . . .*Croton texensis*
Texas panicum . . . . *Panicum texanum*
Thistle . . . . Circium genus, several species
Thyme. . . . .*Thymus vulgaris*
Thyme-leaved sandwort . . . . *Arenaria serpyllifolia*
Thyme-leaved speedwell. . . . . *Veronica serpyllifolia*
Tickle grass. . . . . *Aristida dichotoma*
Toadflax . . . .*Linaria vulgaris*
Toothed spurge. . . . .*Euphorbia dentata*
Torch plant. . . . . see common mullein
Torches. . . . . see common mullein
Trompillo. . . . . see silverleaf nightshade
Trumpet vine . . . . *Campsis radicans*
Trumpet Creeper . . . . *Campsis radicans*
Tufted vetch. . . . .*Vicia cracca*
Tumbleweed (pigweed style). . . . . *Amaranthus albus*
Tumbleweed. . . . . .see Russian thistle
Tumbleweed. . . . . see white pigweed
Turnip weed . . . . *Rapistrum rugosum*
Upright spurge . . . .*Euphorbia hysopifolia*
Velvet dock. . . . . see common mullein
Velvet mullein . . . . see common mullein
Velvet plant . . . . see common mullein

Velvetleaf . . . . *Abutilon theophrasti*
Venice mallow . . . . see flower-of-an-hour
Venus looking glass . . . . *Specularia perfoliata*
Verbena . . . . see hoary vervain
Vetch . . . . Vicia genus, several species
Vinegrass . . . . .see Bermuda grass
Volunteer barley. . . . . *Hordeum vulgare*
Volunteer wheat . . . . *Triticum aestivum*
Volunteer rye . . . . *Secale cereale*
Wall speedwell . . . . *Veronica arvensis*
Water hyacinth. *Eichornia crassipes*
Watercress . . . .*Nasturtium officinale*
Watergrass . . . . .see barnyard grass
Western ragweed . . . . Ambrosia genus, several species
Western wheatgrass .see wheatgrass
Wheatgrass. . . . .*Agropyron cristatum*
White avens . . . . *Geum album*
White campion . . . . *Lychnis vespertina*
White goosefoot. . . . . see lambsquarters
White horsenettle. . . . . see silverleaf nightshade
White mullein . . . .*Verbascum thapsiforme*
White mustard. . . . . *Brassica alba*
White oak bark . . . . Querus genus, several species
White pigweed. . . . . see lambsquarters
White prickly poppy . . . .*Argemone intermedia*
White snakeroot. . . . .*Eupatorium* genus, several species
White top. . . . . see hoary cress
Wild alfalfa. . . . . *Psoralea floribunda*
Wild barley . . . .*Hordeum jubatum*
Wild barley . . . . *Hordeum nodosum*
Wild blue lettuce . . . .*Lactuca pulchella*
Wild buckwheat. . . . . *Polygonum convolvulus*
Wild camomile. *Matricaria chamomilla*
Wild cane. . . . .*Sorghum bicolor*
Wild carrot. . . . . *Daucus carota*
Wild cherry . . . . *Prunus avium*
Wild cherry bark . . . . *Prunus serotina*
Wild chervil . . . . *Anthriscus sylvestris*
Wild cucumber . . . .*Echinocystis lobata*
Wild garlic. . . . .*Allium vineale*
Wild ginger . . . . Zingiber genus, several species
Wild gourd. . . . . see buffalo gourd

Wild grape . . . . *Vitus lambrusca*
Wild indigo . . . . *Baptisia tinctoria*
Wild larkspur . . . . Delphinium genus, several species
Wild lettuce . . . . Lactuca genus, several species
Wild mignonette . . . . *Reseda lutea*
Wild millet. . . . . see yellow foxtail
Wild morning glory . . . . *Ipomoea purpurea*
Wild mustard. . . . . *Brassica kaber*
Wild oats . . . . *Avena fatua*
Wild onion. . . . . *Allium canadense, Allium vineale*
Wild onion. . . . . see garlic
Wild opium . . . . see prickly lettucue
Wild pansy. . . . . *Viola tricolor*
Wild portulaca . . . . see purslane
Wild potato vine . . . . *Ipomoea pandurata*
Wild proso millet . . . . *Panicum miliaceum*
Wild pumpkin . . . . see buffalo gourd
Wild radish . . . . *Raphanus raphanistrum*
Wild rye. . . . . Elymus genus, several species
Wild spinach . . . . see lambsquarters
Wild strawberry . . . . *Fragaria virginiana*
Wild sunflower. . . . . see sunflower
Wildflowers . . . . Various species
Willowweed . . . . *Polygonum persecaria*
Wind witch . . . . see Russian thistle
Winter vetch . . . . *Vicia villosa*
Wintergreen herb . . . . *Gaultheria procumbens*
Winterweed . . . . see chickweed
Wiregrass . . . . see goosegrass, see also Bermuda grass
Wirestem muhly. . . . . *Muhlenbergia frondosa*
Witch Gowan. . . . . see dandelion
Witchgrass . . . . *Panicum capillare*
Woolly cupgrass . . . . *Eriochloa villosa*
Woolly croton . . . . *Croton capitatus*
Woolly loco . . . . *Astragalus mollissimus*
Wormseed . . . . *Cagnopodium ambrosioides*
Wormwood . . . . *Chenopodium ambrosioides*
Yardgrass . . . . see goosegrass
Yarrow . . . . *Achillea millefolium*
Yellow bristlegrass. . . . . see yellow foxtail
Yellow camomile . . . . *Anthemis tinctoria*
Yellow clover . . . . *Trifolium agrarium*

WEEDS BY SCIENTIFIC NAME

Abutilon theophrasti. . . . . velvetleaf, Indian mallow, butterprint
Acanthospermum hispidum . . . . bristly starbur
Achillea millefolium. . . . . yarrow flora
Aegilops cylindrica . . . . goatgrass, jointed goatgrass
Aethusa cynapium . . . . Japanese hedge parsley
Agave lecheguilla . . . . agave
Agropyron cristatum. . . . . .crested wheatgrass
Agropyron repens . . . . Portulaca oleracea
Agropyron repens . . . . quackgrass, couchgrass, crested wheatgrass
Agropyron smithii . . . . .wheatgrass, western wheatgrass
Agrostemma githago. . . . . corn cockle, purple cockle
Agrostis genus and several species. bent grass
Aira caepitosa . . . . huffcaps
Ajuga replans. . . . . sickle pod
Alchemilla arvensis . . . . .lady's mantle
Allium genus, several species. . . . . wild onion, garlic, leek, chives
Allium canadense. . . . . wild onion, garlic
Allium ursinum. . . . . ramsons
Allium vineale. . . . . wild garlic, wild onion
Alopecurus agrestis . . . . .black bent
Alopecurus agrestis . . . . .slender foxtail
Amaranthus albus . . . . tumbleweed
Amaranthus blitoides . . . . prostrate pigweed
Amaranthus genus, several species . . . . pigweed
Amaranthus graecizans. . . . . white pigweed, tumbleweed
Amaranthus hybridus. . . . . .green, palmer, spleen, and red amaranth,
                                              carelessweed, rough pigweed
Amaranthus retroflexus. . . . . .redroot pigweed, pigweed
Amaranthus spinosus . . . . spring amaranth
Amaryllis genus, several species. Amaryllis
Ambrosia artemisiifolia . . . . common ragweed
Ambrosia coronopifolia. . . . . .Western ragweed, perennial ragweed
Ambrosia elatior . . . . ragweed
Ambrosia psilostachya. . . . . ragweed, Western ragweed
Ambrosia trifida .giant ragweed, buffaloweed
Amphiachyris dracunculoides . . . . broomweed

Anagallis arvensis. . . . . scarlet pimpernel
Andropogon virginicus . . . . .broom sedge, poverty weed
Anthemis arvensis . . . . corn camomile
Anthemis cotula. . . . . mayweed, dog fennel, stinking mayweed
Anthemis tinctoria. . . . . .yellow camomile
Anthriscus sylvestris . . . . .wild chervil
Apocynum cannabinum . . . . dogbane, Indian hemp
Arctium lappa . . . . burdock
Arctium minus . . . . .common burdock
Arenaria serpyllifolia . . . . .sandwort, thyme-leaved sandwort
Argemone intermedia. . . . . white prickly poppy, poppy
Arisaema genus, several species . . . . Argentina bahia grass
Aristida dichotoma . . . . tickle grass
Arsium arvense . . . . .creeping thistle
Artemisia fugida . . . . sage grass
Artemisia vulgaris . . . . sage
Asclepias currassavica. . . . . milkweed
Astragalus genus. . . . . There are some 300 species of Astragalus
Astragalus mollissimus . . . . woolly loco, loco weed
Atriplex patula . . . . orache
Avena fatua. . . . . .wild oats
Baptisia tinctoria. . . . . .wild indigo
Barbarea vulgaris. . . . . yellow rocket
Bartsia odontites . . . . .red bartsia
Berberis aquifolium . . . . Oregon grape
Betula lenta. . . . . sweet birch
Bidens bipinnata. . . . . Spanish needle
Bidens frondosa . . . . beggarticks
Brachiaria platyphylla . . . . broadleaf signal grass
Brachypodium sylbaticum. . . . . .false brome
Brassica alba . . . . white mustard
Brassica arvensis . . . . .charlock, mustard
Brassica juncea . . . . .Indian mustard
Brassica kaber . . . . wild mustard
Brassica sinapis . . . . .charlock, field mustard
Bromus japonicus. . . . . Japanese bromegrass
Bromus mollis . . . . soft brome
Bromus secalinus . . . . .cheat, chess
Bromus tectorum . . . . cheat grass, downy brome, downy chess
Brunnichia cirrhosa. . . . . redvine
Buchloo dactyloides . . . . buffalo grass
Cagnopodium ambrosioides . . . . wormweed

Campsis radicans . . . . Canada trumpet creeper, trumpet vine
Cannabis sativa . . . . hemp, Indian hemp, marijuana, Mary Jane
Capsella bursapastoris . . . . shepherd's purse, lady's purse,
                    pepper plant, St. James weed, shepherd's pouch, mother's heart
Cardamine pratensis . . . . lady's smock
Cardiospermum haliccacabum . . . . .balloonvine
Carduus nutans . . . . musk thistle
Carex gravida . . . . .heavy sedge
Carex vulpinoidea . . . . .fox sedge
Cassia obtusifolia . . . . .sickle pod
Cassis fasciculata . . . . partridge pea
Ceanothus americanus . . . . .redroot, wild pepper, mountain sweet
Cenchrus pauciflorus . . . . sandbur, field sandbur
Centaurea cyanus . . . . bachelor's button
Centaurea nigra . . . . .hardhead, knapweed
Centaurea repens . . . . Russian knapweed
Centaurea scabiosa . . . . greater knotweed
Centaurea solstitialis . . . . Barnaby's thistle
Cerastium arvense . . . . mouse-ear-chickweed
Cerastium vulgatum . . . . mouse-ear-chickweed
Chaerophyllum procumbens . . . . chervil
Chamaesyce maculata . . . . spotted spurge, milk spurge
Chelidonium genus, several species . . . . celandine
Chenopodium album . . . . lambsquarters, white goosefoot,
                    pitseed goosefoot, mealweed, baconweed, wild spinach,
            white pigweed, fat hen, frostbite, chou grass, muckweed, dungweed
Chenopodium ambrosioides . . . wormwood, Mexican tea, Jesuit tea, teaweed
Chenopodium arvense . . . . creeping thistles
Chimaphila umbellate . . . . prince's pine herb
Chrysanthemum leucanthemum pinnatifidum . . daisy, oxeye daisy, dog daisy
Chrysanthemum segetum .corn marigold, tansy
Cichorium intybus . . . . .chicory
Cimicifuga racemosa . . . . .black cohosh
Cirsium altissimum . . . . .pasture thistle, field thistle, tall thistle
Cirsium arvense . . . . Canada thistle, Canadian thistle, creeping thistle
Cirsium lanceolatum . . . . bull thistle
Cirsium vulgare . . . . bull thistle
Colchicum genus, several species . . . . autumn crocus
Conium maculatum . . . . .hemlock
Conopodium denudatum . . . . pignut
Conringia orientalis . . . . .hare's ear mustard
Convolvulus arvensis . . . . bindweed, creeping jenny, field bindweed,

	morning glory
Convolvulus repens	bindweed
Convolvulus sepium .... hedge bindweed, creeping bindweed,
	morning glory, climbing false buckwheat
Corynanthe yohimbe	yohimbe
Crotalaria spectabilis	crotalaria
Crepis taraxacifolia	beaked hawksbeard
Croton capitatus .... woolly croton, hogwort
Croton texensis.	Texas croton
Cucurbita foetidissima .... buffalo gourd, wild gourd, wild pumpkin,
	pumpkin vine, gourd vine, calabagilla, chili coyote
Cuscuta genus, several species.	dodder
Cymodon dactylon. .... Bermuda grass, wiregrass, devil grass,
	scutch grass, dogtooth grass, Bahama grass, vinegrass
Cyperus esculentus .... yellow nutsedge, nutsedge, nutshade
Cyperus rotundus .... purple nut sedge, nutsedge
Cytisus scoparius	scotch broom
Dactylis glomerata	orchard grass
Datura stramonium.	Jimson weed
Daucus carota	wild carrot
Delphinium genus, several species .... larkspur, wild larkspur
Descurainia genus, several species.	flaxweed
Descurainia intermedia	tansy mustard
Dichrophyllum marginatum. .... snow-on-the-mountain
Digitalis genus, several species	foxglove
Diodia teres. .... buttonweed, poorjoe
Distichlis stricta.	salt grass
Drosea rotundifolia	sundews
Echinacea genus, several species .... purple coneflower
Echinacea angustifolia .... coneflower, echinacea
Echinocereus genus, several species. .... prickly pear
Echinochloa colonum	junglerice
Echinochloa crusgalli .... barnyard grass, watergrass, panic grass,
	cockspur grass, cocksfoot panicum
Echinocystis lobata.	wild cucumber
Eichornia crassipes.	water hyacinth
Eleusine indica .... goosegrass, yardgrass, silver crabgrass
	wiregrass, goosegrass plantain
Elymus genus, several species .... ryegrass, wild rye
Ephedra nevadenses	Mormon tea
Equisetum arvense.	horsetail
Eragrostis cilianensis. ..... stinkgrass, skunkgrass, lovegrass, matrimony grass

Erianthus contortus . . . . bent awn
Erigeron canadensis . . . . Canada fleabane, mare's tail, horseweed
Erigeron ramosus . . . . fleabane, rough daisy
Eriochloa villosa . . . . woolly cupgrass
Eriodictyon californicum . . . . yerba santa
Eucalyptus globulus . . . . eucalyptus, blue gum
Eupatorium genus, several species. . . . . white snakeroot
Eupatorium perfoliatum. . . . . .boneset
Eupatorium purpureum . . . . Joe-Pye weed
Eupatorium wrightii . . . . no common name
Euphorbia genus, several species. . . . . . caper spurge, pencil tree, poinsettia
Euphorbia corollata . . . . flowering spurge
Euphorbia dentata. . . . . toothed spurge
Euphorbia escula . . . . .flowering spurge, leafy spurge
Euphorbia exigua . . . . .dwarf spurge
Euphorbia glyptosperma. . . . . mat spurge
Euphorbia helioscopia . . . . sun spurge
Euphorbia heterophylla . . . . .spurge
Euphorbia hexagons. . . . . .spurge
Euphorbia hysopifolia . . . . upright spurge
Euphorbia maculata . . . . spotted spurge, milk spurge
Euphorbia marginata. . . . . .snow-on-the-mountain
Euphorbia peplus. . . . . petty spurge
Euphorbia preslii . . . . .spurge
Euphorbia serpens . . . . .spurge
Euphorbia supina . . . . prostrate spurge
Euphrasia officinalis. . . . . eyebright
Festuca elatior . . . . meadow fescue
Festuca octoflora . . . . slender fescue
Filago germanica. . . . . .cudweed
Fragaria virginiana . . . . .wild strawberry
Franseria tomentosa. . . . . bur ragweed, lagoonweed
Fumaria officinalis . . . . .fumitory
Galarrhoeus cyparissias. . . . . .cypress spurge
Galinsoga ciliata . . . . galinsoga
Galinsoga parviflora . . . . smallflower galinsoga
Galium aparine. . . . . bedstraw, cleavers, goosegrass
Gaultheria procumbens . . . . wintergreen herb
Geranium dissectum. cut-leaved geranium
Geranium molle. . . . . .crane's bill, dove's foot, geranium, soft crane's bill
Geranium pratense. . . . . geranium
Geranium pusillum .geranium, small crane's bill

Geum album . . . . white avens
Gonolobus laevis . . . . climbing milkweed, sandvine, common milkweed
Grindella squarrosa . . . . gumweed, tarweed, Grindella
Gnaphalium uliginosum . . . . .marsh cudweed
Gypsophila paniculata . . . . baby's breath flower
Helenium tenuifolium . . . . bitterweed, narrow-leaved sneezeweed
Helianthus annuus . . . . . .sunflower, common sunflower, annual sunflower,
wild sunflower
Helianthus ciliaris . . . . blueweed, blue sunflower
Helianthus petiolaris . . . . prairie sunflower, sand sunflower, plains sunflower
Helianthus tuberosus . . . . .Jerusalem artichoke, girasole
Heracleum sphondylium . . . . hogweed
Hibiscus trionum . . . . flower-of-an-hour, Venice mallow, bladder
ketmia, brown-eyed Susan, shoo-fly
Hieracium aurantiacum . . . . .devil's paint brush
Hieracium pilosella . . . . mouse-ear-hawkweed
Hippocrepis comosa . . . . horse shoe vetch
Holcus lanatus . . . . Yorkshire fog
Hordeum jubatum . . . . wild barley, foxtail barley
Hordeum nodosum . . . . wild barley
Hordeum pusillum . . . . little barley
Hordeum vulgare . . . . volunteer barley
Hydrangea genus, several species . . . . .hydrangea
Hydrastis canadensis . . . . goldenseal root
Hydrocotyle genus, several species . . . . pennywort
Hypericum perforatum . . . . St. Johnswort
Hypochaeris radicata . . . . .cat's ear
Inulahelenium . . . . Helen's tear plant, horse elder
Ipomoea hederacea . . . . morning glory
Ipomoea pandurata . . . . .wild potato vine, man-of-the-earth
Ipomoea purpurea . . . . morning glory, wild morning glory,
common morning glory
Iva xanthifolia . . . . .burweed marsh elder, marsh elder
Kochia scoparia . . . . .kochia, summer cypress, mock cypress,
Mexican fireweed, red belvedere, burning bush
Lactuca genus, several species . . . . . . arrow-leaved wild lettuce, wild lettuce
Lactuca pulchella . . . . wild blue lettuce, perennial lettuce
Lactuca scariola . . . . lantana, prickly lettuce, horse thistle,
English thistle, milk thistle, common wild thistle, Chinese lettuce,
compass plant, wild opium
Lactuca scariola integrata . . . . prickly lettuce, horse thistle,

English thistle, milk thistle, common wild thistle, Chinese lettuce, compass plant, wild opium

Lactuca serriola . . . . prickly lettuce, horse thistle, English thistle, milk thistle, common wild lettuce, Chinese lettuce, compass plant, wild opium

Lactuca virosa . . . . prickly lettuce, horse thistle, English thistle, milk thistle, common wild thistle, Chinese lettuce, compass plant, wild opium

Lamium amplexicaule . . . . henbit, blind nettle, bee nettle, giraffe head, dead nettle

Lamium purpureum . . . . red deadnettle

Lappula echinata . . . . blue bur

Lapsana communis . . . . nipplewort

Larrea mexicana . . . . chaparral

Larrea tridentata . . . . chaparral

Leersia oryzoides . . . . rice cutgrass

Legousia hybrida . . . . corn campanula

Leontodon autumnalis . . . . autumnal hawkbit

Lepadena marginata . . . . snow-on-the-mountain

Lepidium apetalum . . . . peppergrass, green flowered peppergrass

Lepidium campestre . . . . peppergrass

Lepidium densiflorum . . . . peppergrass

Lepidium draba . . . . hoary cress, white top, perennial peppergrass

Lepidium virginicum . . . . peppergrass

Leptochloa filiformis . . . . red sprangletop

Linaria spuria . . . . round leaved toadflax

Linaria vulgaris . . . . toadflax, butter-and-eggs, yellow toadflax

Linum catharticum . . . . purging flax

Lithospermum arvense . . . . corn gromwell

Lobelia inflata . . . . Lobelia herb

Lolium multiflorum . . . . annual ryegrass

Lolium perenne . . . . perennial ryegrass

Lolium temulentum . . . . darnel

Lotus corniculatus . . . . bird's foot trefoil

Lychnis flos-cuculi . . . . ragged robin

Lychnis flos-cuculi . . . . meadow pink, cuckoo flower

Lychnis githago . . . . corn cockle

Lychnis vespertina . . . . white campion

Lycopsis arvensis . . . . field alkanet

Machaeranthera tanacelifolia . . . . tansy aster

Malva neglecta . . . . mallow

Marrubium vulgare . . . . common horehound

Matricaria chamomilla . . . . .camomile, wild camomile
Matricaria inodora . . . . scentless mayweed
Matricaria suaveolens . . . . .pineapple weed
Mentha arvensis . . . . corn mint
Mollugo verticillata . . . . carpetweed
Muhlenbergia frondosa. . . . . wirestem muhly
Myosotis arvensis . . . . field forget-me-not, forget-me-not
Napeta cataria. . . . . .catnip herb
Nasturtium officinale. . . . . .watercress
Neomammilara genus, several species . . . . prickly pear
Nepeta cataria. . . . . .catnip
Neslia paniculata. . . . . ball mustard
Onomis repens . . . . rest harrow
Oplopanax horridum. . . . . devil's club
Opuntia genus, several species . . . . prickly pear
Opuntia humifusa . . . . prickly pear
Oryza sativa . . . . red rice
Oxytropis lambertii . . . . loco, stemless loco
Panax quinquefolium . . . . .ginseng
Panicum capillare . . . . .witchgrass
Panicum dichotomiflorum . . . . fall panicum, facelis
Panicum fasciculatum . . . . browntop panicum
Panicum miliaceum . . . . wild proso millet
Panicum texanum . . . . Texas panicum
Papaver argemone .pale poppy, poppy, papaver
Papaver rhoeas. . . . . red poppy
Parapholis incurva . . . . sickle grass
Paspalum dilatatum. . . . . dallis grass
Paspalum distichum . . . . knotgrass
Paspartum distichum . . . . St. Augustine
Passiflora caerulea . . . . Passion flower herb
Passiflora incarnata . . . . maypop
Pepo foetidissima . . . . buffalo gourd, wild gourd, wild pumpkin,
pumpkin vine, gourd vine, calabagilla, chili coyote
Petroselinum sativum. . . . . .parsley fern
Physalis hetrophylla . . . . ground cherry, bladder cherry,
clammy ground cherry, lanternweed
Phytolacca genus, several species. . . . . pokeweed
Plantago aristata . . bracted plantain, greater plantain, large bracted plantain
Plantago lanceolata . . . . ribbed plantain, ribwort plantain
Plantago major . . . . .greater plantain
Plantago media . . . . hoary plantain

Plantago rugelii . . . . . .blackseed plantain, rugel, purple-stemmed plantain
Poa annua. . . . . annual meadow grass
Podophyllum peltatum .mandrake root, mayapple
Polygala vulgaris . . . . milkwort
Polygonum genus, several species . . . . persecaria
Polygonum augustissimum . . . . .prostrate knotweed
Polygonum aviculare . . . . knotgrass
Polygonum aviculare . . . . .prostrate knotweed
Polygonum coccineum pratincolum . . . . swamp smartweed
Polygonum convolvulus . . . . wild buckwheat, knot bindweed,
black bindweed, bear bind, ivy bindweed,
climbing bindweed, cornblind
Polygonum hydropiperoides. . . . . mild water pepper
Polygonum neglectum. . . . . .prostrate knotweed
Polygonum pensylvanicum . . . .Pennsylvania smartweed, Jim McHale's weed
Polygonum persicaria . . . . spotted knotweed, ladysthumb, willowweed
Portulaca olenacca . . . . purslane, pursley, pussley, common purslane,
common purslane, pursley duckweed, wild purtulaca
Potamogeton americanus . . . . pond weed
Potamogeton fluitans . . . . pond weed
Potamogeton nodosus . . . . pond weed
Potamogeton rotundatus. . . . . pond weed
Potentilla genus, several species. . . . . cinquefoil
Potentilla anserina. . . . . silverweed
Potentilla recta . . . . sulfur cinquefoil
Prunus avium . . . . wild cherry
Prunus serotina . . . . wild cherry
Psoralea floribunda . . . . wild alfalfa
Pteridium acquilinum . . . . bracken
Pteris aquilina. . . . . bracken fern
Pueraria lobata . . . . kudzu
Ranunculus acris. . . . . .buttercup, tall buttercup
Ranunculus arvensis . . . . corn buttercup
Ranunculus repens. . . . . creeping buttercup
Raphanus raphanistrum. . . . . wild radish
Rapistrum rugosum . . . . turnip weed
Reseda lutea. . . . . wild mignonette
Rhamnus purshiana. . . . . cascara segrada bark
Rhinanthus major . . . . yellow rattle
Rhus copallina. . . . . poison sumac
Rhus glabra. . . . . smooth sumac
Rhus quercifolia. . . . . poison oak

Rhus radicans . . . . .poison ivy
Rhus toxicodendron . . . . poison oak
Richardia scabra . . . . Florida purslane
Rosa bracteata . . . . .Cherokee rose
Rosa suffulta . . . . prairie rose
Rottboellia exalta. . . . . Itchgrass
Rumex acetosella . . . . red sorrel, sheep's sorrel, dock
Rumex altissimus. . . . . tall or pale dock
Rumex crispus . . . . yellow dock, curly dock, dock, sour dock,
              curly leaf dock, narrow leaf dock, curly
Rumex obtusifolius . . . . broad dock, broadleaf dock
Rumex sanguineus . . . . .dock
Sagittaria latifolia. . . . . .arrowhead
Salix nigra . . . . pussywillow
Salsola kali . . . . Russian thistle, tumbleweed, Russian cactus,
              saltwort, prickly glaswort, wind witch
Sambucus genus, several species . . . . .elder flower
Sanguinaria canadensis . . . . bloodroot
Saponaria officinalis . . . . bouncing bet
Sassafras albium . . . . sassafras
Scabiosa arvensis . . . . scabious, field scabious
Scandix pecten. . . . . shepherd's needle
Scleranthus annuus . . . . annual knawel
Secale cereale. . . . . Volunteer rye
Senebiera coronopus. . . . . .swinecress
Senecio jacobaea . . . . .stinking Willie, tansy ragwort
Senecio vulgaris. . . . . groundsel
Serenoa repens . . . . saw palmetto berries
Serenoa serrulata . . . . saw palmetto
Setaria faberi. . . . . .giant foxtail, foxtail
Setaria geniculata . . . . knotroot foxtail, perennial bristlegrass
Setaria glauca . . . . yellow foxtail
Setaria lutescens. . . . . .yellow foxtail, yellow bristlegrass, wild millet
Setaria verticillata . . . . bristly foxtail
Setaria viridis . . . . .green bristlegrass
Sheradia arvensis. . . . . .field madder
Sicyos angulatus . . . . .bur cucumber
Sida spinosa. . . . . .prickly sida
Silene inflata. . . . . .bladder campion
Sinapis arvensis . . . . mustard
Sitanion hystrix. . . . . squirreltail
Solanum carolinense . . . . .horse nettle

Solanum carolinense . . .horse nettle, nettle, Carolina nightshade, bull nettle
Solanum dulcamara. . . . . nightshade
Solanum elaeagnifolium. . . . . silverleaf nightshade, nightshade, bull nettle, prairie berry, sand briar, silver horsenettle, trompillo, white horsenettle
Solanum nigrum . . . . black or garden nightshade
Solanum rostratum . . . . .prickly nightshade, buffalo bur
Solidago genus, several species . . . . .goldenrod
Solidago canadensis . . . . Canada goldenrod, goldenrod
Solidago glaberrima. . . . . Missouri goldenrod
Sonchus genus, several species . . . . sowthistle
Sonchus arvensis . . . . corn sowthistle
Sorghum bicolor . . . . .shattercane, wild cane
Sorghum halepense. . . . . Johnson grass
Specularia perfoliata . . . . .Venus looking glass
Spergula arvensis. . . . . corn spurry, spurry
Spiraea genus, several species . . . . meadowsweet
Sporobolus neglectus. . . . . .dropseed
Stellaria media . . . . .chickweed, common chickweed, starwort, starweed, winter weed, satin flower, mouse-ear-chickweed
Symphoricarpos orbiculatus .buckbrush, coralberry
Tanacetum vulgare. . . . . .tansy
Taraxacum officinale . . . . dandelion, blowball, lion's tooth, puffball, milk witch, yellow Gowan, witch Gowan, door-head clock, common dandelion, caukerwort
Taraxacum vulgare . . . . dandelion
Tetradymia genus, several species . . . . horsebrush
Thlaspi arvense . . . . .pennycress, French weed, stinkweed
Thymus vulgaris . . . . .thyme
Tragopogon arrifolius . . . . purple flowered oyster, salsify, goatsbeard
Tragopogon pratensis . . . . purple flowered oyster, salsify, goatsbeard, yellow salsify, yellow goatsbeard, oysterplant
Tribulus terrestris. . . . . puncture vine, goathead, bullhead, caltrop, puncture weed, burnut, ground burnut
Triticum aestivum . . . . volunteer wheat
Tussilago farfara . . . . coltsfoot
Typha latifolia. . . . . cattails
Ulmus fulva . . . . slippery elm
Ulmus rubra. . . . . slippery elm bark
Umbellularia californica . . . . bay laurel
Urtica procera . . . . .stinging nettle
Urtica urens . . . . .small nettle

Vaccinium ovatum. . . . . huckleberry foliage
Valerianella olitoria . . . . lamb's lettuce
Veratrum viride . . . . .hellebore, false hellebore
Verbascum thapsus . . . . common mullein, velvet dock, great mullein,
flannel leaf, big taper, candle wick, torches, Aaron's rod, Jacob's staff,
hedge table, velvet plant, mullein, velvet mullein, torch plant
Verbena bracteata . . . . prostrate vervain, large bracted verbena
Veronica fasciculata . . . . ironweed
Veronica alrissima . . . . ironweed
Veronica agrestis. . . . . field speedwell
Veronica arvensis . . . . .wall speedwell
Veronica hederaefolia . . . . ivy-leaved speedwell
Veronica interior . . . . ironweed
Veronica officinalis. . . . . field speedwell
Veronica peregrina . . . . purslane speedwell
Veronica persica. . . . . .corn growwell
Veronica serpyllifolia . . . . thyme-leaved speedwell
Veronica stricta . . . . hoary vervain, verbena
Veronica tournefortii . . . . large field speedwell
Viburnum prunifolium . . . . .black haw
Vicia angustifolia. . . . . vetch
Vicia cracca. . . . . tufted vetch
Vicia villosa. . . . . winter vetch
Viola genus, several species . . . . Confederate violet
Viola odorata. . . . . youth root, amomum, orris root, iris
Viola tricolor. . . . . field pansy, wild pansy
Vitus lambrusca. . . . . .wild grape
Xanthium canalense. . . . . .cocklebur, common cocklebur, clotbur
Xanthium Chinense. . . . . .cocklebur, common cocklebur, clotbur
Xanthium commune . . . . .cocklebur, common cocklebur, clotbur
Xanthium italicum . . . . .cocklebur, common cocklebur, clotbur
Xanthium orientale . . . . .cocklebur, common cocklebur, clotbur
Xanthium pennsylvanicum. . . . . .cocklebur, common cocklebur, clotbur
Xanthium speciosum . . . . .cocklebur, common cocklebur, clotbur
Xanthium spinosum. . . . . .cocklebur, common cocklebur, clotbur
Xanthium strumarium. . . . . .cocklebur, common cocklebur, clotbur
Zigadenus genus, several species . . . . death camas
Zingiber genus, several species . . . . wild ginger

PICTORAL GLOSSARY

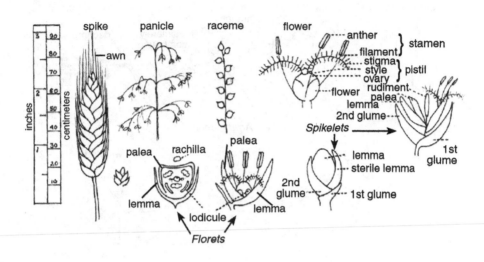

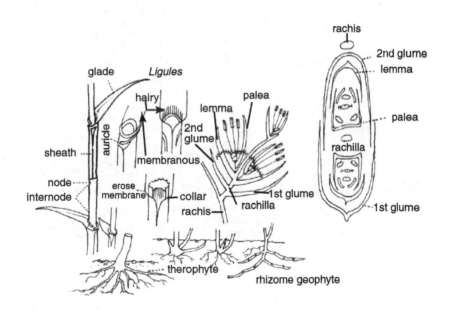

Leaves

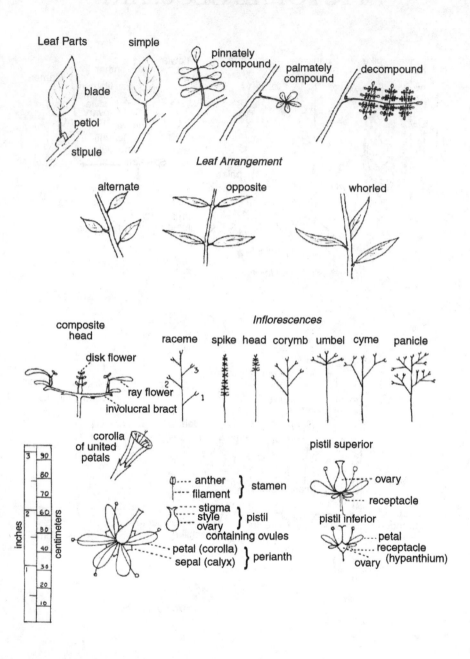

Leaf Parts

blade

petiol

stipule

simple

pinnately compound

palmately compound

decompound

Leaf Arrangement

alternate

opposite

whorled

Inflorescences

composite head

disk flower

ray flower

involucral bract

raceme   spike   head   corymb   umbel   cyme   panicle

corolla of united petals

inches   centimeters

anther
filament } stamen

stigma
style } pistil
ovary
containing ovules

petal (corolla)
sepal (calyx) } perianth

pistil superior

ovary

receptacle

pistil inferior

petal
receptacle
ovary (hypanthium)

Fruits

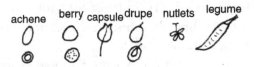

achene   berry   capsule   drupe   nutlets   legume

Leaf Shape

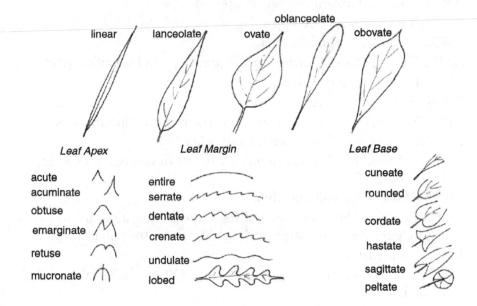

linear   lanceolate   ovate   oblanceolate   obovate

Leaf Apex

acute
acuminate
obtuse
emarginate
retuse
mucronate

Leaf Margin

entire
serrate
dentate
crenate
undulate
lobed

Leaf Base

cuneate
rounded
cordate
hastate
sagittate
peltate

GLOSSARY

ACAULESCENT. Stemless or apparently so. In some cases the stem may be below ground.

ACUMINATE. Tapering to a sharp point.

ACUTE. Sharp pointed, albeit less tapering than acuminate.

ACHENE. A single seeded, dry, indehiscent fruit.

ALTERNATE. Leaves, branches, buds, etc., scattered singly along the stem, and not opposite each other.

ANNUAL. Growing one season. A winter annual grows from a seed in the autumn, and flowers and fruits the following spring.

ANTHER. The part of the stamen containing the pollen.

ARTICULATE. Having a node or a joint.

ASCENDING. Growing obliquely upward.

AURICLE. An ear-shaped appendage.

AWN. A slender bristle-like organ.

AXIL. The upper angle formed by the juncture of a leaf with a stem.

AXIS. The center line of an organ.

BIENNIAL. Growing for two years.

BIPINNATIFID. Having similar parts arranged on opposite sides.

BISEXUAL. Having both stamens and pistils.

BRACT. A modified head subtending a flower or belonging to an inflorescence.

BRANCHLET. A small branch; a twig.

BULBIL. A small bulblike organ of vegetative propagation, in size and weight similar to a large seed, that drops off the parent plant.

BUR. A spiny fruit.

CALYX. The outer part of a perianth. The set of sepals. Usually green in color.

CAPILLARY. Hairlike in form.

CAPSULE. A dry fruit of more than one carpel which splits at maturity to release the seeds.

CARPELS. A simple pistil, or one member of a compound pistil.

CARYOPSIS. The grain or fruit of grasses. The seed coat is grown fast to the pericarp as in the grain of wheat or corn. In some few grasses the seed is free within the pericarp, as in the case of drop-seed and goosegrass.

CAULINE. Pertaining to the stem.

CELL. A cavity of an anther or ovary.

COMPOSITE. A plant having few to many flowers on a common receptacle, the group of flowers surrounded by involucral bracts. A member of the Compositae.

COMPOUND. Composed of two or more similar parts united into a whole.

CONE. A fruit with woody, overlapping scales.

CORDATE. Heart-shaped, with point upwards.

COROLLA. The inner part of a perianth, composed of petals, usually bright colored.

COTYLEDON. The first leaf or one of the first pair or whorl of leaves developed by the embryo of a seed plant or of some lower plants.

CROWN. An inner appendage to a petal, or to the throat of a corolla.

CULM. The jointed stem of grasses.

DEHISCENT. Opening by valves or slits to emit the contents.

DISC. A development of the receptacle at or around the base of the pistil. In Compositae, the tubular flowers of the head as distinct from the ray.

DIVIDED. Cleft to the base or to the midrib.

DORSAL. On the back; pertaining to the back.

DRUPE. A fleshy or pulpy fruit in which the inner portion is hard or stony.

EMBRYO. A rudimentary plant in the seed.

ENDOSPERM. The substance surrounding the embryo of a seed; albumen.

FLOWER. An axis bearing stamens or pistils or both (calyx and corolla usually accompany these).

GENUS. A group of related species; a subdivision of a family.

GLABROUS. Without hairs.

HOARY. Gray-white with a fine, close pubescence.

HYDROPHYTE. A water plant.

INDEHISCENT. Not opening by valves or slits; remaining persistently closed.

INVOLUCRE. One or more whorls of bracts situated below and close to a flower, flower cluster, or fruit.

LANCEOLATE. Lance-shaped, broadest above the base and tapering to the apex, but several times longer than wide.

LATERAL. Situated on the side of a branch.

LEGUME. A podlike fruit composed of a solitary carpel and usually splitting open by both sutures.

LIGULE. A strap-shaped corolla, as in the ray-flowers of Compositae; a thin scarious projection from the summit of the sheath in grasses.

MIDRIB. The central vein of a leaf of leaflet.

MONOCOTYLEDONOUS (embryo). Having only one cotyledon.

NODE. The place upon a stem which normally bears a leaf or whorl of leaves.

NUT. A hard and indehiscent, one-celled, one-seeded fruit.

OBOVATE. Ovate, with the broadest part toward the apex.

OVAL. Broadly elliptical.

OVARY, OVULARY. The part of a pistil that contains the ovules.

OVATE. Egg-shaped, with the broad end basal.

PANICLE. A loose, irregularly compound inflorescence with pedicellate flowers.

PAPPUS. The modified calyx limb in composites, forming a crown of various character at the summit of the achene.

PEDUNCLE. A stalk bearing a flower of flower cluster or a fructification.

PEPO. An indehiscent flashy 1-celled, or falsely 3-celled many-seeded berry that has a hard rind and is the characteristic fruit of the gourd family.

PERIANTH. The calyx and corolla of a flower considered as a whole.

PERICARP. The ripened walls of the ovary when it becomes a fruit.

PETIOLE. A slender stem that supports the blade of a foliage leaf.

PISTIL. The seed-bearing organ of a flower, normally consisting of ovary, style and stigma, containing the megasporangia (ovules).

PISTILLATE. Provided with pistil, but usually without the stamens.

PLACENTA. An ovule-bearing surface.

POD. Any dry and dehiscent fruit.

POLLEN. The microspores (dustlike substance in the anthers of the flower) which on a suitable stigma may grow into the pollen tube (male gametophyte) and produce the male gametes (male sex units).

POME. A fleshy fruit, as the apple.

PROSTRATE. Lying flat on the ground.

PYXIS. A capsule whose dehiscence is circumscissile, or which opens by a circular, horizontal line, so that the upper part comes off like a lid.

RACEME. A simple inflorescence of flowers on pedicels of equal length arranged on a common, elongated axis (rachis).

RACEMOSE. Resembling a raceme.

RADIATE. Bearing ray-flowers; spreading from or arranged around a common center.

RAY. One of the peduncles or branches of an umbel; the flat marginal flowers in composites.

RHIZOME. A rootstock; an underground stem.

RIB. A primary or prominent vein of a leaf.

ROSETTE. A cluster of spreading or radiating basal leaves, as in the overwintering stage of certain panicums, or of mullein.

RUNNER. A filiform or very slender stolon.

SCABROUS. Rough to the touch.

SCIENTIFIC NAME. Two Latin or Latinized words denoting respectively the genus and species, e.g., Salsola kali.

SEPAL. One of the divisions of a calyx.

SERRATE. Toothed, the teeth sharp and pointing forward.

SESSILE. Attached directly by the base; not raised upon a stalk or peduncle.

SILIQUE. The peculiar pod of Brassicaceae (mustard family).

SPECIES. A group of like individuals, as soft maples.

SPIKE. A simple inflorescence of sessile flowersl arranged on a common elongated axis (rachis).

SPIKELETS. The units of the inflorescence in grasses, consisting of two glumes and one or more florets, or in sedges of a series of glumes each with a flower in its axil.

SPINE. A sharp, woody outgrowth from a stem.

STAMEN. The pollen-bearing organ of a flower, normally consisting of filament and anther; the microsporophyll.

STIGMA. The part of a pistil which receives the pollen.

STIPE. The stalklike lower portion of a pistil; the leaf-stalk of a fern.

STOLON. A basal branch rooting at the nodes.

STRIATE. Marked with fine longitudinal stripes or ridges.

STYLE. The part of a pistil connecting ovary with stigma.

SUCCULENT. Soft and juicy.

SUCKER. A shooting arising from a subterranean part of a plant.

TENDRIL. A thread-shaped process used for climbing.

TUBER. A thickened and short subterranean branch, having numerou buds.

UTRICLE. A small, thin-walled, one-seeded fruit.

WHORL. An arrangement of three or more leaves or branches in a circle round an axis.

WOOLLY. Covered with long and matted or tangled hairs.

INDEX

Amaranthus genus, 55, 120
Amaranthus graecizans, 38, 244
Amaranthus hybridis, 38, 88, 220, 244
Amaranthus palmeri, 88
Amaranthus retroflexus, viii, 88,119, 244-245
Amaranthus ruberculatos, 88
Amaranthus spinosus, 88
Amaryllis, 38
Ambrosia artemisifolia, 87, 120, 253-254
Ambrosia elatior, 81, 251, 253-254
Ambrosia genus, 119
Ambrosia psilostachya, 58
Ambrosia trifida, 81, 87, 253
American Cyanamid, 182
ammonia, 270
ammonium sulfate, 201, 208, 270
amomum, 155
Amphiachyris dracunculoides, 199
Amway, 278
amygdalin, 148, 149
Anagallis arvensis, 75
Anatomy of Life and Energy in Agriculture, The, xii, 7, 85
Ancient Mysteries, Modern Visions, x
Andersen, Arden, xii, 7, 85
Anderes, Robert L., 37
Andropogon virginicus, 39, 118
Angry Testament, 168
anhydrous ammonia, 123, 217
annual grasses, insects harbored, 51
annual knawel, 72, 76
annual meadow grass, 76, 83
annual ryegrass, 256
annual sunflower, 265
annuals, 6
Anoda cristata, 88
Anthemis arvensis, 75
Anthemis cotula, 75-81, 119

Anthemis tinctoria, 64
aphids, 10, 43, 53-52
aphrodine, 146
Apocynum cannabinum, 213-214
Apocynum sibericum, 214
Arabian jasmine, 37
Arabic numbers, 138
arable weeds, spread of, 32
Aramite, 171
Arctium lapa, 157, 165, 201
Arctium minus, 119, 154, 201
Are We Going to Grass?, 188
Arenaria serpyllifolia, 75
Argemone intermedia, 275
Argentina bahia grass, 55
army cutworm, 52
army worms, 51-52
Arntzen, Charles, 182
arrow leaved wild lettuce, 64
arrowhead, 135
Artemisia fugida, 119
Artemisia vulgaris, 120
Asclepias genus, 55, 119
Asclepias syriaca, 87, 235
ash, 223
Asia, 280
asparagus, 85
aster yellow, 53, 55
Astragalus genus, 143, 145
Astragalus mollissimus, 234
Astragalus recemosus, 234
Atomic Energy Commission, 111
atomic fallout, 60
atomic tests, ground zero, 59
atrazine, 60, 182-183, 187
Atriplex patula, 75, 83
Australia, 3, 43
Australian ryegrass, 256
autumn crocus, 135
autumnal hawkbit, 33

black haw root, 157
black nightshade, 53, 55, 87, 237-238
black vetchling, 64
blackbodies, 47
blackseed plantain, 245
bladder campion, 76, 84
bladder cherry, 221
bladder ketmia, 215
blading, 247
Blepharida rhois, 50
blessed thistle, 269
blind nettle, 223
blind staggers, 145, 234
blister beetles, 51
blister rust, 168
bloodroot, 157, 163
blowball, 210
blue bur, 32
blue morning glory, 236
blue sunflower, 198
blueberries, 85
bluegrass, 256
blueweed, 198
Bogorad, Lawrence, 182
boneset, 82
Bordeaux mixture, 224
boron, 196,199, 204, 211, 215, 220, 227-228, 233, 235-236, 238, 241, 253, 256-259, 266, 271-272, 280-283
bouncing bet, 149
Brachiaria platyphylla, 258
Brachypodium sylvaticum, 135
Brachypodium pinnatum, 135
bracken, 148
bracted plantain, 245-246
Brassica alba, 75
Brassica arvensis, 276
Brassica juncea, 124, 276
Brassica kaber, 120, 276

Brassica kaber, pinnatifida variety, 124
Brassica sinapis, 75, 119
Brenchley, W. E., 63
briar, 65, 188
bristly foxtail, 219
bristly star bur, xiv, 87, 118
broad dock, 76
broadleaf dock, 32
broadleaf signalgrass, xiv, 258
broadleaf weeds, xiv, 7, 24, 89
Bromus commutalus, 204
Bromus hordcaccus, 204
Bromus japonicus, 198-199
Bromus mollis, 135, 204
Bromus racemosus, 204
Bromus secalinus, 56, 119, 203
Bromus sterilis, 204
Bromus tectorum, 204
broom sedge, 10, 39, 61-62, 118, 190
broomcorn millet, 280
broomweed, 199-200
brown-eyed Susan, 215
browntop panicum, 242
Brunnichia cirrhosa, 88, 255
Buchloe dactyloides, 56
buckbrush, 200
buckhorn, 206, 261-262
buckwheat, 149
buckwheatvine, 255
buffalo bur, 87, 239
buffalo gourd, 200-201
buffalo grass, 54, 56
buffalo wallows, 239
buffalo weed, 253
bulbet, definition of, 194
bulbous buttercup, 74
bull nettle, 238-239
bull nettle, insects harbored, 51
bull thistle, 118, 267
Bullet, x

devil's club root, 157
devils paint brush, 18
devilsclaw, 87
diamond-back moth, 52
Dichrophyllum marginatum, 260
dicots, xiv
digitalis, 149
Digitaria filiformis, 208
Digitaria ischaemum, 208
Digitaria sanguinalis, 119, 207
Dilldrin, 171
Diodia teres, 38, 88, 118, 246
dioxin, 170
discing, 204, 218, 259, 278-279
Distichlis stricta, 38
DNA, 109, 111, 138, 149, 158,
   186, 204, 209, 211, 220, 230
dock, 64, 134, 188, 261
dock, insects harbored, 51
docks, 63, 135
dodder, 137, 212-213
dog daisy, 74, 135
dog fennel, 81
dogbane, 213-214
dogs, 224
dogtooth grass, 196
dolomite, 217
Doomsday Mountain, 156
door-head clock, 210
Double Helix, The, 111
dove's foot, 85
Dow Chemical, 169, 170
downy brome, 204
downy chess, 204
dowsing, 115, 131-133
Doyle, Jack, 171-188
drainage, soil, 241, 211, 223, 225,
   227-228, 230, 235, 241-242,
   248-250, 255, 257, 260, 277-
   280
drainage problem weeds, 64
dropseed, 214

drought, 3-4, 199, 204, 215, 229-
   230, 244, 248, 252-253, 257,
   270
Drown, Ruth, 113
drupe, definition of, 194
dry gangrene, 55
dryland weeds, 14, 16
Dual, xiv, 182
duckfoot, 247
Dugger, B. M., 61
dungweed, 230
DuPont, 182, 184, 185, 186
Dust Bowl, 1, 5, 13, 239, 248
dwarf spurge, 32, 75

early blight of potato, 56
Earp, Wyatt, 142, 156
earthworms, 210
East coast, the, 219, 263
Eastern black nightshade, 87
ecdysone, 42
echinacea, 157
Echinacea angustifolia, 164
Echinochloa colonum, 228
Echinochloa crusgalli, 119-195
eggplant, 53
eggs, 257
Einstein, Albert, 77, 80
elder flower, 156
electrolytes, 235
electromagnetic spectrum, 44, 45,
   121
Eleusine indica, 220
eloptic energy, 117, 118
Elymus genus, 56
Emenhiser, Keith, 11
Energy Refractors, 121
Energy Law of Similars, 117
English grain aphid, 51-52
English ryegrass, 256
English thistle, 231
enzymes, 218, 244, 254

magnesium, 94-107, 196, 199, 201, 203, 207, 211-215, 217-218, 225, 228, 231-236, 238-242, 245, 247, 249-250, 252-266, 269, 271-272, 276, 278, 280-283
magnesium carbonate, 201
Maier, John, 156
Maine, 199, 229
Mainline Farming for Century 21, 79
mallow, 63-64
man-of-the-earth, 280
Mandragora officanarum, 156
mandrake root, 156
manganese, 89, 196, 202 211-212, 220, 225, 227-228, 230, 232, 235, 238, 240, 242, 244, 249, 251-253, 257-259, 265-271, 281, 283
manure, 205, 228
manure, horse, 262
manure, undigested, 245
manure salts, 219
manures, character of, 26
mare's tail, 88, 215
marigold, 135
marijuana, 222
marsh cudweed, 75
marsh elder, 202-203
Marshall, C. E., 103
Mary Jane, 222
masses, 137
Masterson, Bat, 142
mat spurge, 193
Matricaria chamomilla, 76
Matricaria inodora, 76
matrimony grass, 264
mayapple, 163
maypop, 164
mayweed, 32, 34, 81, 85, 119

McCamam, Jay, 122, 123, 230, 281-282
McCoy, David C., 134
McHale, James A., v
meadow fescue, 56
meadow pink, 64
meadowsweet, 135
mealweed, 230
Medicago, 32
Medical Botany, 30
Melitara dengala, 44
Melochia corchorifolia, 88
melon aphid, 51
Mendeleyeff, Dmitri I., 174
Mentha arvensis, 76, 83
methane, 17, 86, 226, 271
Mexican clover, 250
Mexican fireweed, 229
Mexicanweed, 88
microbes, 237
microorganisms, 91, 213, 271, 279-280
Midwest United States, 157, 164, 201
mild water pepper, 64
mildew, 224
milk, 232, 242-243, 252, 279
milk sickness, 147
milk spurge, 263
milk thistle, 231
milk witch, 210
milkweed, 53, 55, 64, 119, 147, 213
milkwort, 135
Miller, Richard A., 156, 158
millet, 65, 217
milliequivalents (ME), 94-107
milo, 204-205, 211-212, 276
Milocep, 182
mineral release, 210
mint, 135
Miracle Worker, The, 79

perekatipole, 3
perennial bristlegrass, 56
perennial lettuce, 232
perennial peppergrass, 208
perennial ragweed, 254
perennial ryegrass, 256
perennials, 6
Periodic Chart of Elements, 174-175
persecaria, 34
Perthane, 171
pesticides, 227
petty spurge, 73-75
Pfeiffer, Ehrenfried, E., 62, 64, 67, 111, 159, 224
pH, 24, 26, 28, 66-68, 197-198, 201-202, 204-207, 210, 212-213, 217, 226-227, 232, 250, 269, 272, 278-279
Phaltan, 60
Phenomena of Life, The, 111
phenoxy herbicides, 198
phosphate, 12, 196, 199, 201-204, 206-207, 209-210, 212, 214-215, 220-221, 227, 230-231, 233, 236, 238-241, 244-245, 247-250, 252-253, 255, 257-263, 265-266, 271-272, 276, 279, 281-282
phosphate conversion, 24
phosphate-potash imbalance, 89
phosphate-potash ratio, 7
phosphorus, 94-107, 196-197, 206, 210-211, 245, 253, 272, 276
phosphorus-potassium ration, 121
photosynthesis, 210
Physalis anagulata, 87, 221
Physalis genus, 55-56
Physalis heterophylla, 221
Physalis laceifolia, 87
Physalis lanceolata, 221

Physalis longifolia, 221
Physalis pumila, 221
Physalis rotundata, 221
Physalis virginiana, 221
Phytolacca americana, 156, 163
Phytolacca decandra, 55
pignut, 135
pigs, 232, 250
pigweed, xiv, 6, 14-15, 55, 63, 81, 120, 188, 220-221, 231, 243
pigweed, insects harbored,51
pineapple weed, 63
Pinnacle, x
Piperonyl Butoxide, 171
Piperonyl Sulfoxide, 171
pitseed goosefoot, 230
plains sunflower, 266
plant lice, 53
Plantago aristata, 245
Plantago lanceolata, 74, 76
Plantago major, 76
Plantago media, 76
Plantago rugelii, 245
plantain, 63, 206
Plinius, 159
Pliny the Elder, 35
plowing, 211, 279
plowpan, 204, 211
Poa annua, 76, 83
Podopyllum peltatum, 163
pods, 157
poinsettia, 145
Poirot, Gene, 189, 190
poison ivy, 143, 144
poison oak, 143, 246
poison sumac, 143
poisoning, 144
Poisonous Plants of the United States and Canada, 144
pokeweed, 53, 55, 64, 156, 163
polio, 85
pollen, 89, 247

stalk borer, 43
Starr, Belle, 142
starweed, 205
starwort, 205
Steiner, Rudolf, 21, 111, 117, 128, 131-132
Stellaria media, 74, 76, 83, 119, 205
stem rust, 53, 55, 277
stemless loco, 233
steroid, 148
Steroidal sapogenins, 145
sticky soil, 197, 214, 225, 227, 238, 242, 255, 257, 262-263, 272, 276, 281-282
stinging nettle, 120
stinkgrass, xiv, 119, 264-265
stinking mayweed, 75
stinking willie, 64
stinkweed, 242
Stomp, xiv
stover, 277
Strasburger, Jackie, 149, 151
strawberry leaf spot, 53, 56
Strobane, 171
subsoil weeds, 18
succulents, 7, 89
Sudan grass, 239
sudan grass, insects harbored, 52
sugar, 227, 231, 252, 252, 276
sugar cane, 227
sugar cane rootstock borer, 51
sugarbeet leafhopper, 270
sugarbeet root aphid, 52
sulfate, 196, 203, 207, 211-212, 219-220, 227, 231, 235-238, 240-242, 247-249, 251, 253, 257-260, 265-266, 271-272, 283
sulfate salt, 270
sulfur, 207-208, 210, 270
sulfur, deionized, 270

sulfur cinquefoil, 120
sumac, 50, 225
summer annuals, 6
summer cypress, 2, 229
sun spurge, 75, 84, 144
sundews, 64
sunflower, xvi, 7, 9, 43, 225-226, 265-266
sunflower leaf beetle, 52
surfactants, 279
Sutton, Fred, 141, 142
swamp smartweed, 66, 259-260
swamp weeds, 18
swampy horsetail, 64
sweet birch, 163
sweet clover, 65
sweet potato flea beetle, 51
swinecress, 32, 76
sword fern, 157
symbiosis, 231
Symphoricarpos occidentalis, 200
Symphoricarpos orbiculatus, 200
synanthropes, 31

take-all of wheat, 56
tall buttercup, 76
tall dock, 212
tall morning glory, 236
tall thistle, 268
tall waterhemp, 88
tansy, 64, 82, 159
tansy aster, 266-267
tansy mustard, 266
tansy ragwort, 135, 150-152
Taraxacum officinale, 87, 157, 162, 210
Taraxacum vulgare, 76, 119
tarweed, 222
Tasmanian Organic Growers Association, 128
tea, 224
teaweed, 120, 247

ACKNOWLEDGMENTS

The sources used to construct this study have been many, and for the most part have been made a matter of record in the paragraphs and chapters of this book. Special thanks go to Hugh Lovel, Sarah Hieronymus, Arden Andersen, and Richard Alan Miller, whose quoted paragraphs helped backbone this study. Jay McCaman gave this project a special assist by providing a number of soil fertility readouts for weed patterns in his computerized catalog. Jack Doyle's quotes in Chapter 12 have been acknowledged amply, I hope, in the context of that presentation. The art used to illustrate this volume came from old texts now in the public domain, namely *Selected Weeds of the United States*, Regina Hughes, artist; and from *Weeds in Kansas*. *Selected Weeds* is now kept in print by Dover Publications, New York, as *Common Weeds of the United States*. Professor Phil Callahan read the manuscript critically and provided numerous improving suggestions.

It is not likely that this updated version would have come to fruition without the dedicated help of Diane Vance and Laura Thorn, production staff at the *Acres U.S.A.* office.

Finally, a farm editor and writer cannot live by weeds alone. He, too, needs compassion and gentleness, which Ann T. Walters and *Acres U.S.A.* staffers provided above and beyond the call of duty. I thank them all warmly.

— *Charles Walters, 1999*